Your Time Is My Time

Table of Contents

Foreword

Annika Toots &
Merilin Talumaa

1 COVID-19 paused this kind of comfortable and nomadic lifestyle, mainly seen through Instagram filters, which has been well described, for example, in the novel *Cold East* (first published in 2017) by Lithuanian writer Gabija Grušaitė. For a while, this kind of life that Grušaitė describes seemed like an era that had come to an end.

2 Although from the Baltic perspective this applies only to a handful of artists who have been included in the global art world and art market, most of them have been living in North America or Western Europe for a while and are being represented by internationally renowned galleries.

Your Time Is My Time is an attempt to capture a specific moment in the lives of contemporary artists from the Baltics. The focus of the book is on the notions of migration and belonging as both part of the artistic practices of these artists and the way they identify and define themselves. Due to globalisation, contemporary artists have been able to move between countries quite freely, often migrating and commuting between different cities, countries, and even continents,[1] giving them better access to the global art market and the international network of exhibitions and art fairs,[2] but also often resulting in mental exhaustion from the constant demand to be visible in many places at the same time.

All of this came to a certain *pause* during the COVID-19 pandemic, which is also why "time" plays such an important role in this book. The common routes and ways of migration came to a halt, and the suspended state of isolation and confinement that followed often resulted in rethinking artistic practices, notions of belonging and of home, and questions of sustainability in art-making for these artists. This suspended time was, however, temporary, and three years later we can see that only some of the changes that the pandemic promised have actually been executed. It's part of human nature to seek for pleasure and avoid the unpleasant, meaning that people don't easily give up the comforts in their lives and that any kind of "freedom" often results in acts that might be damaging to our ecological system.

There is one thing that the pandemic, together with the energy and climate crises, certainly did change, and that is the understanding of the concept of time, particularly in arts and literature. *Your Time Is My Time*

3 David Farrier, *Anthropocene Poetics: Deep Time, Sacrifice Zones, and Extinction* (Minnesota: University of Minnesota Press, 2019), 1–2.

acknowledges the heterogeneity of time. There is no one time that we would all experience the same way: time is a construct, time is not linear, time is subjective. Our perception of time constantly changes. The so-called era of crises, something that we have witnessed especially during the last four years, is also the period the idea behind this book has been forming, and *Time* has taken on new meanings and new perceptions. The Anthropocene era that we are living in, our addiction to fossil fuels, the climate crisis, etc., has broadened our sense of time, introducing notions of deep pasts and deep futures.[3] In art, literature, and culture in general, we are obliged to think beyond our lifetime, about geological time, altered ecosystems, and possible dystopian futures.

While ecological issues and concerns have been steadily building during these past few years, the period of research for this book has also witnessed the "suspended time" of the COVID-19 pandemic as well as the enlivening of the traumatic past in the present in Baltic countries by Russia's aggression towards Ukraine. Our time is a time of continuous and growing eco-anxiety, as well as a time in which latent layers of past and present become more and more visible. The acknowledgement of the damage that has been done to the planet has become inevitable, as well as the understanding that the present is something fleeting that is always being constructed by the past. Our time is full of complexities, and this also affects artists and their practices.

In the midst of these turbulent times, we started making a book on the artistic practices of Baltic artists who have lived between many countries and have constantly travelled around, with a studio in one place and a home in another, not to mention exhibition

4 Restoration of the fully independent republics of Estonia, Latvia, and Lithuania took place respectively on August 20, 1991, May 4, 1990, and March 11, 1990.

openings around the world. For many artists, the period of stillness, isolation, and "suspended time" of the pandemic meant returning to their homeland where they felt the safest. The ruptures in the seeming homogeneity of the fabric of time during the past four years, as well as escalating climate worries, not only have influenced the way artists define "home" or migrate between different countries, but also manifested itself in the materials and methods they use in their practices. Several artists have turned to more eco-friendly materials, trying to practise thinking-with inorganic and non-human objects, shifting away from the physical heaviness of artworks toward more ephemeral, non-burdening, sustainable practices.

These changes are reflected in this book. In 2020, we set out to photograph the studios of Baltic artists abroad, but after going through all these incredibly stressful and paralysing events like the pandemic and the war, it seemed a better and more suitable option that the artists themselves contribute visual essays to this book. Some of these contributions are reproductions of earlier works, some of them are studio views, and some of them unedited materials and reflective diary entries, or visual narratives of the process of art-making itself. This means that the visual material for this book is very diverse, but the focus of the book has remained unchanged since the beginning—to map Baltic artists that have emigrated (and returned), to analyse the reasons behind these processes, and to bring out how this is also reflected in their art.

Baltic countries[4]—Estonia, Latvia, and Lithuania—have experienced increased emigration since the 1990s due to the transition to market economies and significant economic and social changes, including a rise in unemployment, inflation, and social unrest. Additionally,

5 Nancy L. Green, Mirjana Morokvasic, and Marie Poinsot, "L'engagement au féminin: retour sur l'expérience scientifique de deux chercheuses," *Hommes & Migrations* 1331 (October-December 2020): 201–202.

there has been an exodus of artists from Baltic countries, with many moving to established art markets in London, Paris, Berlin, New York, and Los Angeles. This migration has been facilitated by the increasing globalisation of the art world and limited opportunities for artists in Baltic countries, where many artists continue to struggle to make a living from their work. This has led them to seek out opportunities in more established art markets, where they can access a wider audience and more lucrative commercial opportunities.

During our research, which is not conclusive and definitely deserves further exploration, we observed that there is a significant number of women artists from Baltic states who have emigrated to other countries or are living between various places. This is particularly true for the generation of artists born at the end of the Soviet period and the beginning of the 1990s, who grew up in independent countries and witnessed the ruins of the Soviet regime. They also experienced the significant economic boost that took place in Baltic states in the 2000s, including the entry into the European Union. In a way, emigration can be seen as a form of emancipation that reveals unequal power dynamics within communities, and has the potential to disrupt established orders and challenge traditional gender roles. For women, especially those who leave alone, migration can be a way to escape moral stigmas and seek social and economic stability and mobility.[5] Overall, in addition to gender inequalities, such as the wage gap, limited (job) opportunities have been a driving factor in migration for Baltic artists. This does not necessarily mean that it has been easy to find better possibilities and circumstances elsewhere. The fact that the art historical canon is still evidently inclined to

6 Full title of the essay: "From Surviving to Thriving: Notes on Migration, and Shared Cities, and Moments with Viktor Timofeev, Ella Kruglyanskaya, Daiga Grantiņa, and Ingel Vaikla."

the West mirrors the complexity of injustices that artists inevitably face.

Your Time Is My Time consists of three chapters. The first chapter "(Re)placed/(Re)connected/(Re)-routed" offers an overview of migration processes that have taken place in Baltic countries since the restoration of their independence from the Soviet Union in the early 1990s. This chapter considers migratory processes through artists from different generations who, for various reasons, moved away from their native countries. In her essay "I as a Readymade," art historian, curator, and art critic Sandra Skurvida takes a look into a particular phenomenon: the generation of Lithuanian artists who moved to New York and Paris during the 1990s. The flourishing metropolis of New York was an appealing destination for many Lithuanian artists who struggled at first but now thrive and have established themselves as important voices in the international art world.

The visual contributions in this book by Vytenis Jankūnas and Žilvinas Kempinas serve as a testament to a generation of Lithuanian artists who were part of the first wave of voluntary migration from a newly independent state to a bustling metropolis. Their migration was not so much of necessity, but rather of possibility—a chance to spread their wings and to explore the limitless potential of a world beyond their borders. Their work reflects not only the experiences of migration but also the unique cultural perspectives and artistic visions that arise from it.

In her essay "From Surviving to Thriving,"[6] art historian, curator, and critic Inga Lāce analyses the practices of three Latvian-born artists—Viktor Timofeev, Ella Kruglyanskaya, and Daiga Grantiņa—whose families escaped the economic uncertainty and political instability that haunted the Baltic region in the early post-Soviet years, and subsequently found their way to New York and Hamburg. These artists share a desire to position themselves as global artists and have built supportive communities around them. On the other hand, they also wish to stay connected to their respective home countries. The most recently (re)placed artist in this chapter is Estonian artist Ingel Vaikla, who moved to Belgium for her studies, and during these years has almost unwittingly grown a professional life, community, and roots in Brussels.

Throughout the first chapter, questions of (re)placement, (re)connection, and (re)routing recur in the artists' visual contributions, highlighting the impact that migration and travel have on an artist's sense of identity and place in the world. Today, it is widely expected that artists must travel extensively as an integral aspect of their work. Artists are seen as well-connected individuals who are constantly seeking out significant interactions by living in unfamiliar locations and immersing themselves in diverse environments. Thanks to the internet and social media, it has become easier for artists to promote their work and connect with galleries and collectors all over the world. This has also enabled Baltic artists to gain greater exposure for their work and to establish themselves in international art scenes, sometimes without the necessity to fly to the other side of the globe.

Although blending the terms "migrants" and "nomads" into a hybrid concept has become quite common today, we have made a distinction between these two terms in this book. This differentiation is rooted in the relationship between an individual and the place they inhabit at a given moment. "Migrants" are people who belong to a particular place but move due to exceptional circumstances, often involving conflict or upheaval. "Nomads" engage in a lifestyle that involves movement and is characterised by such movement.

7 Pascal Gielen, "Nomadeology: The aestheticisation of nomadic existence," in *Life Between Borders: The Nomadic Life of Curators and Artists*, eds. Steven Rand and Heather Felty (New York: apexart, 2013), 1–112.

8 Niels Van Tomme, "The trouble with the migrant metaphor," in *Life Between Borders: The Nomadic Life of Curators and Artists*, eds. Steven Rand and Heather Felty (New York: apexart, 2013), 1–112.

Contemporary nomadic artists take advantage of inexpensive air travel to move freely between fairs, biennials, and exhibitions. Their motivations for doing so are not based on survival but on networking and exposure.[7] The movement of migrants, who are excluded from this book, is marked by existential disruption. In contrast, the movement of artist nomads is characterised by a privileged, free choice. This difference can also be articulated as the contrast between movement guided by a "life" and movement guided by a "lifestyle."[8] Of course, it is important to note that artists who have migrated also sometimes lead a nomadic lifestyle, and that nomadic artists have decided to migrate at a certain point during their career.

The second chapter in the book, "Contemporary Nomadism," aims to take a look into the practices of Baltic artists who despite the turbulent circumstances are living and working in nomadic settings. Emma Duester's essay "Artists' Geographies of Home and Belonging" and Neringa Černiauskaitė's essay "A Love Letter to the Non-Belonger" give an insight into the joys and hardships of a nomadic lifestyle: building and staying in touch with various communities and a sense of belonging and commitment to different people and places along the road. Although living between different countries can be challenging, as one needs to navigate unfamiliar customs, languages, and social norms, it is often a very enriching experience that forms the identity of artists and their work. Nomadic identity involves a sense of fluidity and adaptability as well as a relationship with different environments.

Throughout our research and interviews with artists it became clear that nomadic identity can also create a sense of displacement and lack of rootedness, as artists may not have a permanent home or sense of belonging in a specific place. Living between various countries, cities, and cultures can be challenging to build and maintain long-term relationships, which can lead to feelings of isolation and loneliness. It can also be expensive, with costs such as travel, housing, and visas adding up quickly, especially if the artist has a family to support. This altogether shows the precariousness and vulnerability of such artistic practices and the misunderstanding of a nomadic life as a carefree and privileged way of working. Visual contributions by Pakui Hardware, Evita Vasiļjeva, Emilija Škarnulytė, Katja Novitskova, Agnė Juodvalkytė, Lina Lapelytė, Merike Estna, and Dorota Gawęda and Eglė Kulbokaitė offer personal reflections on the myriad ways of being this contemporary nomadic lifestyle entails.

In recent years, a trend has emerged among Baltic artists to return to their home countries, seeking to contribute to the vibrant arts scenes in Estonia, Latvia, and Lithuania. One of the main factors for this are the dynamic contemporary arts scenes in Baltic countries. As these scenes have developed and gained international recognition, more and more artists have been inspired to return home to contribute to these communities and help shape their future direction. They see themselves as playing an important role in shaping the artistic identity of their countries. In addition, important aspects behind these moves are often connected to social and financial reasons: being able to find stable employment, receive free health care services, and gain easier access to local cultural fundings.

The last chapter, "The Second Migration," considers this moment of the return, the reasons behind it, and the struggle for the ease of finding a supportive community and more sustainable artistic methods. This chapter includes interviews conducted by Annika Toots and Merilin Talumaa and visual essays by artists

Laura Põld and Maria Kapajeva. After spending time living and working in various cities—Vienna and London, respectively—these artists have decided to return to their home countries. The decision to switch from a nomadic life to the stability of a home country has been a response not only to the COVID-19 pandemic but also to a deepening economic and ecological crisis. Most importantly, though, this return is due to the urge to find a more secure setting, be it either for social, healthcare, or financial circumstances. Regardless of their choices, the experiences of these artists highlight the dynamic and ever-changing nature of artistic migration, and the ongoing dialogue between local and global cultures that shape the artistic landscape of our time.

Artists interviewed for the book between 2020–2023: Viktor Timofeev, Ella Kruglyanskaya, Ingel Vaikla, Vytenis Jankūnas, Žilvinas Kempinas, Evita Vasiļjeva, Laura Põld, Maria Kapajeva, Katja Novitskova, Agnė Juodvalkytė, Dorota Gawęda and Eglė Kulbokaitė, Lina Lapelytė, and Merike Estna.

I

(Re)placed
(Re)connected
(Re)routed

From Surviving to Thriving: Notes on Migration, and Shared Cities, and Moments with Viktor Timofeev, Ella Kruglyanskaya, Daiga Grantiņa, and Ingel Vaikla

Inga Lāce

1 The news stated that it is expected that Latvia will receive 237 asylum seekers from Hungary, 221 from Greece, and 68 from Italy. "Straujuma: Latvijai paredzēts papildus uzņemt 526 bēgļus, kopumā 776 cilvēkus," editorial, *LSM.lv*, September 9, 2015, https://www.lsm.lv/raksts/zinas/latvija/straujuma-latvijai-paredzets-papildus-uznemt-526-beglus-kopuma-776-cilvekus.a144904.

Notes on Migration in the Region

Over the last years, together with colleagues in Riga and across several countries and continents, we have been looking into different traces of migration and exile, transnational connections, diaspora, and contemporary nomadism, most notably through the research project *Portable Landscapes* that followed Latvian exile and emigration communities in New York, Paris, Berlin, Montreal, and Gotland. One of the reasons that triggered us to start that research in Riga, around 2015, was the European refugee crisis, which is a phrasing that describes the processes where migration from African and Middle Eastern countries reached a level of crisis within the European Union. In Latvia, at the semi-periphery of Europe, where people rarely decide to move even if no other choice is provided, instead of a refugee crisis, there was a political crisis related to the potential idea that refugees may arrive. People were stressed as to what a migration of this magnitude might mean for their lives, their jobs, and otherwise. With a population of nearly 2 million, the decision was made for Latvia to take in 776 asylum seekers;[1] as we can imagine, nothing much changed. However, in that tense political climate of popular nationalism, we wanted to show that this recent migration could in many ways be compared to the Latvian exodus during WWII, when people fled from the Soviet Union and found homes elsewhere in Europe, as well as in the United States, Brazil, and Australia, among many other places.

These last few years also proved to be dramatic in relation to migration in the region with at least two significant crises. In one case, refugees from Syria, Afghanistan, Iraqi Kurdistan, and other Middle Eastern and African countries were trafficked through Belarus to the borders with Latvia, Lithuania, and Poland, only to then be violently pushed back by our border guards. In defence of this inhuman action, our government cited the excuse of guarding the outside border of the EU. And then, in February 2022, the full-scale invasion of Ukraine by Russia began, creating an immediate departure of thousands and thousands of people fleeing Ukraine. These war refugees of various nationalities were quickly welcomed by the EU, especially by neighbouring Eastern European countries. Refugees of colour who had been living and studying in Ukraine, but without Ukrainian citizenship, faced more difficulties on the borders, a reminder once again of the racism permeating Europe's infrastructures of power. But the mere fact that so many people could be so quickly accepted in such a short time proves that there is an administrative mechanism to offer safe haven to people from non-EU countries (this time Ukraine), an example that should be used to push for more open border policies.

In April 2022, curator Masha Veits and artist Yevgeniy Fiks, organized a small gathering of curators and artists in the Latvian Pavilion in Venice, as part of their nomadic initiative the *Yiddishland Pavilion*, asking whether other times and spaces of exile—for example, the one I had been researching that took place during WWII—could somehow be compared, maybe even offer some consolation, to the current mass exodus of people fleeing the Russia-Ukraine war. Yet, where one crisis is for our generation an art historical project, with most of the protagonists either well-settled or already passed away after fulsome lives, the other is an ongoing tragedy, a rupture that continues to tear apart lives, including those of so many artists and friends.

In fact, the current war dramatically affected all of us, those living in the region and those inhabiting different places across the world, and it made us realize quite painfully how very Eastern European we still are. Really, you could distinguish where one was coming from by how shaken they were at the beginning of the full-scale invasion of Ukraine, regardless if they were in New York, Brussels, or Paris. An Eastern European couldn't escape the nervous looks from constantly checking for news, or the grim overall mood and saddened gazes that would inevitably follow.

The generation of Latvian and Estonian artists that I focus on in this text I'm sure were shaken as well, and with some of them we even shared moments at the collective Ukraine support events over the last year. But their story is certainly different from the fleeing people of today, or the war-torn generations before them, as they are refugees of neither conflict. In most cases, these artists left the Baltics in the early 1990s, after the collapse of the Soviet Union, or later in the 2000s, as children or teenagers with their families, or even later on to pursue their studies. The choice of their parents' generations, born in the 1950s or 1960s, to leave was often geared by economic reasons since Latvia and Estonia alike were turbulent places at the time. Staying was difficult and leaving wasn't always easy, but after so many years behind the Iron Curtain, it was a choice at least.

Viktor Timofeev and Ella Kruglyanskaya in New York

The 1990s were difficult economically and filled with ethnic tensions between Latvians celebrating their renewed independence and the Russian-speaking population in Latvia who were firmly excluded from this regained national identity. Russian language and culture was indelibly tied to occupation and oppression for many Latvians, a reality that took time to redress and repair. From then onwards, there have been several more waves of emigration from Latvia, mostly following economic pressures.

Viktor Timofeev's and Ella Kruglyanskaya's families left Latvia in the 1990s. Both families had diverse backgrounds but fell under the simplifying "Russian-speaking" label. Viktor (b. 1984) grew up in the suburbs of Riga, and when his family moved to New York they lived in Brooklyn. He studied at the Hunter College in New York and lived in London and Berlin until a move to the Netherlands to study at the Piet Zwart Institute, which is where we first met. Somewhere in between he reconnected with the art scene in Riga and has been back in New York since 2019.

In New York, there's never time. There's no time to meet, no time to work, to do art or to write emails. No time to go to parties, nor to do research. No time to buy a nice shampoo, so you get one at the local bodega. There's no time for sex, and if there is, then there's no time to watch a film. One needs to choose. There is always an early appointment and everyone's meeting a deadline. Or not meeting it, but it is always approaching.

But in this city, when something happens, it is magical. When you meet someone at that party you had no time to go to, and they tell you about an activist who went to Tashkent in the 1960s, and whom you should meet, though of course, you don't have time for that. But it is part of your research, and you give her a call and when you have that meeting, those are the most amazing, concentrated, inspiring four hours of your life with stories from the Black Arts Movement of the 1960s, migration of artists from Africa to New York, the Harlem Renaissance, and much more. You may even meet again soon.

2 Bonaventure Soh Bejeng Ndikung, "Black, Queer and Holy: The Many Shapes of Black Multiplicity," *Frieze.com*, June 9, 2020, https://www.frieze.com/article/black-queer-and-holy-many-shapes-black-multiplicity.

3 Mirdza Zīvere (b. 1953) is a Latvian singer, producer, entrepreneur, and director.

It is in this context that Viktor survives and thrives as an artist, a teacher, and an assistant to experimental filmmaker Ken Jacobs. Thinking about Viktor and his work, I want to introduce the phrase brought to my attention by curator Bonaventure Soh Bejeng Ndikung, who talks about a conversation between writer Édouard Glissant and writer, filmmaker, and cultural theorist Manthia Diawara that took place aboard the transatlantic liner *Queen Mary II* en route from Southampton to Brooklyn in 2009. "Asked what 'departure' means to him, Glissant responds: 'It's the moment when one consents not to be a single being and attempts to be many beings at the same time. In other words, for me, every diaspora is the passage from unity to multiplicity.'"[2] Glissant talks about the multiple diasporas of Africa. It's not a comparison, but I'm thinking of the many Eastern Europe's across the world, that exist in different locations and time zones.

When I spend time with Viktor, I feel that he embodies that variable state of being part of multiple worlds at the same time. With his family in upstate New York and his friends and colleagues in New York, Viktor's career spans Europe and the US, and of course includes lively connections to Latvia. For example, when we go to an exhibition opening together in New York, we may be the only ones speaking Latvian. Or when there is a party that I didn't have the time to attend, he sends me a message when someone surprisingly plays Mirdza Zīvere.[3] It warms my heart because that's another world we can share within the myriad of overlapping universes that is the city of New York.

Viktor's work is also full of these worlds: mutating computer-plant-beings, programmed armies of red and blue warriors, drawings and paintings that swarm

4 In the group exhibition *Riga Notebook. Following the Lines of Wacław Szpakowski*, featuring artists Wacław Szpakowski, Andrés Galeano, Navine G. Khan-Dossos, Hana Miletić, Evita Vasiļjeva, Janek Simon, Viktor Timofeev, Zanis Waldheims, Amanda Ziemele, and Viktor Timofeev, organized by the Latvian Centre for Contemporary Art and presented at Muzeum Sztuki from October 23 to April 30, 2021, https://msl.org.pl/riga-notebook-following-the-lines-of-waclaw-szpakowski.

from gothic floral compositions to more abstract constellations where Viktor is trying to escape figuration. It then sneaks back in, however, in the form of a tree of life, for example, or other, more apocalyptic shapes. The world of video games is also not far from Viktor's practice. He first studied computer science at Hunter College, but switched to visual art, and during his time in London he entered the video game world through a community of artist friends. Now in his work, Viktor often programs scenarios of no escape, where characters have no salvation. Instead of the pleasure of progress, action, or solution in a standard video game, Viktor's characters are stuck in endless loops; they may be fighting each other, following one another, but never find resolution.

In *Abecedary Clock* (2020), a ticking clock is placed in the upper corner of a room. On the clock's face there are characters that deteriorate faster than anyone can decipher them. The version of the work Viktor showed at the Muzeum Sztuki, Łódź,[4] was a new variation of an ongoing work that he calls a "degenerative alphabet." In this version, the letters of the standard Roman alphabet were placed in a new, clock-like arrangement and then systematically scrambled. A phrase made of the same letters was displayed under the clock hands, changing faster than the viewer's ability to decrypt it. These sorts of dystopian elements mark Viktor's worlds, suggesting that the shared being and multiplicity gained by migration is not always a joyful one. It contains darker corners or shadows that recall

5 Working title.

the opaque bureaucracies of immigration, of daily misunderstandings and political disagreements, perhaps running deeper than the language itself.

Ella (b. 1978) left Latvia with her family in the 1990s when she was a teenager. She has lived and studied in London, in Los Angeles, and now is based in New York. Her works are colourful, and full of women who are rushing, doing errands, fighting, or gossiping. They are curvy but also flat, and look like they are from a collage, just cut out, or a series of drawings. Sometimes when I look at them, I think about a cartoon that I have seen somewhere but cannot remember where exactly. These women are also whimsical, and the titles of Ella's works add to the play.

When I visited Ella's studio, a painting called *The cat is out of the bag* (2019)[5] caught my attention. It depicts a drawing of a woman sticking out of a brown purse. I was thinking how we are using this title phrase a lot in the art world to announce our upcoming projects and successes that need to be shared with peers. Another painting that I remember vividly from her show that I visited earlier at Bortolami Gallery in New York is titled *Good Intentions* (2021) with five different brush strokes—in green, red, very thin blue, yellow, and light grey—set horizontally across the drawing of a women's torso. What intentions are those and by whom? I didn't ask but I keep thinking that Ella's subtle game with words is her way of inhabiting the language, trying it out, as she also tries out if the dress she wants to draw will fit the woman she is drawing or whether the brushstrokes will fit her in the first place.

Daiga Grantiņa in Paris

I haven't been to Paris since March 2022, and I miss it. I've confessed multiple times that, despite the banality of the fact, it remains my favourite city of them all. Daiga (b. 1985) was born in Saldus, moved to Germany with her family when she was seven, studied there, as well as spending some exchange semesters in Vienna, and has been based in Paris since 2015.

Our common journey started when I worked on the Paris chapter of the exhibition *Portable Landscapes* where Daiga made a new work referring to the eccentric couple of Latvian dancer, weaver, and organizer Aia Bertrand and American dancer, philosopher, and artist Raymond Duncan, and their commune called Akademia formed in the centre of Paris. We continued to work together at the Latvian Pavilion at the Venice Biennale in 2019, the last Biennale before the pandemic and before the war. We co-curated the pavilion together with Lithuanian curator Valentinas Klimašauskas, and Daiga created the installation *Saules Suns*. The different objects swirling and twisting in that garden of joyful becoming still act like a memory machine in my head. The dark red spiral suspended at the centre of the room, the mild pink one on the right. They bring me to the paintings of Mikalojus Čiurlionis (1875–1911), and the sun dog phenomena that Daiga refers to in the title. A pastel pink one with feathers inside brings me to another major event of becoming—pregnancy and childbirth.

Daiga's stories are always material. They come in plastic, in threads, in wood, and in the combination of those materials; they come in colours that go from synthetic to natural and back. Words are equally important as her titles spin them around, different

6 Svetlana Boym, "Immigrant Arts, Diasporic Intimacy, and Alternative Solidarity," in Niels Van Tomme, ed., *Where Do We Migrate To?* (Baltimore: Center for Art, Design and Visual Culture at the University of Maryland, 2011), https://pdf.mailinglijst.nl/?m=147526&hash=FEC41C46111C32E84D000685975982340E5111428DB6FF086DB68537A5016229.

languages mingling to create new phrases akin to short poems.

In Latvian, *Saules Suns* means a "sun dog." But *Suns* also sounds like sons. Whether the sons of the sun or the meteorological phenomenon called sun dog, which is a member of the family of halos where bright spots appear on both sides of the sun, it is all a reference to light, another element prominent in Daiga's work.

Daiga's usage of words reminds me of a text by cultural theorist Svetlana Boym, where she refers to Polish-American artist Krzystof Wodiczko. "[He] wrote that an immigrant in today's cities is an 'unintentional prophet'," notes Boym, "who dreams of a better private refuge, but also of a better public democracy that could welcome strangers like himself… Such a modern immigrant, who speaks with an accent in both foreign and native languages, is a bit of a trickster, who teases us with her tongue-tied confessions that tamper with our sense of intimacy and estrangement, of cultural differences and alternative solidarities in the contemporary world."[6] Between Latvian, German, English, and French, Daiga teases out what is important—for her, and likely for others as well.

I also remember someone asking at the Latvian Pavilion opening in Venice, what is Latvian about her installation since it's in the national pavilion? Luckily the question caught my colleague instead of me. But now I think that I could finally answer as this is exactly the sense of intimacy and estrangement that Daiga brings forward through her visual language, a sense that it is at once Latvian and not.

Ingel Vaikla in Brussels

I know the artist Ingel (b. 1992) mostly through the stories of our common artist friend Diāna Tamane. They studied together in the post-graduate program at HISK (Higher Institute for Fine Arts) in Ghent, Belgium, and share common interest in our region, its troubled history, and the human and material traces it has left.

In 2015, Ingel made a work titled *The House Guard*, referring to the abandoned Linnahall in Tallinn, built as the Lenin Palace of Culture and Sport to host regatta during the 1980 Summer Olympic Games in Moscow. Ingel describes her video as a double portrait of the Linnahall and its caretaker Peter, both being bound by seclusion. It still haunts me, the slow pace of time leading powerfully through the decline of infrastructures meant for joy and the building of communism. The work speaks as much to the failed utopia of communism as it does about its ruins and the period that followed, the 1990s, that era of economic shifts and circumstances so difficult that resulted in the waves of emigration that Daiga, Ella, Viktor, and their families were part of.

That abandoned hall is, however, also a marker, waiting for our generation to finally notice it, to build new ecosystems of trust, of human and non-human kinship, equal rights, and diverse co-habitation. Ingel's video is like a first step in making that happen.

Back in Riga

When theorist Rosi Braidotti speaks about her lifelong "engagement in the project of nomadic subjectivity" she says that "[it] has been partly motivated by the conviction that, in these globalized times of accelerating technologically mediated changes, many traditional points of reference and age-old habits of thought are being re-composed, albeit in contradictory ways. Paradoxically,

7 Rosi Braidotti, "Writing as a Nomadic Subject," *Comparative Critical Studies* 11, no. 2–3 (October 2014): 163–184, https://rosibraidotti.com/wp-content/uploads/2018/06/Braidotti-Rosi-Writing-as-a-Nomadic-Subject.pdf.

old power relations are not only confirmed but, in many ways, exacerbated in the new geo-political context."[7] In relation to migration, we can only agree, witnessing as we are what has happened at EU borders, for example.

For me, looking at the questions of migration have been important because growing up in Latvia—a country with one nation-building story—I would always want to look sideways. Were there really just the brave Latvians fighting for their nation, and surviving through German, Russian, and Soviet oppression? What are the stories that lead one astray, where did people migrate and ended up fleeing, who were the curious wanderers, and who are the incomers to Latvia itself and why are they so often excluded from this story?

I'm finishing this text in Riga, where I've slipped comfortably into my apartment that I never sublet even when I go to New York for longer periods of time. When I travel, I move swiftly and effortlessly, with my EU passport as a privilege that many don't have. Passports are one of those absurd causes of inequality that make it difficult to speak about contemporary diasporic artists without talking about war and climate refugees, and those artists who will never be able to come to their own exhibition opening because of visa procedures between countries.

Thus, I think that looking at the older and younger generations of diasporic artists from the Baltics (and elsewhere) is even more important since we can then open threads that connect sideways, that weave a network of stories that are non-linear, that go beyond accepted narratives of nation building, that open up multiplicities, and that can help artists move from surviving to thriving in whatever new environment they find themselves in.

I as a Readymade

Sandra Skurvida

I was a functional object once. Now I carry vestiges of my former function—an accent, a certain unease in establishments where I am being redefined, and a foreign air about me that prompts strangers to ask where I am from. I am constantly dodging the question. Where I am from cannot define me in their eyes, since that what shaped me is actually—historically—gone. So what can I say to my interrogators?

I am an immigrant—like a readymade, I lost my former place and function in order to gain new meaning. I dematerialized. The emergence of a new meaning via a transfer of self from one context to another institutionally sanctioned context is a common experience of immigration—there's nothing otherworldly about it. Transgressing social, economic, political, institutional, linguistic, and discursive boundaries is an immigrant's right of passage, acquired in exchange for most previously held rights—to work, to vote, and to be taken for granted. These transformative transgressions are relative to the radicality of the change—if it happens during historical upheaval, its effect on the personal is amplified, and may be irreversible. There is often a name change involved too.

To assure you that I am not making things up—as it happens sometimes along the way, in order to ensure a smoother passage—take a look at my history, which is well-documented. My inventor, Marcel Duchamp, was a perpetual immigrant. During his sojourn in New York during WWI, he chose his transitional object—a urinal—and estranged it from its sanitary function. Erasing its old history, if any, he cleaned it up and made it new, signing it with the new name, "R. Mutt." This made me super strange and elevated in the new environment of a promised exhibition. After having my mugshot done by Alfred Stieglitz, he let me be lost.

What Duchamp did is not unthinkable to an immigrant. And if you were to ever navigate the process,

1 T.J. Demos, "Duchamp's Labyrinth: *First Papers of Surrealism*, 1942" *October* vol. 97 (Summer 2001): 91–119.

Duchamp's *Sixteen Miles of String* (1942) at *First Papers of Surrealism*, a benefit exhibition he co-organized in order to help exiled surrealists in New York with their immigration papers, will be very familiar to you, this web in which you are caught, dodging questions.

In his own version of *Sixteen Miles of String*, New York–based Lithuanian artist Žilvinas Kempinas made a loop of obsolete magnetic tape—his *Double O* (2010)—dance in the air at the Museum of Modern Art. Freed from recording duty, this twist of tape transfixed museum audiences with its purposeful indeterminacy. Shapeshifting, functionless form held aloft by air streams from two commercial-grade ventilators, it was writing on air. Not quite—it called out to the old readymades housed upstairs at the museum, and recalled the absent labyrinthine string installation. Duchamp's contemporary, Georges Bataille, evoked the labyrinth as a trope for a disoriented Europe in the late 1930s and '40s—a disorientation also familiar to us in Eastern Europe in the 1990s—as an "ontological and epistemological model of identity, structure, and space, in which all are radically decentered."[1] A readymade is produced via disidentification extending beyond objects to signs and identities. *Double O* evokes contingent identity in its fugitive form. In this installation, Kempinas constructed a structure defying structure, just an airwave away from hitting the ground, failing to meet expectations of perpetually upward mobility. Experience of immigration bears on the reconditioning of place as space. Place is concrete, space is transient; place can be pinned down, whereas space is everywhere. Making double loops

2 Georges Bataille, "The Labyrinth," in *Visions of Excess: Selected Writings, 1927–1939*, ed. Allan Stoekl, trans. Allan Stoekl, Carl R. Lovitt, and Donald M. Leslie Jr. (Minneapolis: University of Minnesota Press, 1985), 171–177.

3 "Oral History Interview with Ruth Asawa and Albert Lanier, 2002 June 21 – July 5," Smithsonian Archives of American Art, https://www.aaa.si.edu/download_pdf_transcript/ajax?record_id=edanmdm-AAADCD_oh_230409. *The Faces of Ruth Asawa* is a long-term installation at the Cantor Arts Center, Stanford University, Stanford, California, https://museum.stanford.edu/exhibitions/faces-ruth-asawa.

in space is not quite "being nowhere," as Bataille has claimed in his essay "The Labyrinth."[2]

As we emerge from the labyrinth of immigration, we look back to the point of entry. Kempinas made dozens of life masks of friends and acquaintances in Vilnius in 1996, as we were leaving the place at the end of the era, in search of space. He started the second casting in New York at the end of 2022, and continued in Vilnius at the MO Museum. Most of the masks from the first casting perished, plaster being more fragile than flesh. My first moult is rather vague, whereas the second one holds time imprinted in the negative space of the cast. We have mentally recast ourselves—in the same ways that Duchamp remade his *Fountain* numerous times after purchasing a urinal from a plumbing store. Kempinas's *Fossils* resemble Duchamp's *Fountains* in their eerie negativity procuring stopgaps in time—in our presence. In photos, these negative casts appear as positives, caught between matter and image. Their continuing negotiation of space and presence in the negative keeps them apart from sculpture and representation, and closer to the readymade realm of contingency. Materiality of an imprint transcends the ephemerality of an image, making time itself real. When Ruth Asawa, a Japanese American artist who survived internment during WWII, had cast the faces of the people in her life over the period of thirty years, up until 2000, and hung these life masks on the exterior wall of her house, she, too, was rehabilitating her space—as she said, "Our life as immigrants was much harder than the internment… Just surviving was much more intense."[3] Even though the pretext and technical process of making the cast are similar, outcomes of Asawa's and Kempinas's castings differ—he stops at making the shell, a vessel of time that remains open, whereas she filled the mould with clay of varying tones, resembling skin tones, making the positives and thus completing the process as portraiture. Kempinas and Asawa, far apart in time and space, and certainly unaware of each other, both encircled their respective communities—she, in the positive; he, in the negative—seeking each other out like a yin and yang of history.

Being away is being both here and there at the same time—this doubling loosens a meaning from its discursive moorings yet projects the affective power of absence outwards. S&P Stanikas, a Lithuanian artist duo living in Paris, have been working since the early 1990s with vestiges of representation embedded in their historical DNA—the Soviet aesthetics twisted into grotesque forms in their performative photography and video, grand-scale drawings unhinged from the academic tradition, and ready-made paraphernalia. For the exhibition I curated for the Soros Center for Contemporary Art – Lithuania in 1995, Stanikas created a multimedia installation *History?!*, comprising giant photographs and ceramic sculptures. The two photographic panels resemble crime scene photos blown-up to monumental proportions. Two figures appear in both, in variable configurations—a girl in a party dress and golden sandals is cast down on a dirty concrete floor, her thighs smeared in purple blood; and a statue of Lenin, also cast down, hovering over her. They are switching sides from one panel to the other, like playing cards. At the time, the future was unclear—what will go, and what will stay? This uncertainty rears up again after Russia's invasion of Ukraine in 2022. The artists permit the relics of ideological dominance to possess their bodies and faces in nightmarish apparitions of history—as in *Cinema X* (2004). In their dioramas, S&P

Stanikas transfer themselves into a zone of readymade history. They are wilfully present in their works, engaging history via spectres of their appearances, acting as shifters. Their visual language is caught in a vicious cycle of contingency—their being and the meaning of the works depends on mediation of readymade relativity on the shifting grounds of history. This indeterminacy is even more apparent when compared to the works of artists who, like Stanikas, emerged out of the post-1989 pandemonium, but chose to stay put—for instance, in the films of Lithuanian artist Deimantas Narkevičius, the experience of Soviet occupation remains intact, it is reperformed and transposed toward the future as a kind of fiction, it is thus conceivable and well received. But a life away shatters chronology and continuity—messages become complex, ambivalent, sometimes contradictory. Stanikas takes ready-made bits and pieces of art practices existing outside the framework of the "contemporary"—such as the academic nude, socialist realism, Russian imperialist tropes—and injects them into the white cubes of the world.

Epilogue

A long time ago, I knew an eternal wanderer, a cobbler who would go from village to village, door to door, mending shoes, and making new ones, for new wanderers. I wanted to follow him, yet could not cross borders then, only he and his people could. I jumped into his sack and found good old lost friends there—two Bicycle Wheels, the whole bunch of Bottleracks, a snow shovel, Comb, Traveler's Folding Item, Trap, and some other stuff. After a long while in the dark, I peeked out of the sack, and saw the city of signs—New York imagined by many immigrants, as in Vytenis Jankūnas's photographs. The photos show the outside—big buildings, bright lights, crazy hair, a subway crowd

4 Sla307 Art Space (2015–2019), co-directed with Bareikis, Mediodia, and Laura Zaveckaite; and Undercurrent (2019–2022), co-directed with Daina Mattis, Zaveckaite, and two anonymous co-directors.

frozen in waiting—this city of spectacle dissolves in the eyes of its inhabitants, in the daily looking, from the inside out. Inside, in the downtown lofts of the nineties, I found those who were swept away from Lithuania by WWII, landed before us, and inscribed their histories into the mental map of the city—they have welcomed, shared, and cared for us. Kes Zapkus, a painter of the archaeology of knowledge, who sees it from a global perspective. Rudolf Baranik (1920–1998), an artist activist who transferred unrepresentable suffering of the Shoah into his *Napalm Elegies*, forever mourns the victims of war and oppression. Aleksandra Kasuba (1923–2019), an indomitable spirit who left an imprint of her brick mosaics on the prominent walls of the city, and designed lightweight, stretchable dwellings that can spring up anywhere in a matter of days, providing shelters. Jonas Mekas (1922–2019), who's Anthology Film Archives served after hours as Lithuanian Social Club. We found ourselves in the city of many—Aidas Bareikis, a maker of precious installations from castaways; Ieva Mediodia, a painter of neural networks shimmering in neon colours sapped from the World Wide Web; Kempinas, a conjuror of time loops; Julius Ludavičius, a mixer of art and life as art in several galleries he co-directed;[4] Nomeda and Gediminas Urbonas, a short distance away in Boston, connecting their Lithuanian roots to planetary networks in their visions of a habitable world; and myself, writing this autofiction, finally able to face my life through a mask of an immigrant. For us, history itself was a readymade, and that's how it made us.

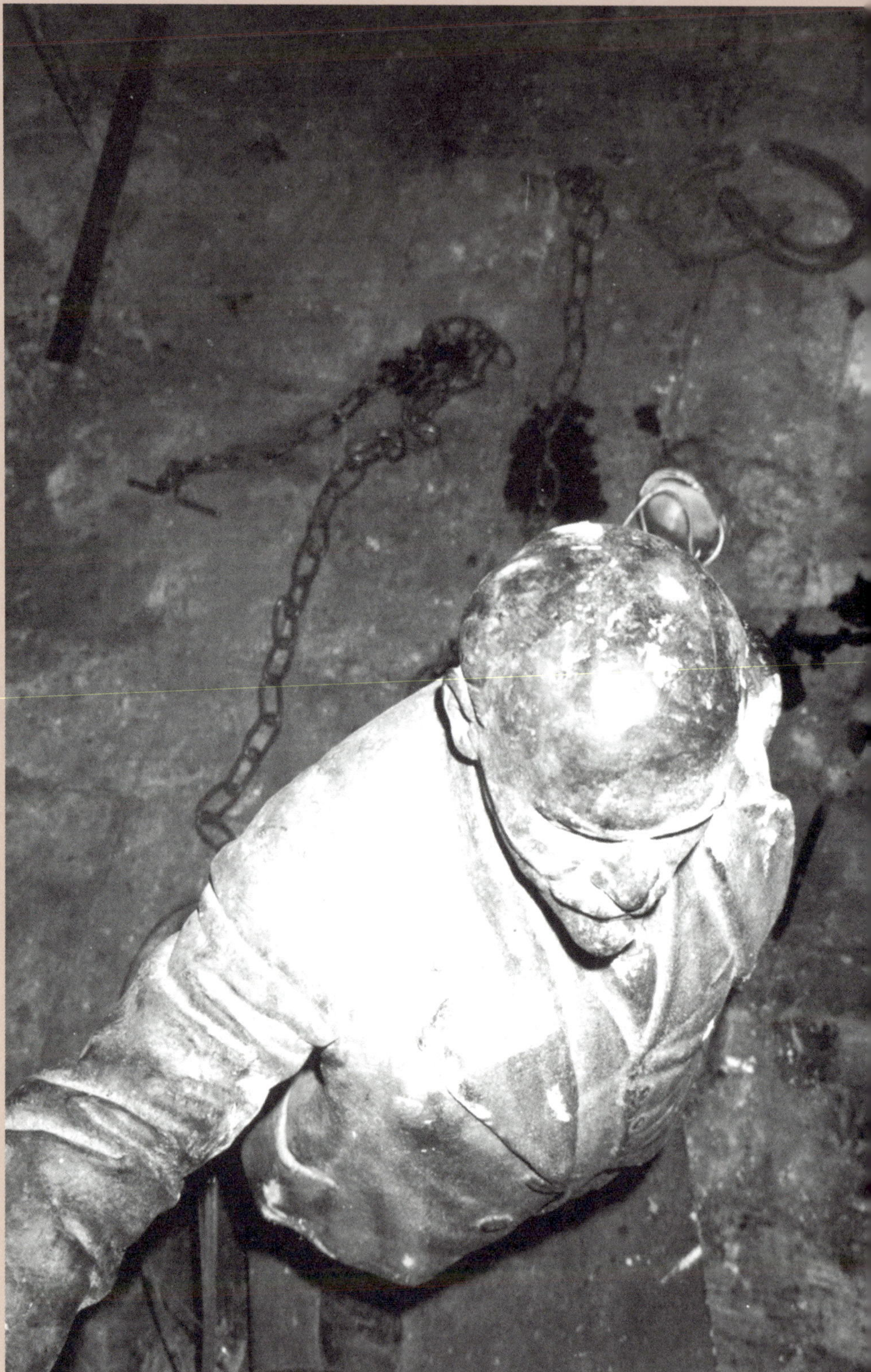

S&P Stanikas, *History!?*, 1992
Installation detail, photo print, 270 x 180 cm

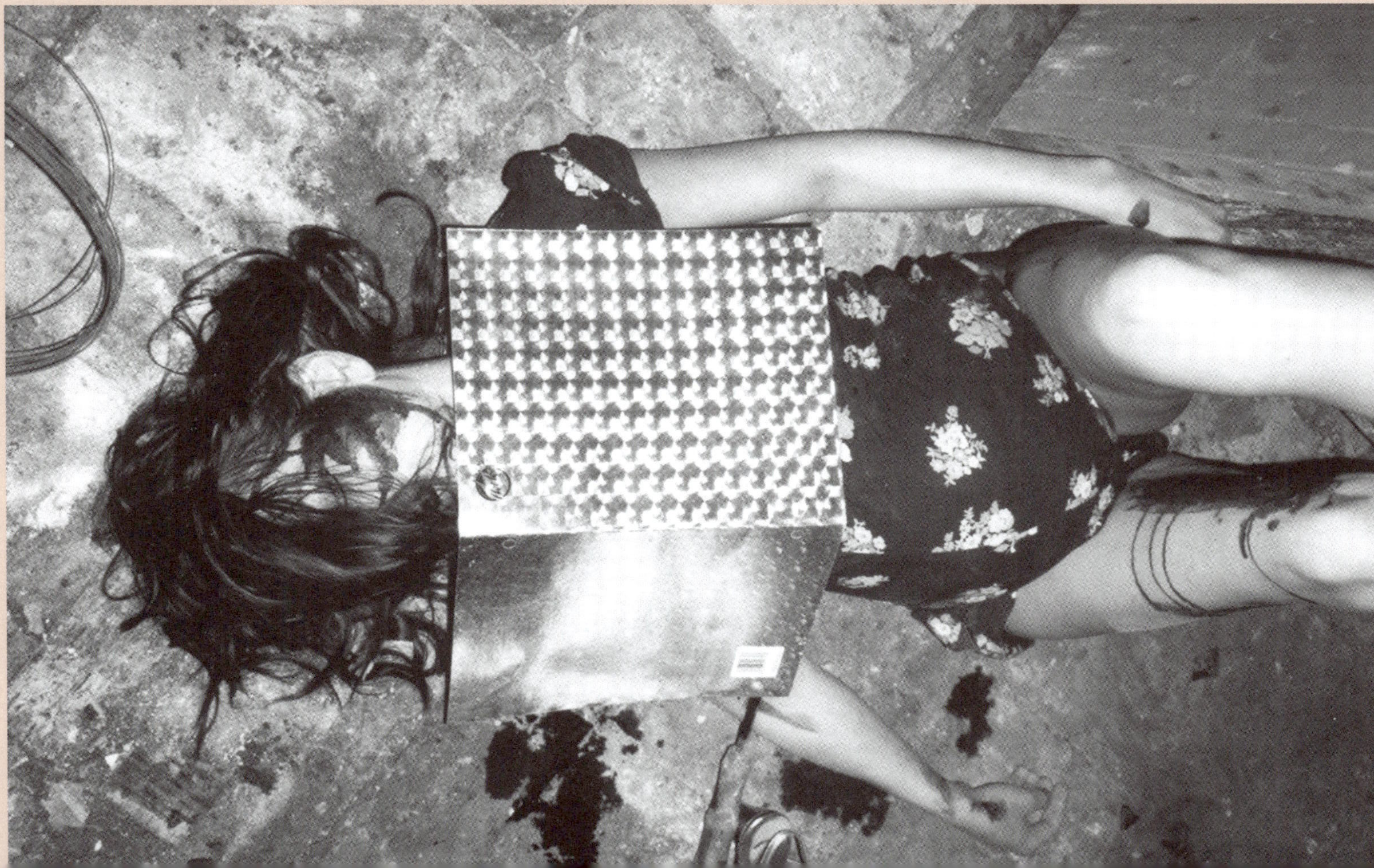

Žilvinas Kempinas

Žilvinas Kempinas (b. 1969, Plunge, Lithuania) is an artist living and working in New York City since 1997. He graduated from the Vilnius Art Academy in 1993 and received his MFA from Hunter College, City University of New York, in 2002. Kempinas is known for employing non-traditional materials to create active and dynamic artwork mostly consisting of installations, kinetic or minimalistic sculptures, and optical art. Many of his works employ a signature material—unwound magnetic tape—which affects the viewer through different senses. Kempinas's use of natural laws, air-fan winds, and gravitation can be perceived as a certain expansion of the field of sculpture. At the same time, his mathematical approach, highlighting the accuracy, detail, and fragility of the objects created, raises questions of poeticism, spatial relationships between viewers and the objects, and the delicate balance between matter and consciousness.

Photos: Ryis Šeškaitis

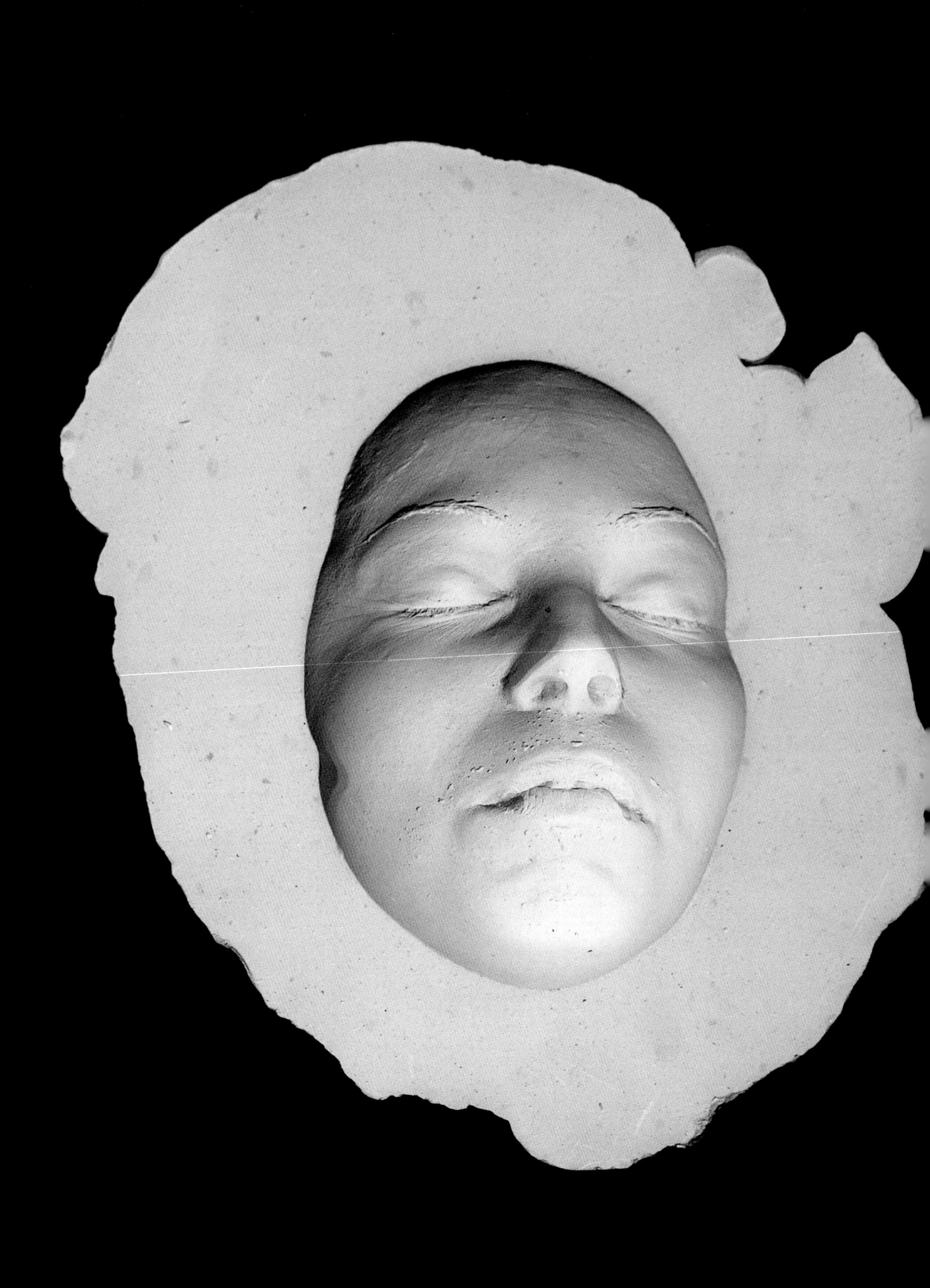

Portraits-Fossils, 1996
(Sandra Skurvida)

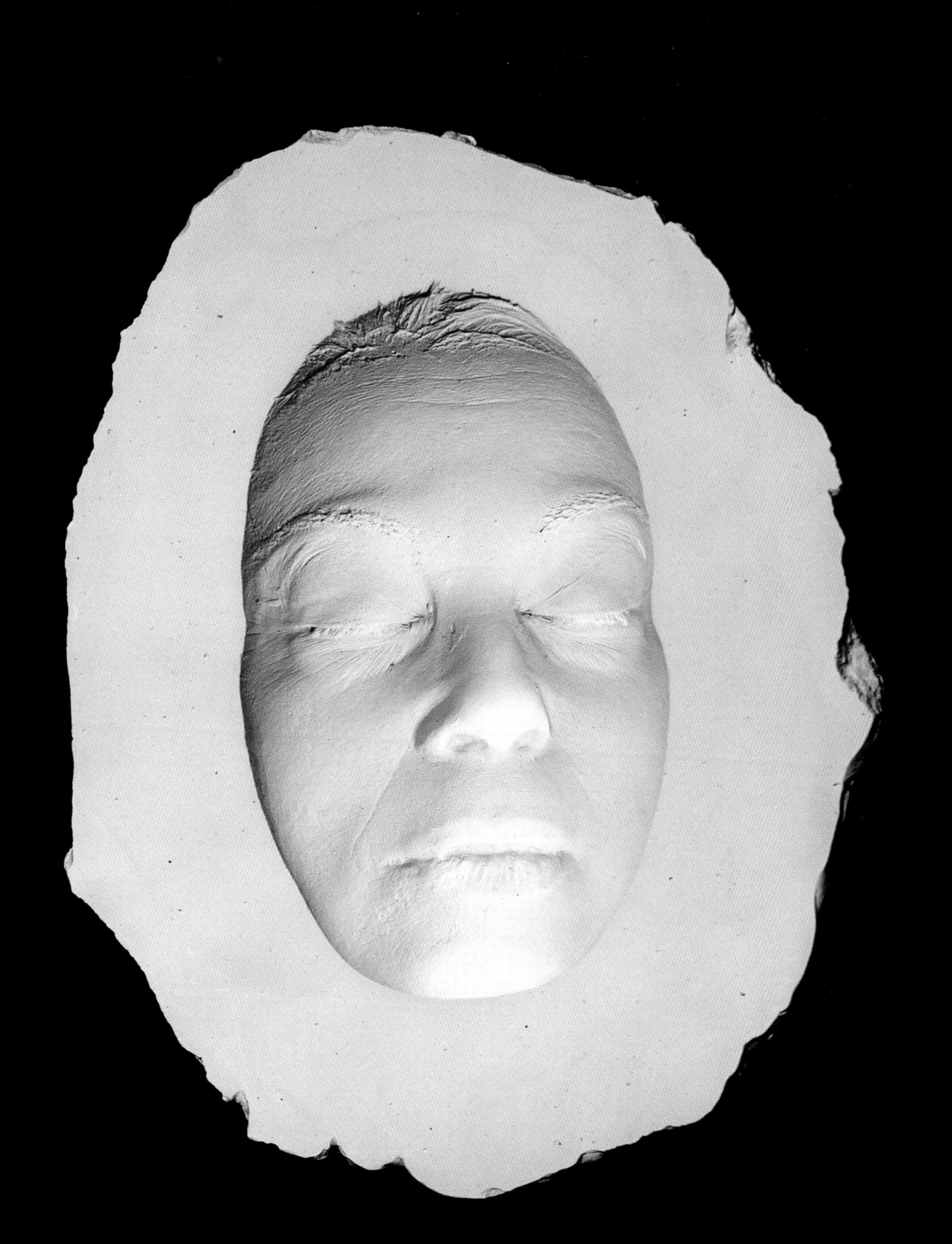

Portraits-Fossils, 2023
(Sandra Skurvida)

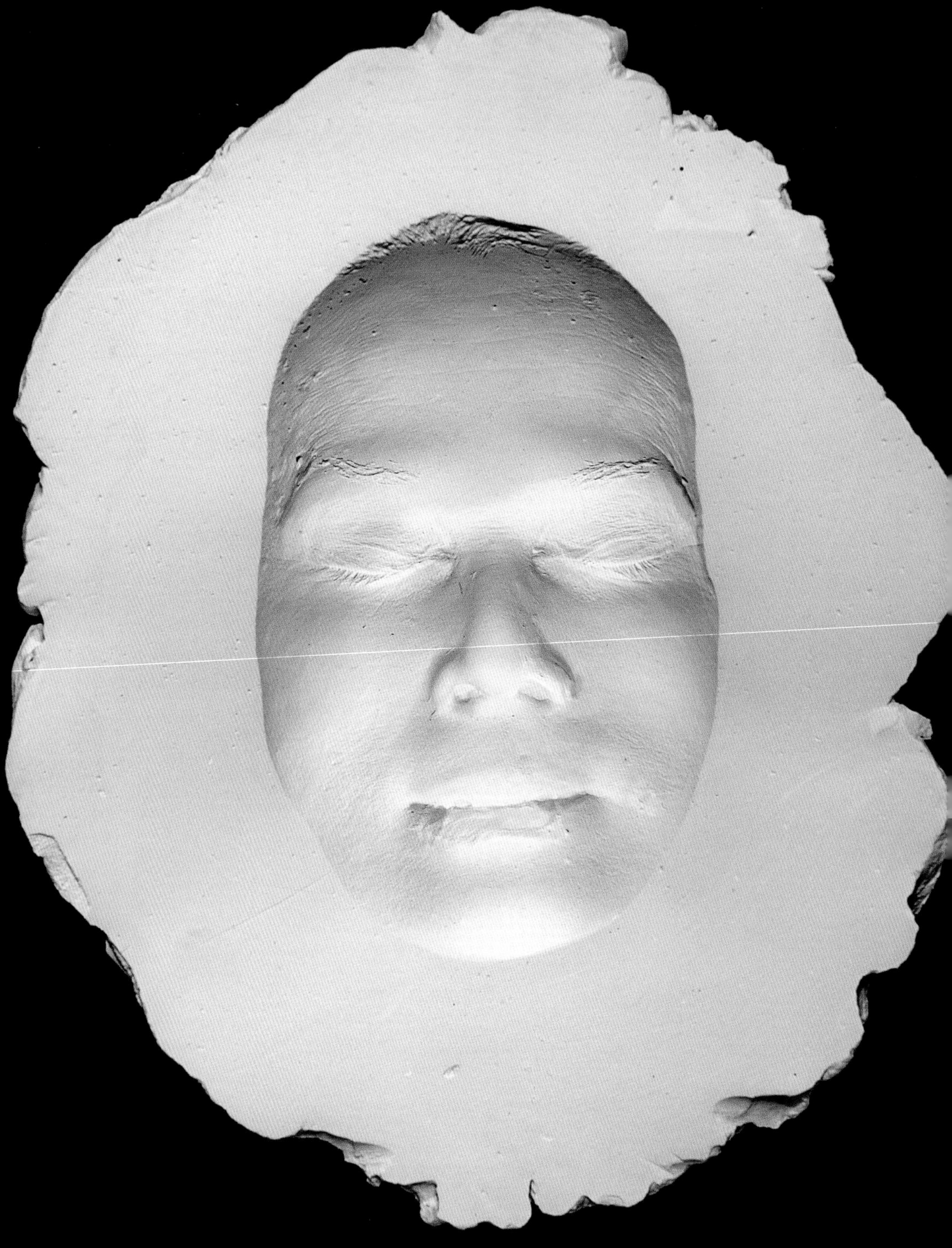

Portraits-Fossils, 2023
(Ieva Mediodia)

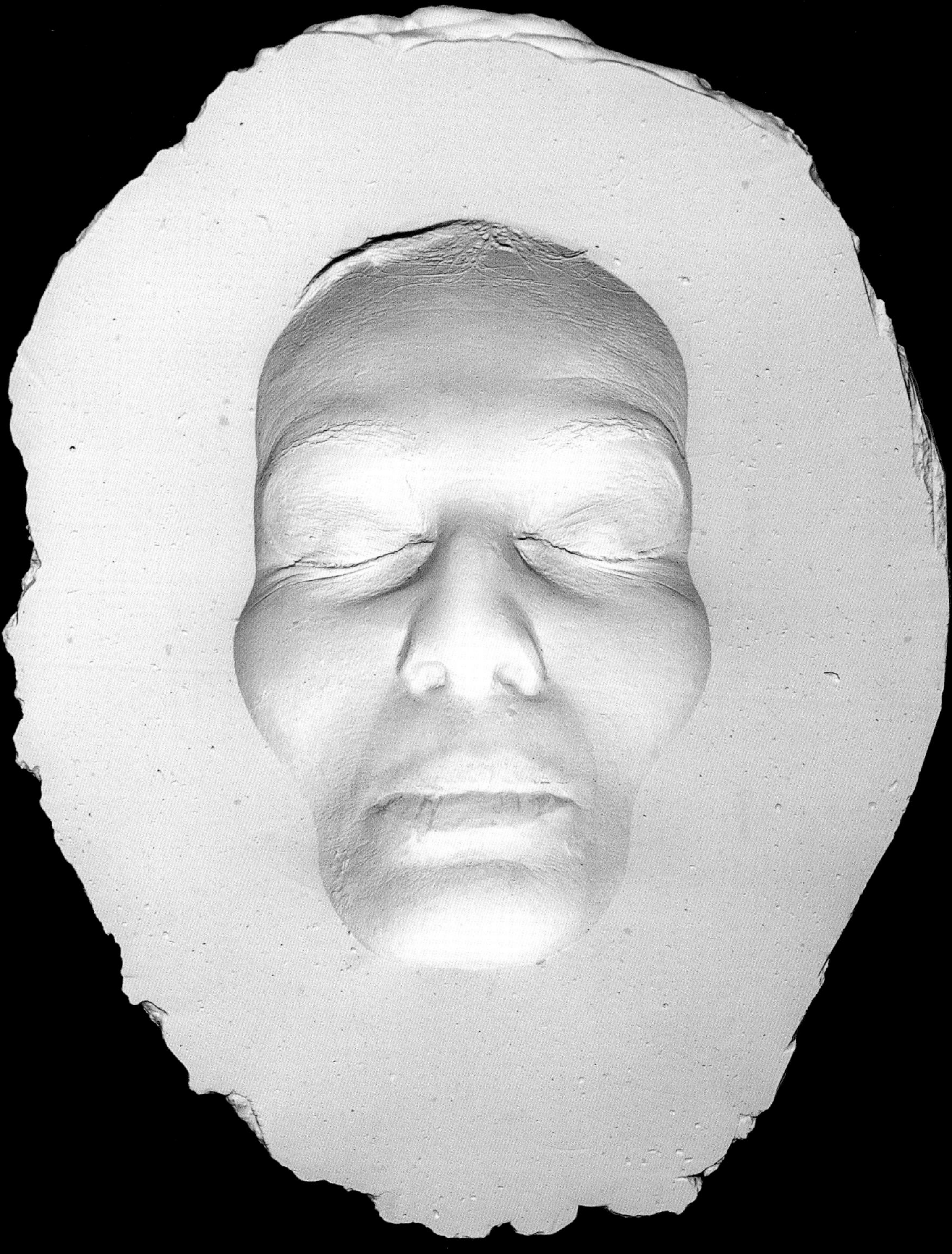

Portraits-Fossils, 2023
(Leila Kasputiene Sukiur)

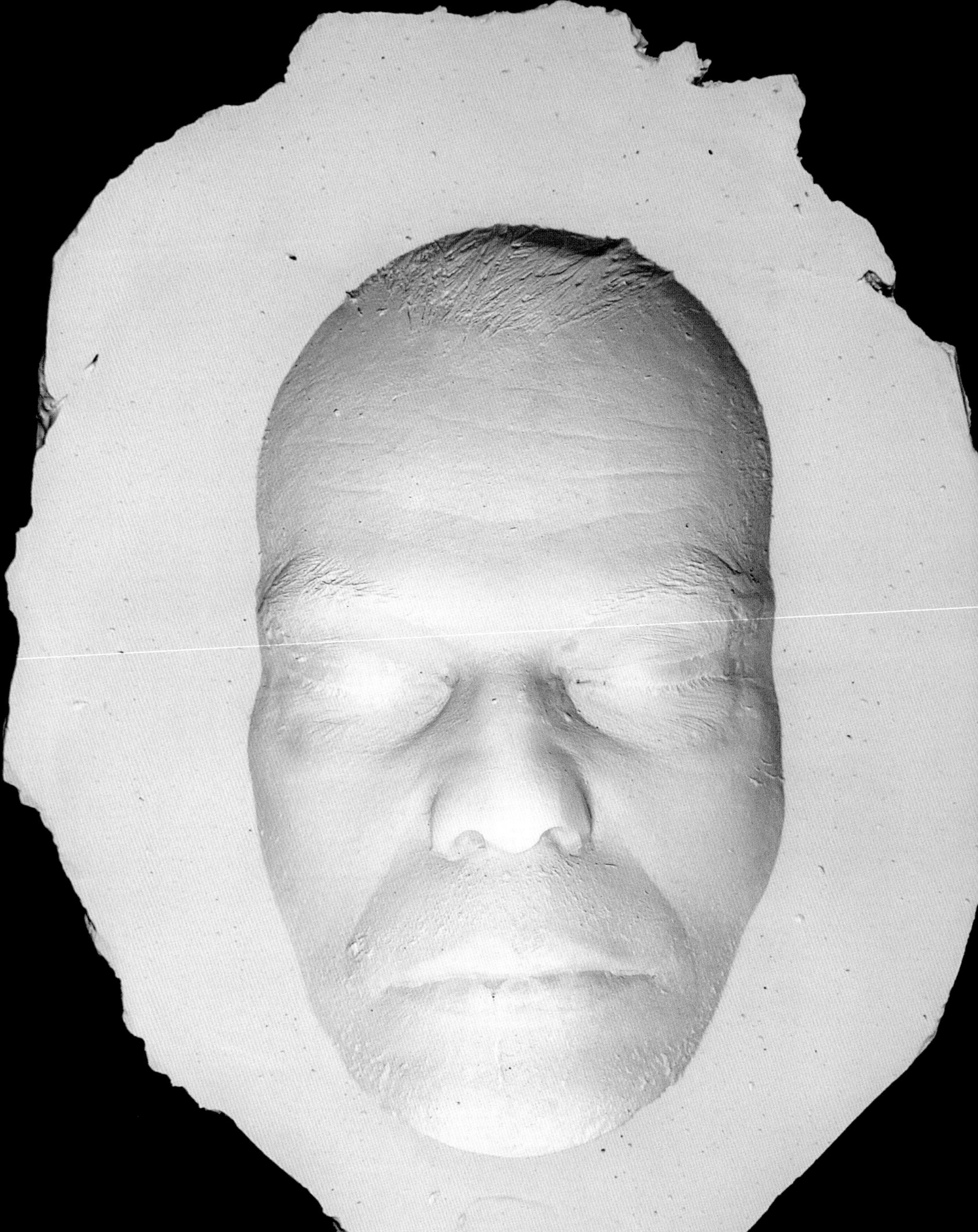

Portraits-Fossils, 2023
(Aidas Bareikis)

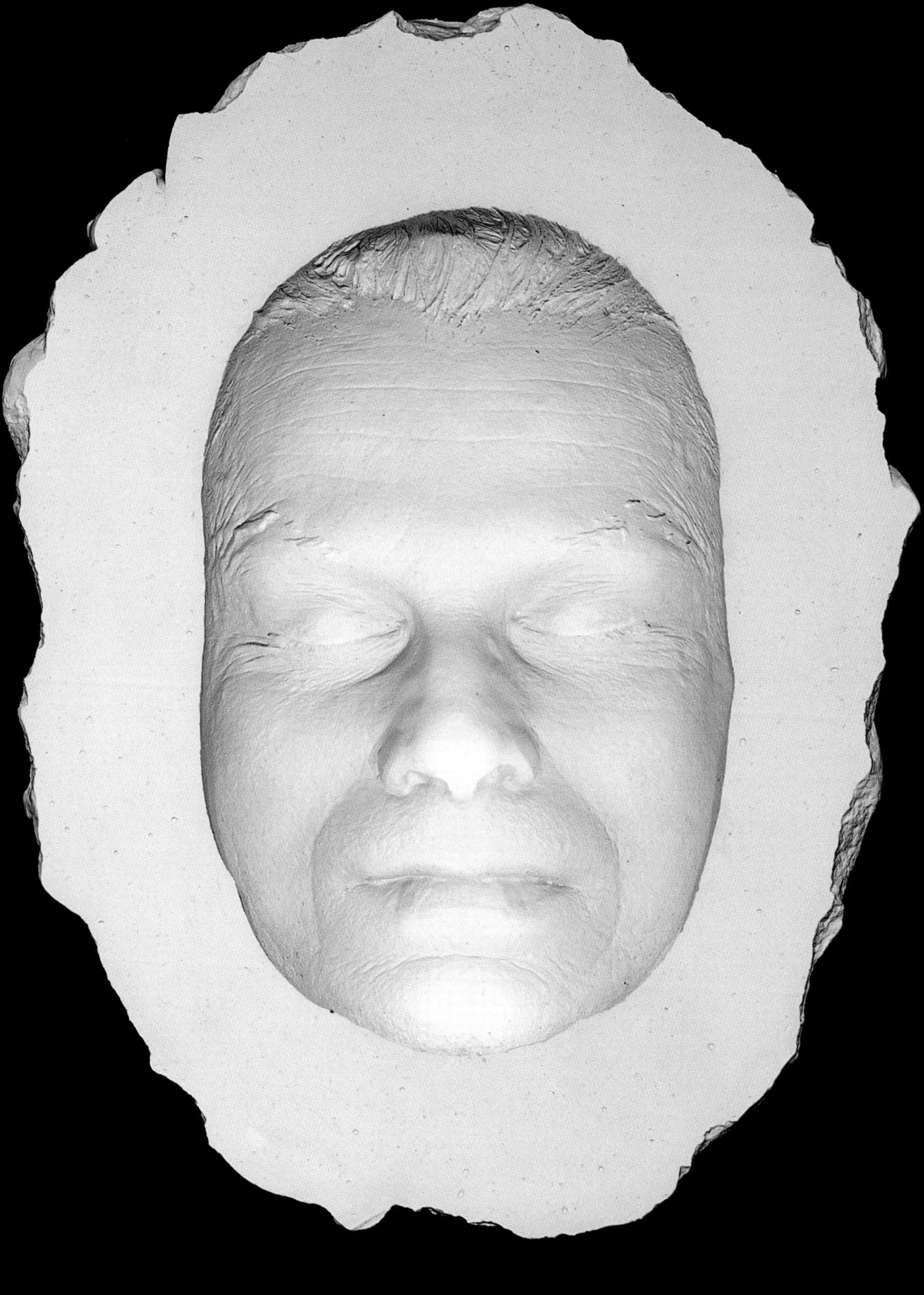

Portraits-Fossils, 2023
(Vytenis Jankūnas)

Vytenis Jankūnas

Vytenis Jankūnas (b. 1961, Kaunas, Lithuania) is a Lithuanian-American artist who has lived and worked in New York City since 1996. Jankūnas graduated from the National M. K. Čiurlionis School of Art in Vilnius. He received his MFA and BFA from Vilnius Academy of Arts. His latest work uses mostly photography as a medium for his artistic projects, which include books, photography, and video installations. Recent exhibitions include: Prospekto Gallery, Vilnius (2021); Undercurrent Gallery, New York City (2017); Tallinn Art Hall Gallery (2016); and Contemporary Art Centre, Vilnius (2015). In 2020, Jankūnas won first place in the Self Published Books category of the International Photography Awards. He has been a recipient of the Fellowship Award from the New York Foundation for the Arts in 2000, and was awarded a residency in 1995 at Nordic Arts Centre (HIAP), Helsinki.

My New York Minute (Decades Long...), 2013–2022

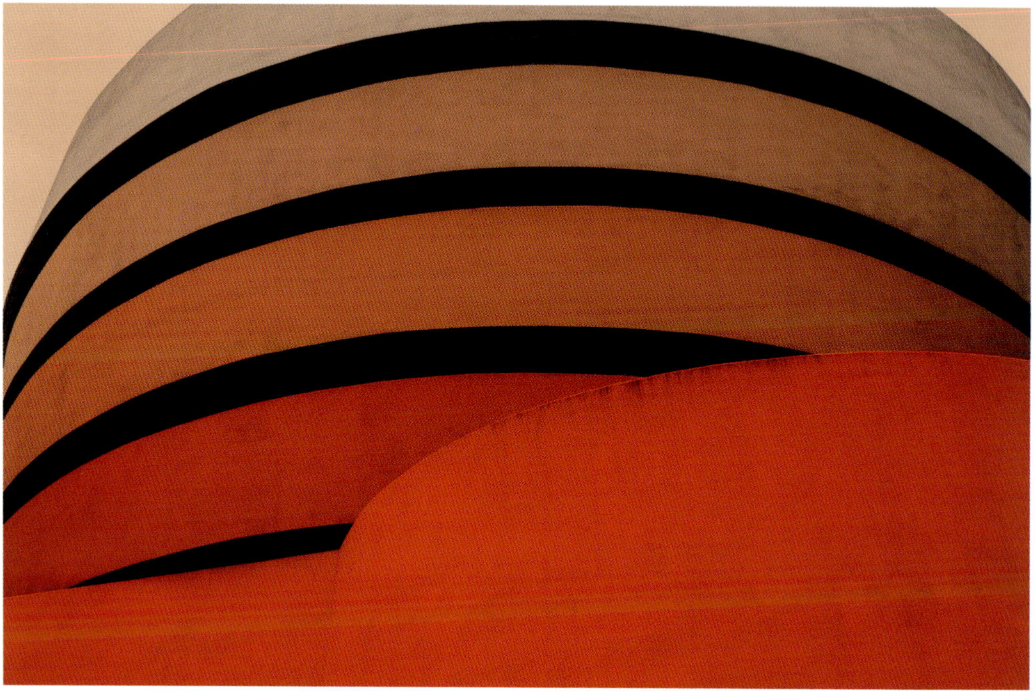

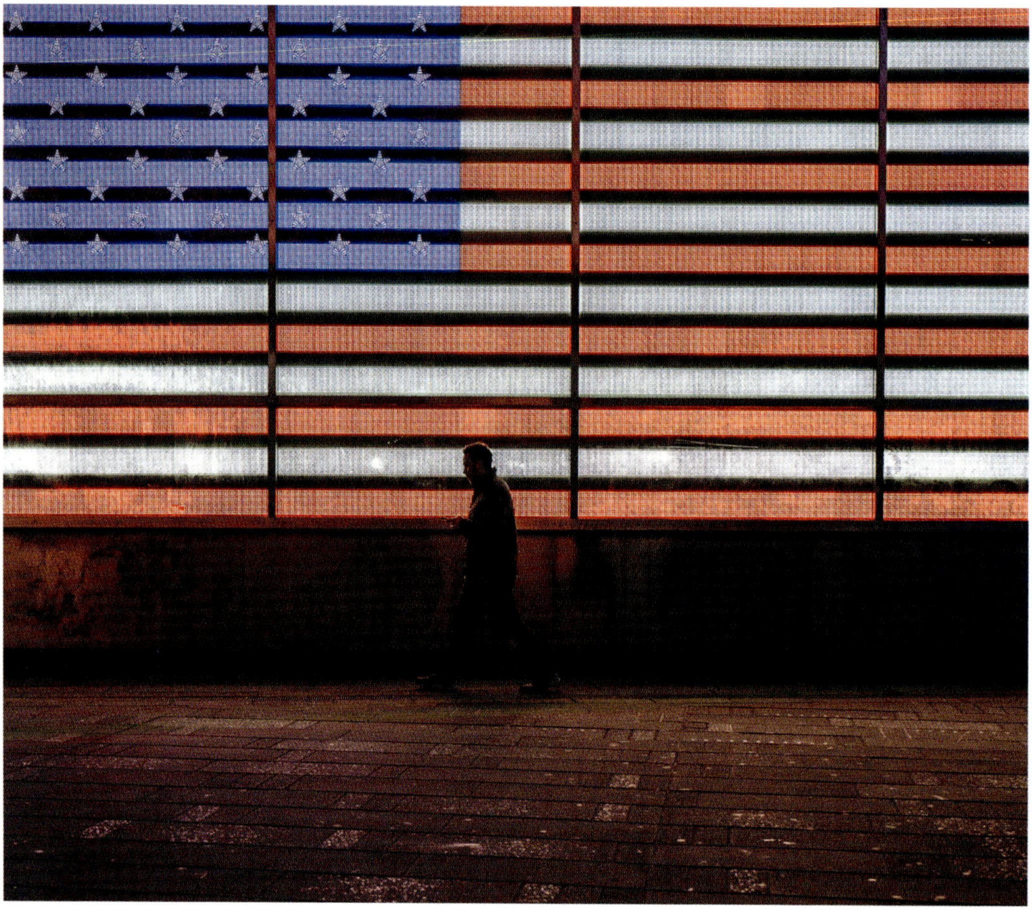

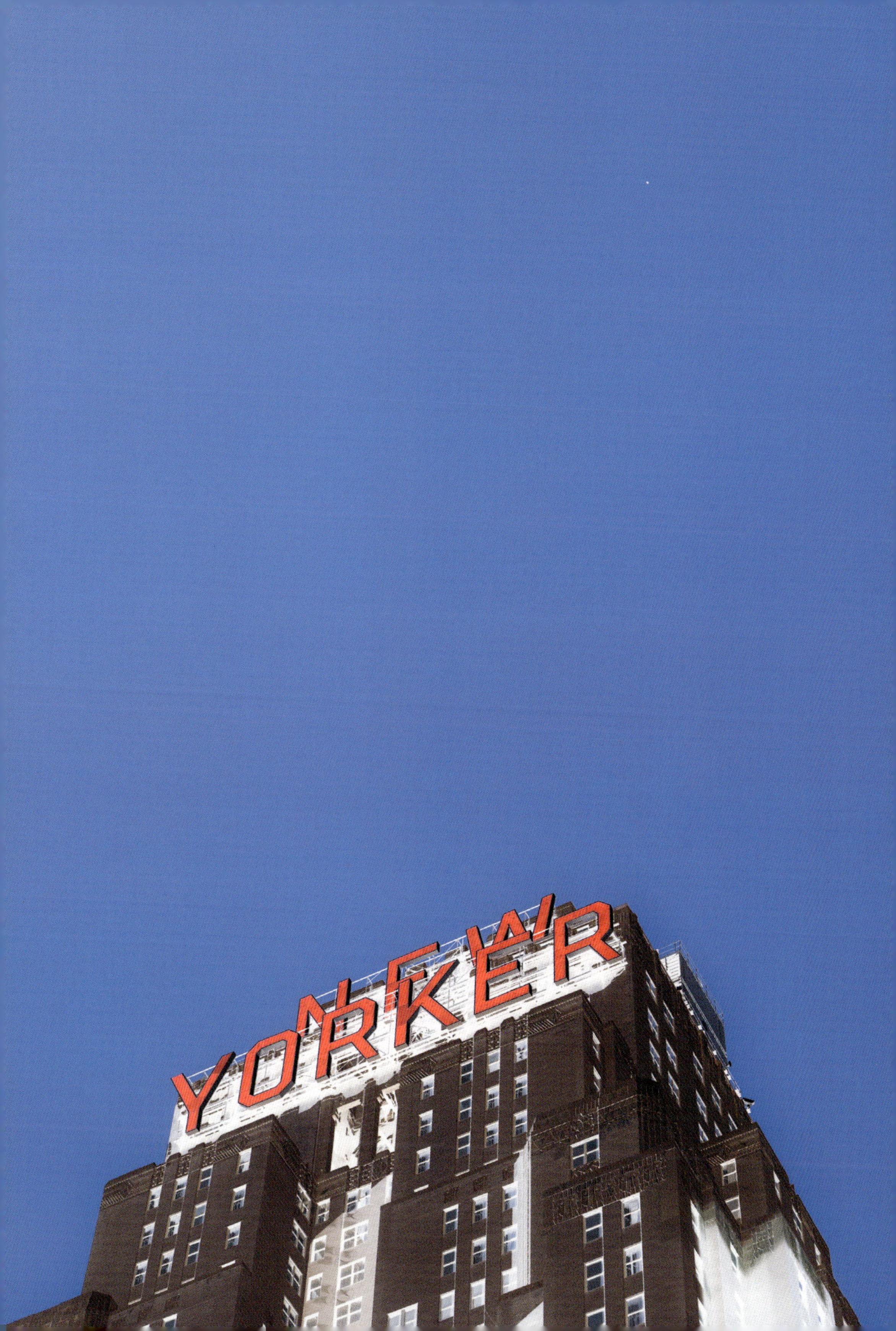
NEW
YORKER

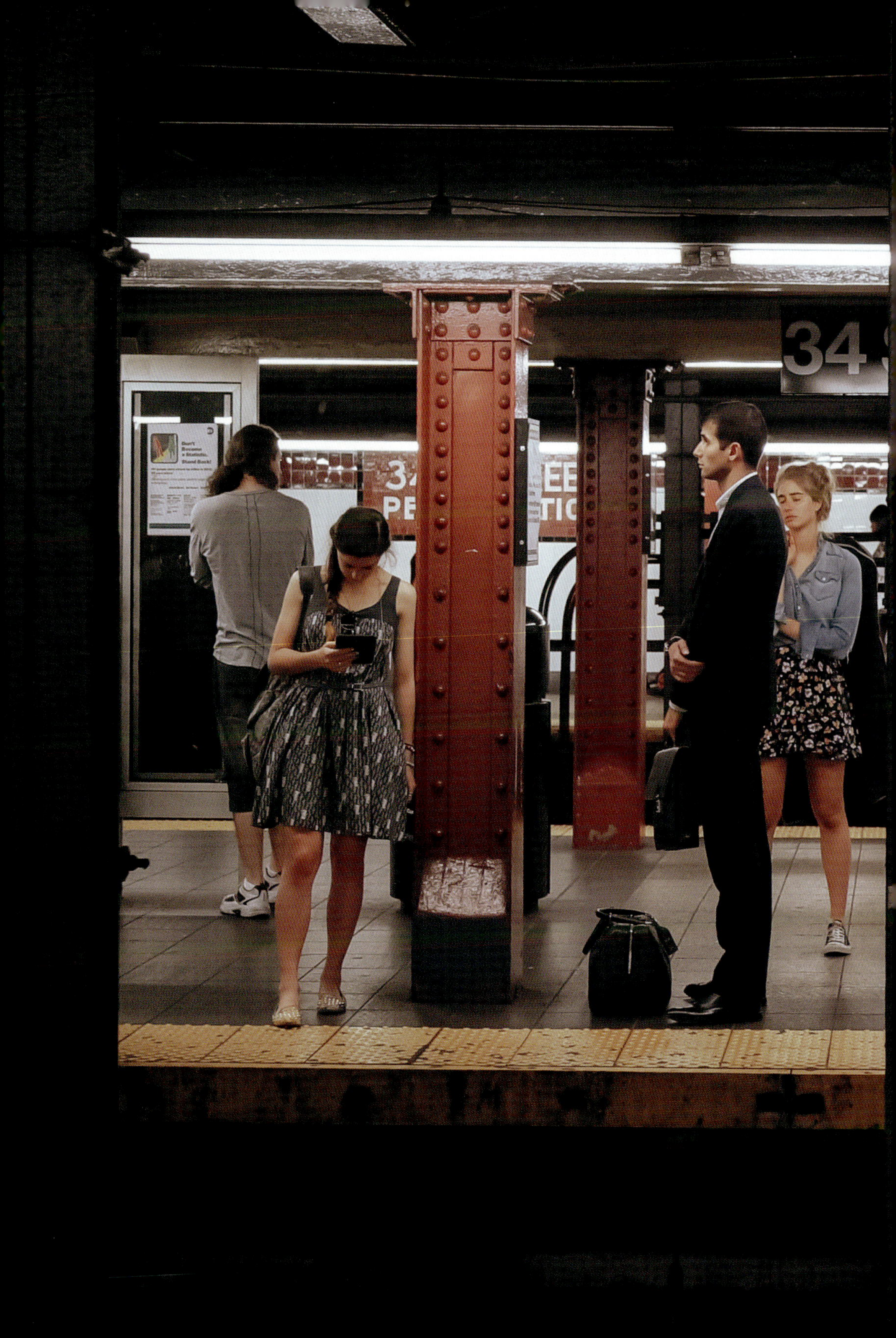
34

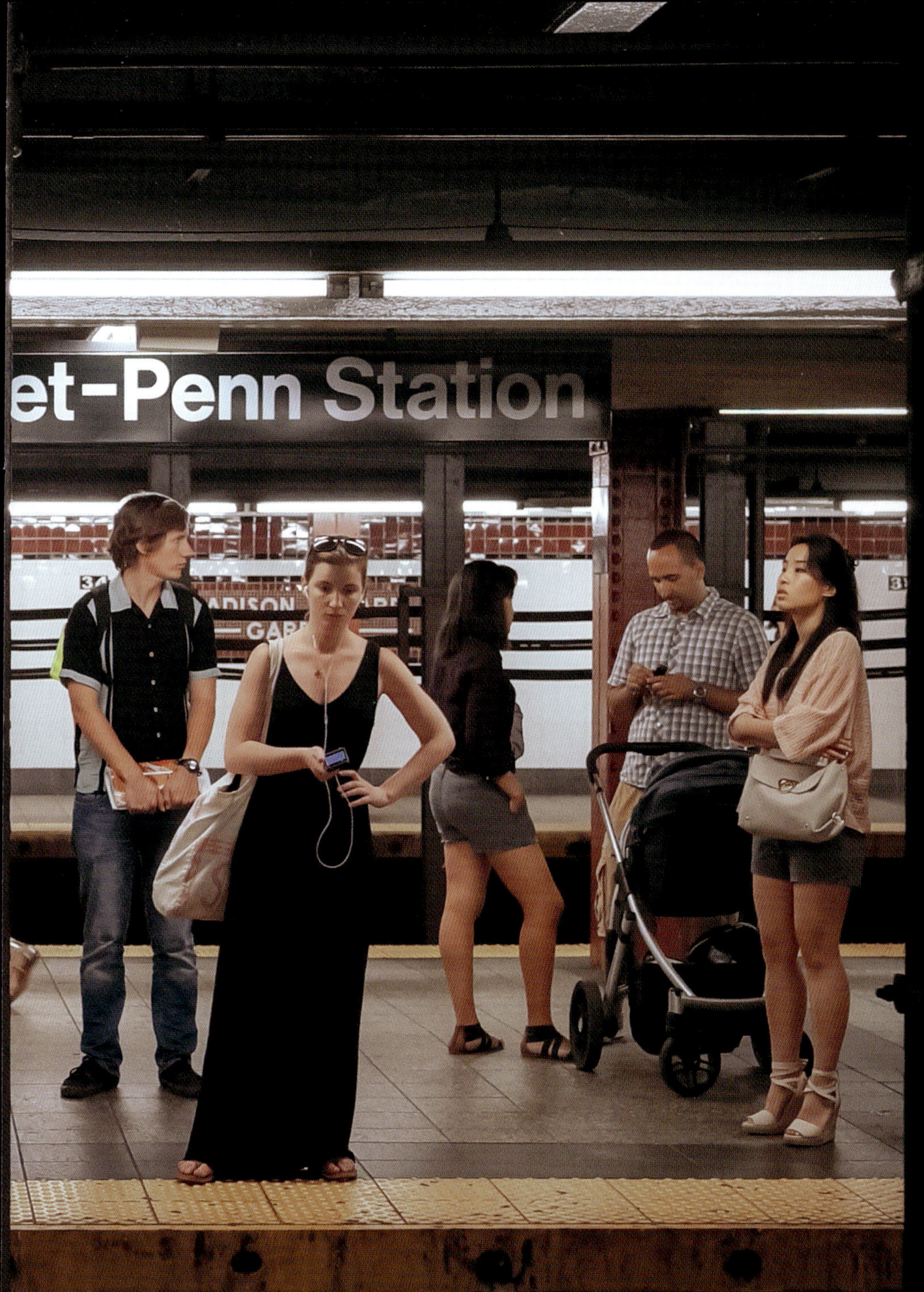
et–Penn Station

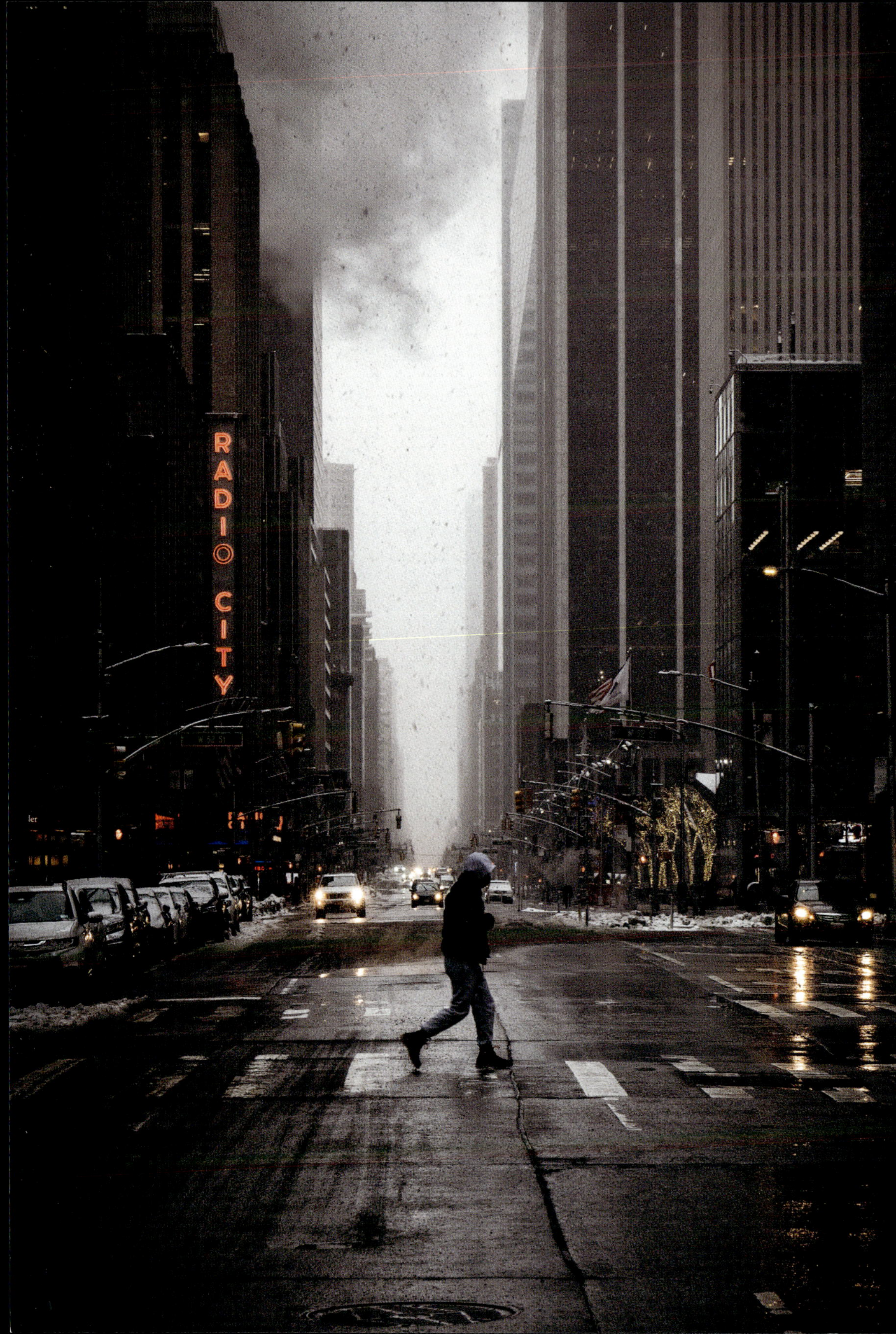
RADIO CITY

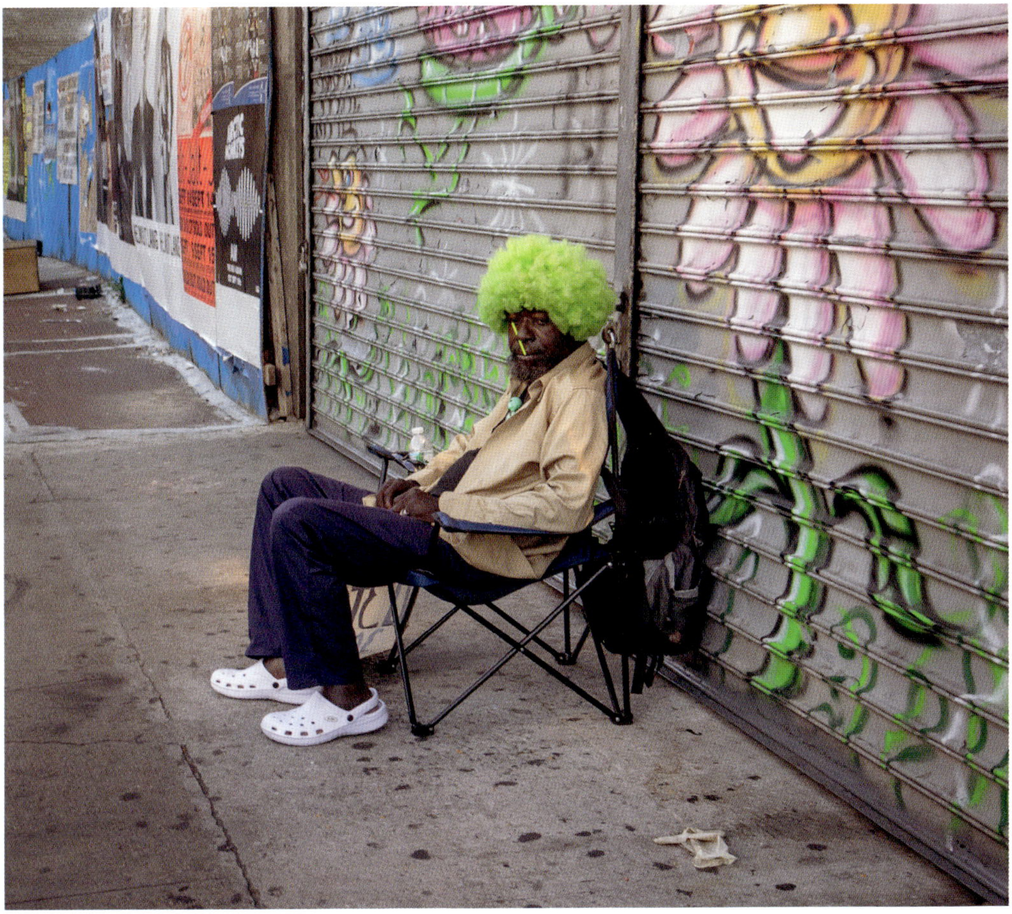

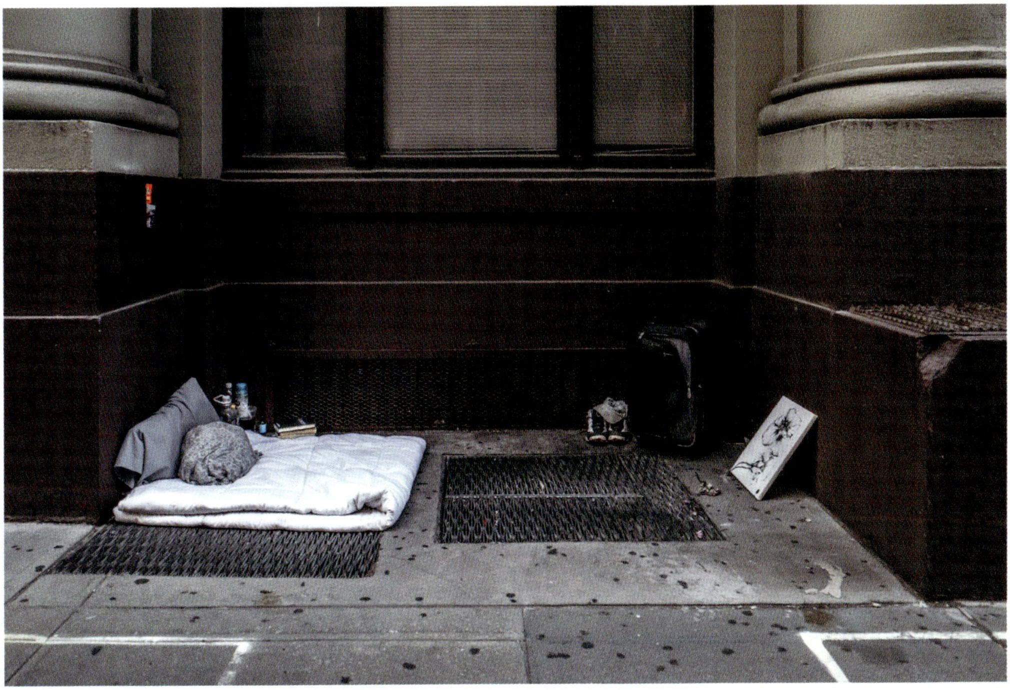

Viktor Timofeev

Viktor Timofeev (b. 1984, Riga, Latvia) is an artist based in New York City. Timofeev's multidisciplinary practice is informed by personal experiences, speculative imaginings, and everything in between. He hosts monthly events that include screenings, performances, and sensory deprivation listening sessions at No Moon, a project space in Brooklyn he co-founded in 2018. He has exhibited at the National Gallery, Prague (2022); 14th Baltic Triennial, Vilnius (2021); Ludwig Museum, Budapest (2020); Bozar, Brussels (2020); and the Latvian National Museum of Art, Riga (2020).

Viktor Timofeev's studio, New York, 2023

Photos: Anna Dave

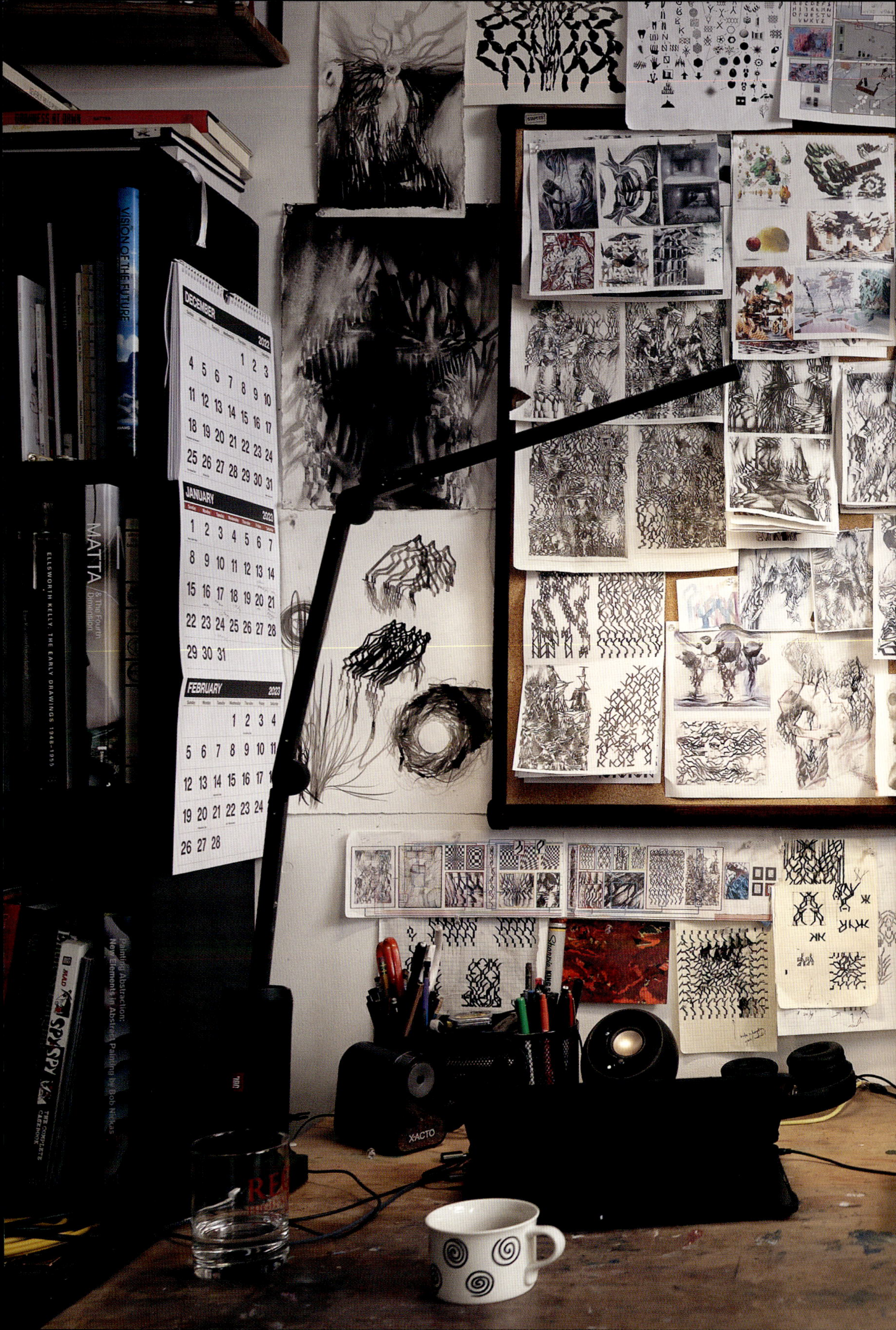
VISION OF THE FUTURE
DECEMBER 2022
JANUARY 2023
FEBRUARY 2023
MATTA
ELLSWORTH KELLY THE EARLY DRAWINGS 1948–1955
Painting Abstraction: New Elements in Abstract Painting by Bob Nickas
SPY VS SPY
X-ACTO

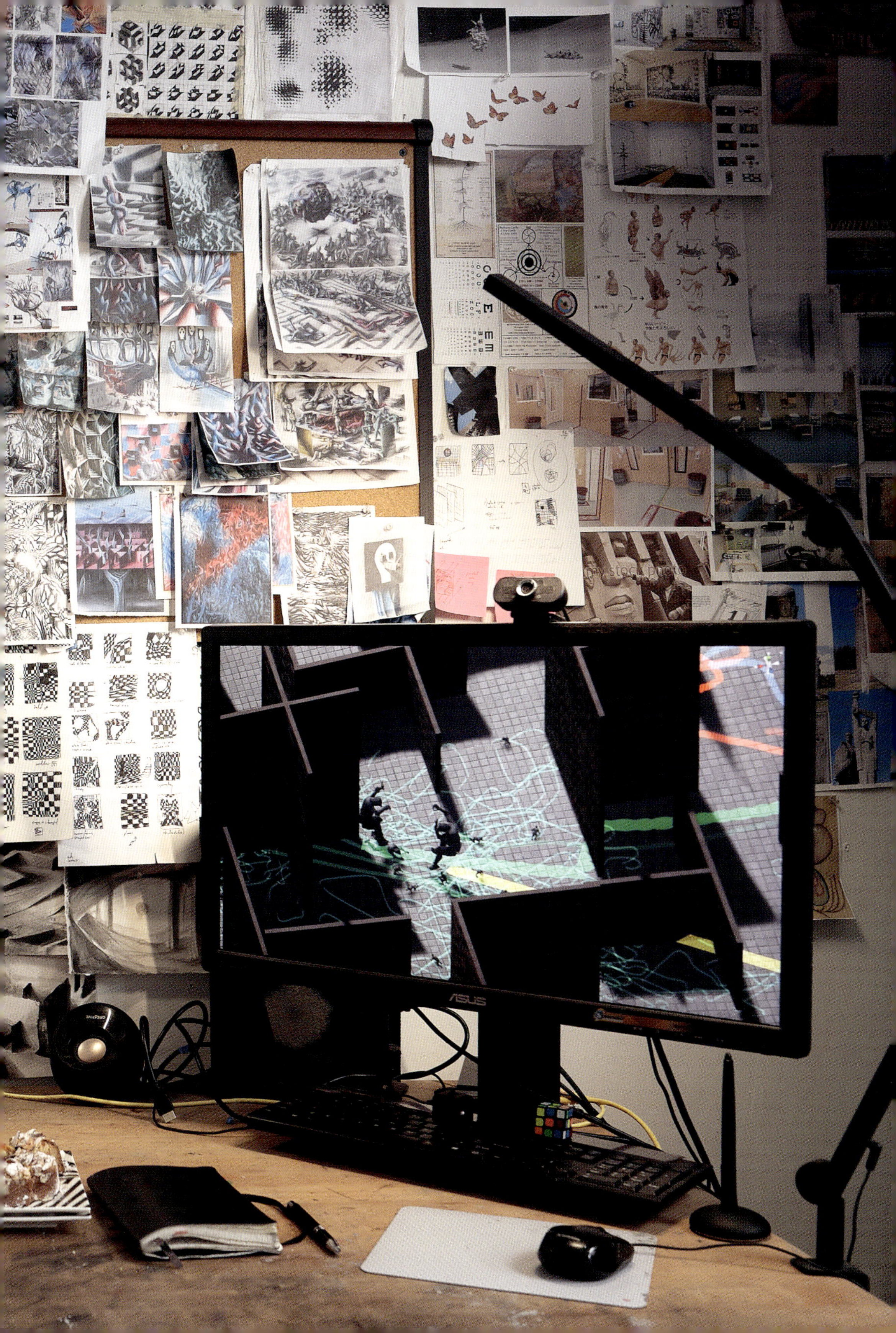

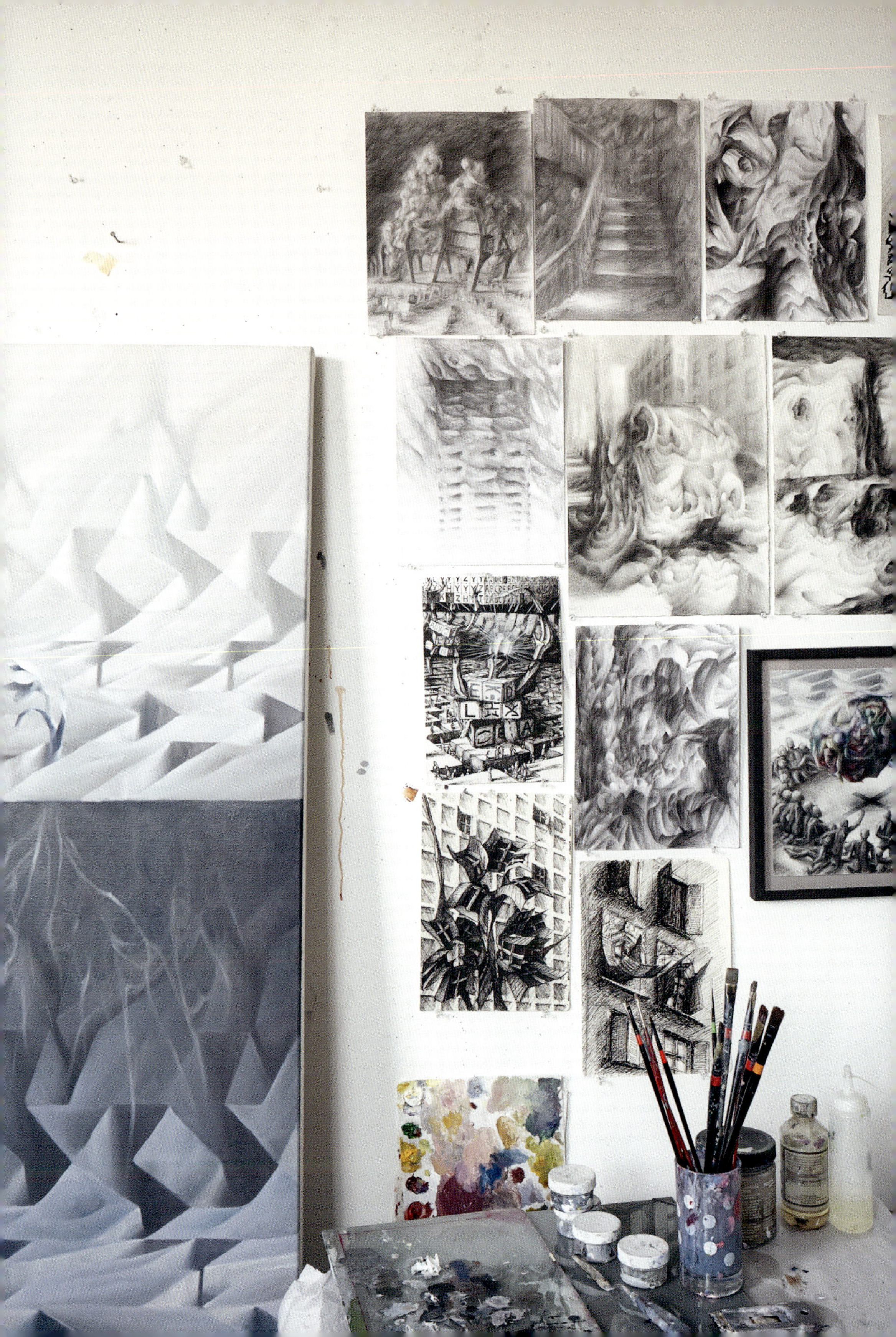

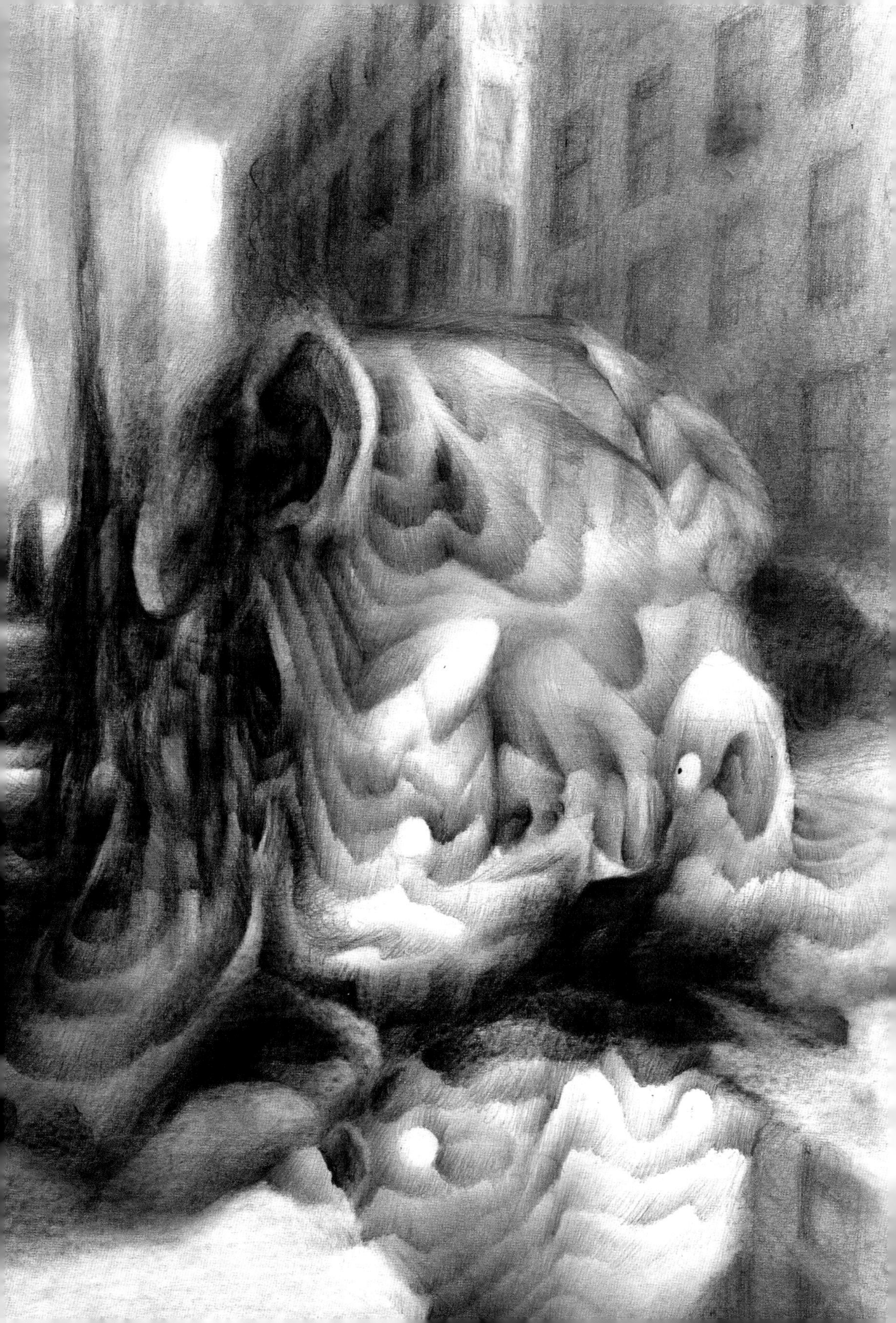

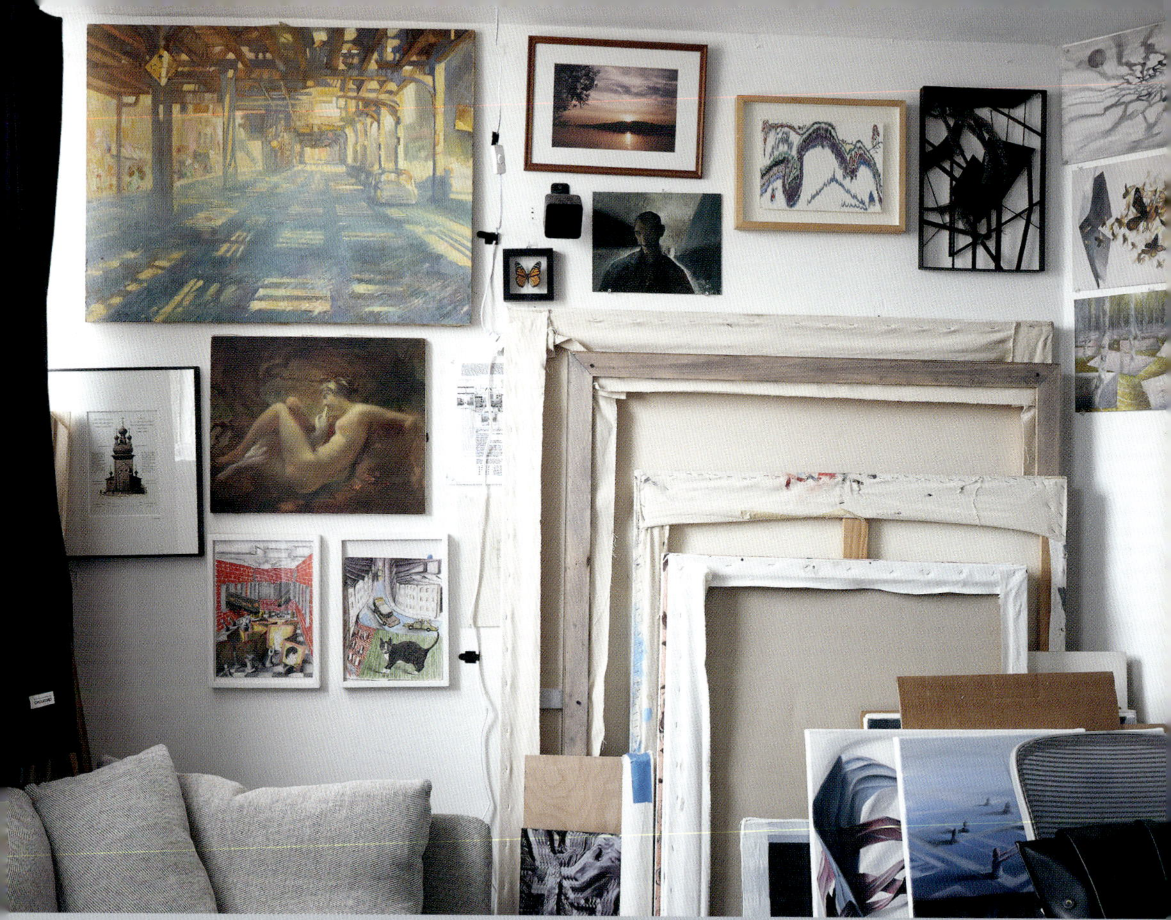

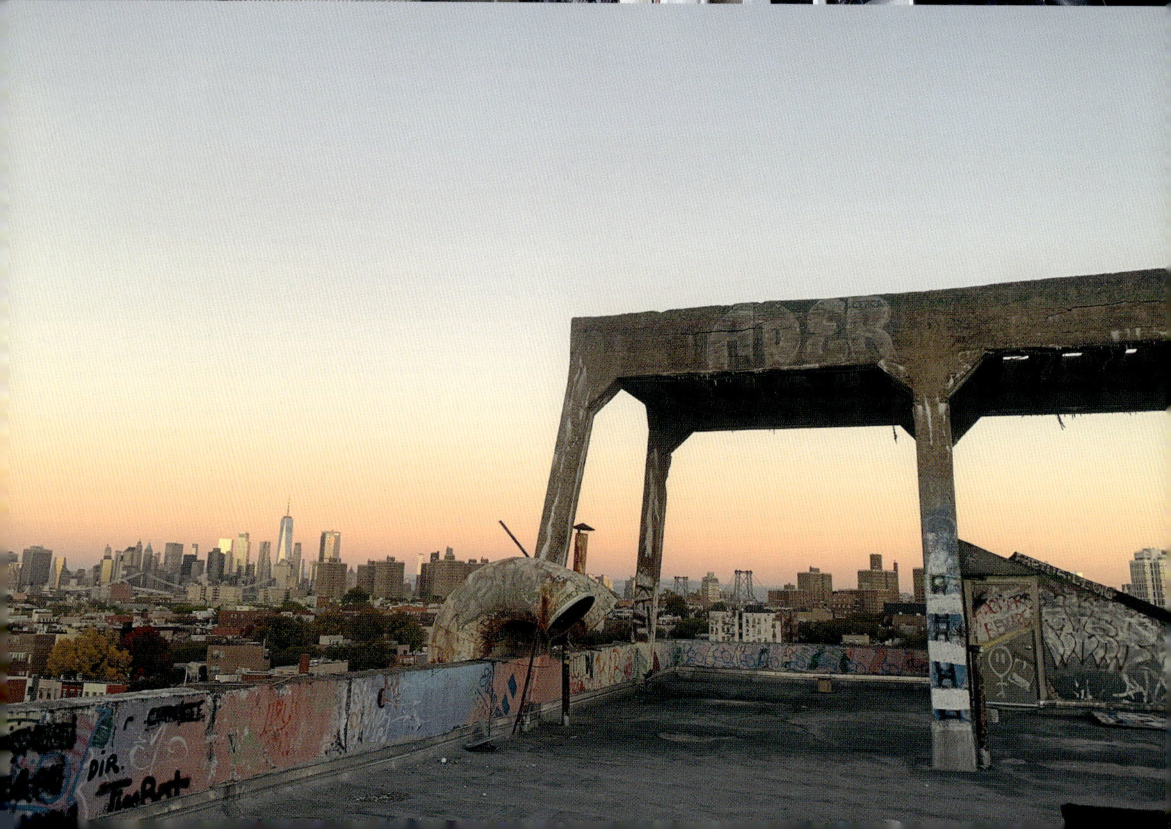

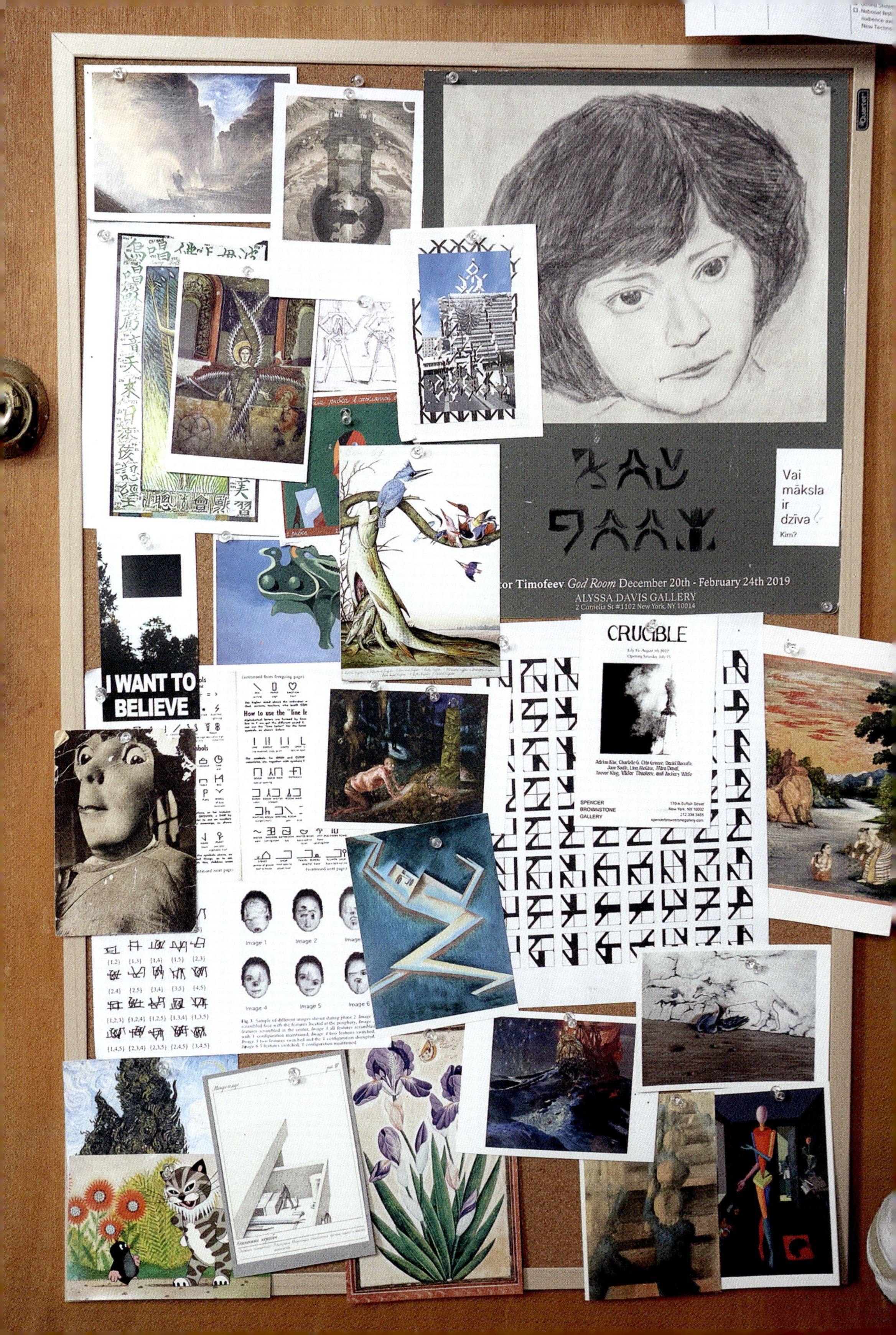

Vai māksla ir dzīva
Kim?
tor Timofeev God Room December 20th - February 24th 2019
ALYSSA DAVIS GALLERY
2 Cornelia St #1102 New York, NY 10014
I WANT TO BELIEVE
CRUCIBLE
SPENCER BROWNSTONE GALLERY

Ella Kruglyanskaya

Ella Kruglyanskaya (b. 1978, Riga, Latvia) lives and works in New York City. Kruglyanskaya was raised in Latvia, where she studied at the Jan Rosenthal Secondary Art School in Riga. After immigrating to the United States with her mother and grandmother in 1995, Kruglyanskaya attended the Cooper Union in New York City before completing her MFA at the Yale School of Art in 2006. Working as a freelance graphic designer until 2011, Kruglyanskaya references the myriad ways that visual culture has depicted modern womanhood, celebrating and exploring the complexities of female identity and experience. Her figures exude a sense of power and confidence, while also conveying a range of emotions, from joy and pleasure to vulnerability and defiance. Her work often references popular culture and art history but reinterprets these influences through a contemporary feminist lens. Blurring hierarchies between drawing and painting, Kruglyanskaya's work simultaneously recalls vanitas still lifes and the walls of her studio, employing trompe l'oeil to juxtapose torn paper edges and dirty paintbrushes against lurid plaids and gestural illustrations of her protagonists. Recent solo exhibitions include Bortolami, New York (2021); Thomas Dane Gallery, London (2020); Feuilleton (2020), Los Angeles; and Real Pain (2020), Los Angeles.

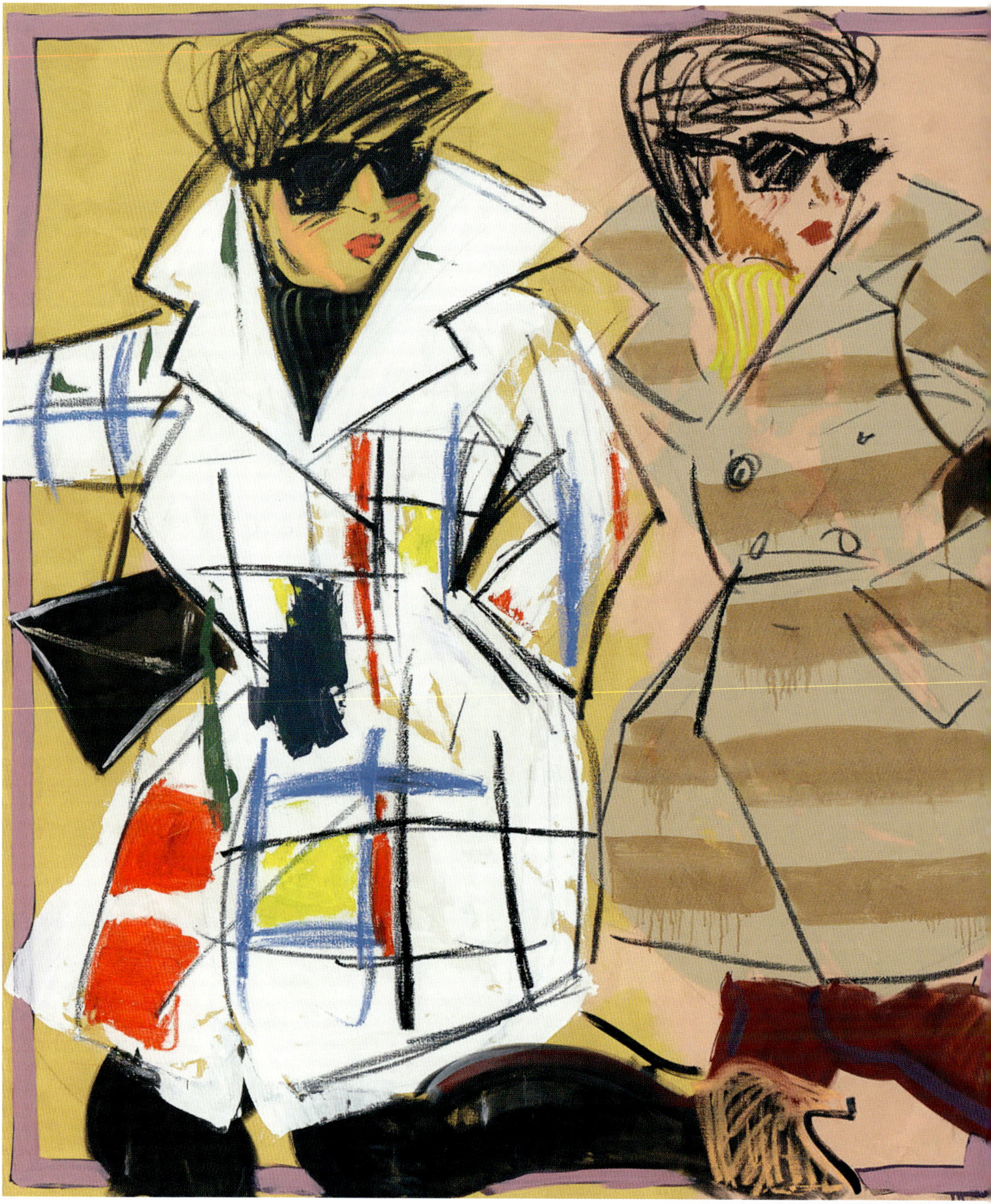

Entrenched, 2020
Oil, oil stick, and graphite on linen, 213.4 x 187.9 cm

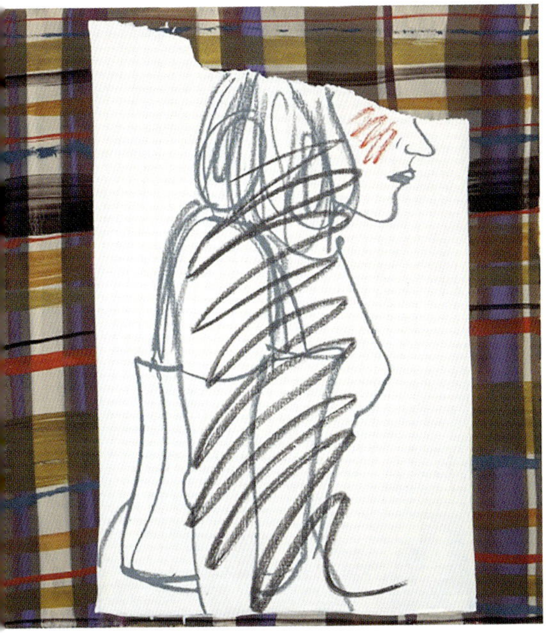

Burden in Plaid (Groceries), 2021
Oil on linen, 97 × 86 cm

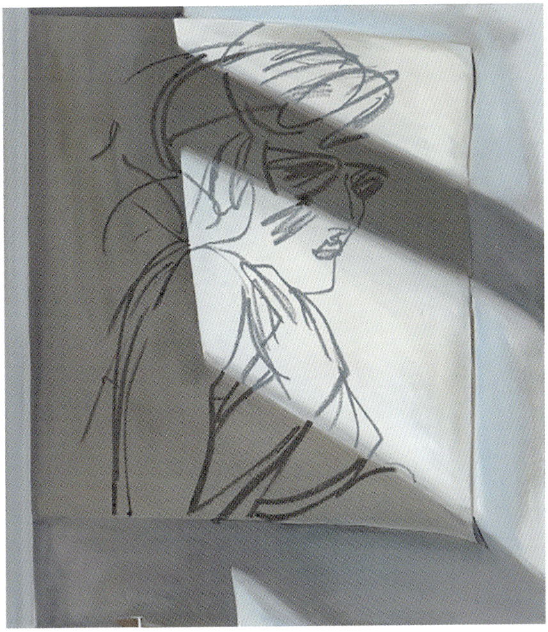

Grey Light, 2021
Oil on linen, 97 × 86 cm

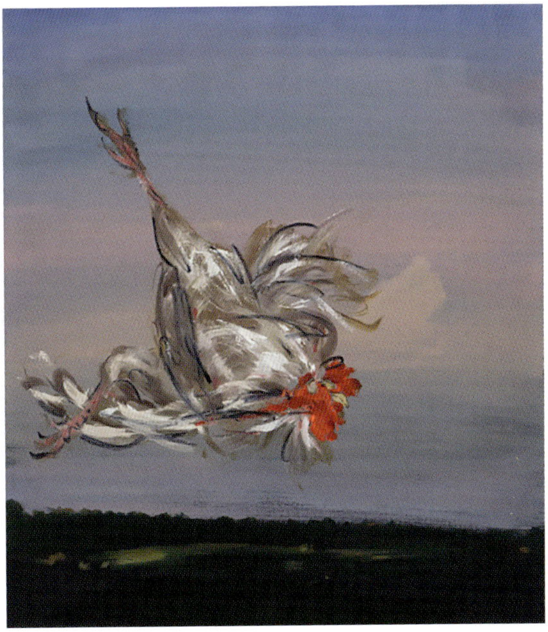

Untitled (Last Flight), 2021
Oil on linen, 97 × 86 cm

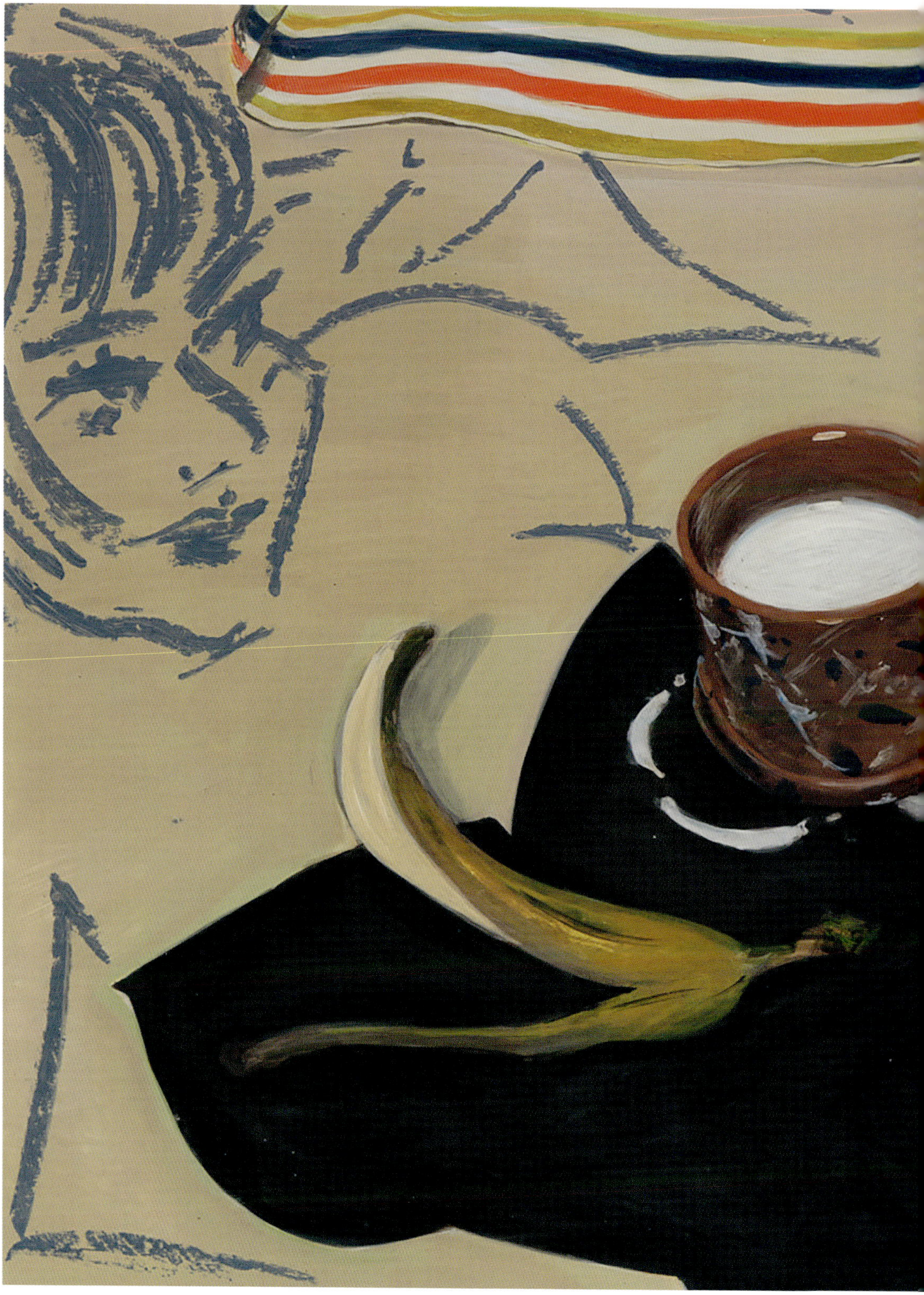

Lemon, Peel, Milk, 2019
Tempera and oil stick on panel, 50.2 x 65.1 cm

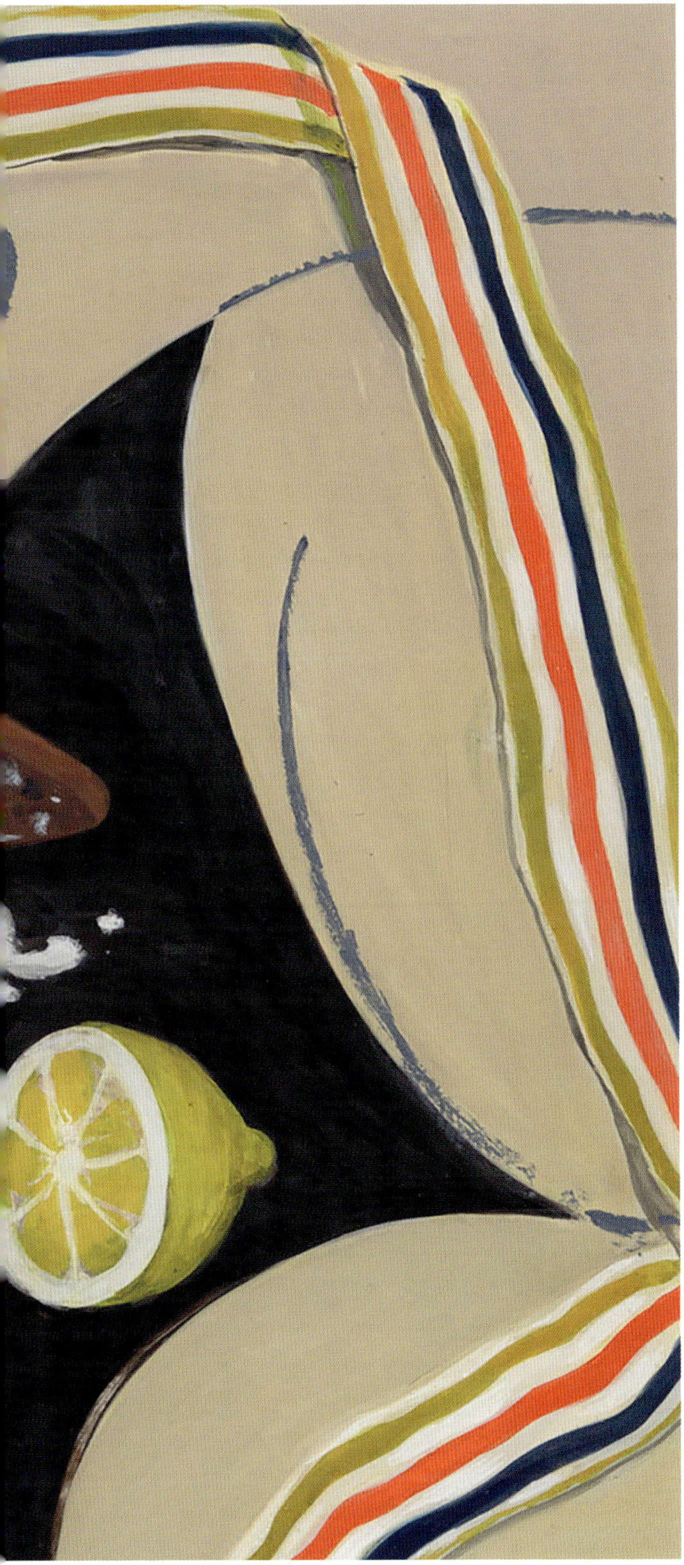

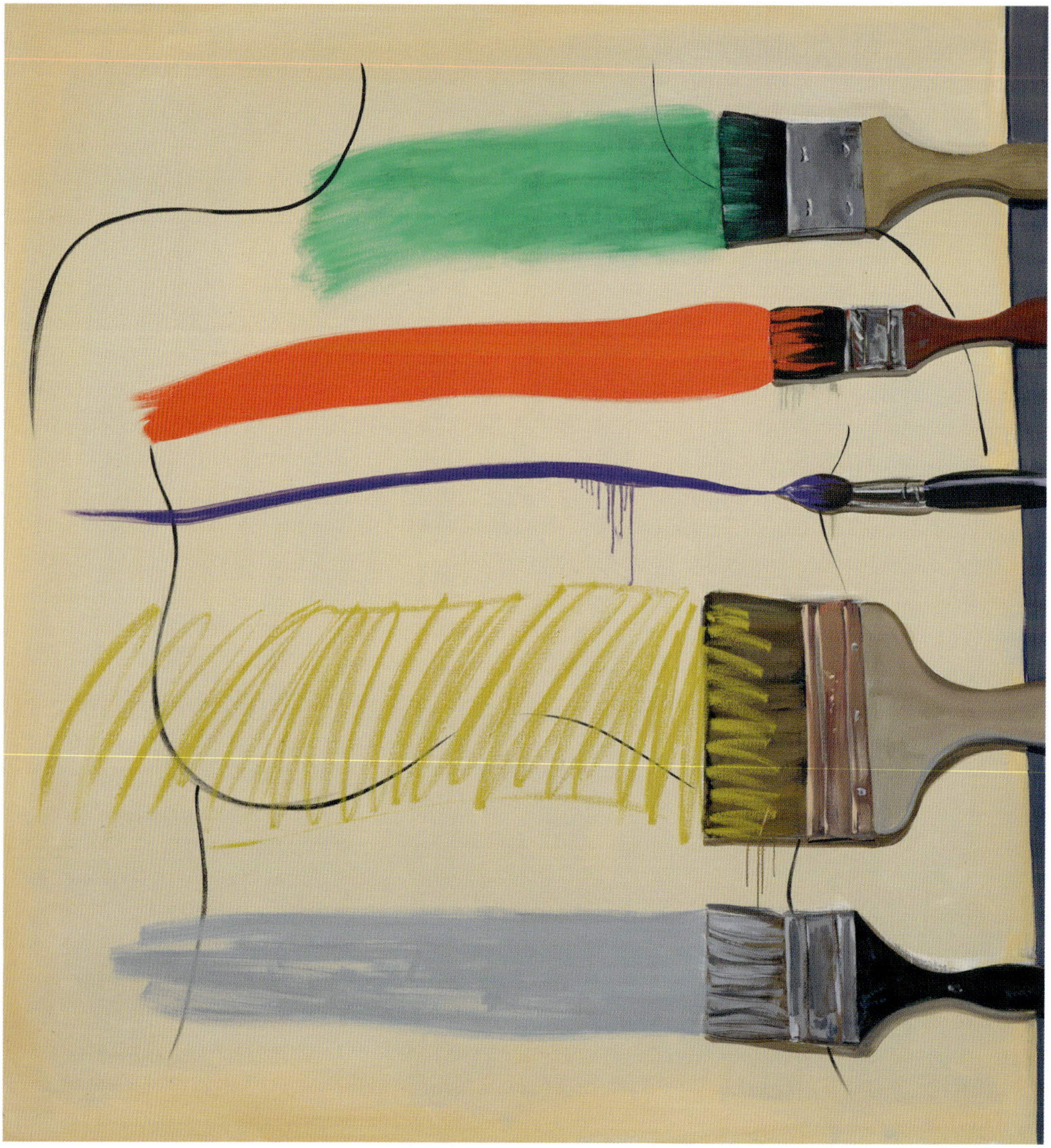

Good Intentions, 2021
Oil on linen, 167.6 x 157.5 cm
Courtesy the artist and Bortolami Gallery, New York

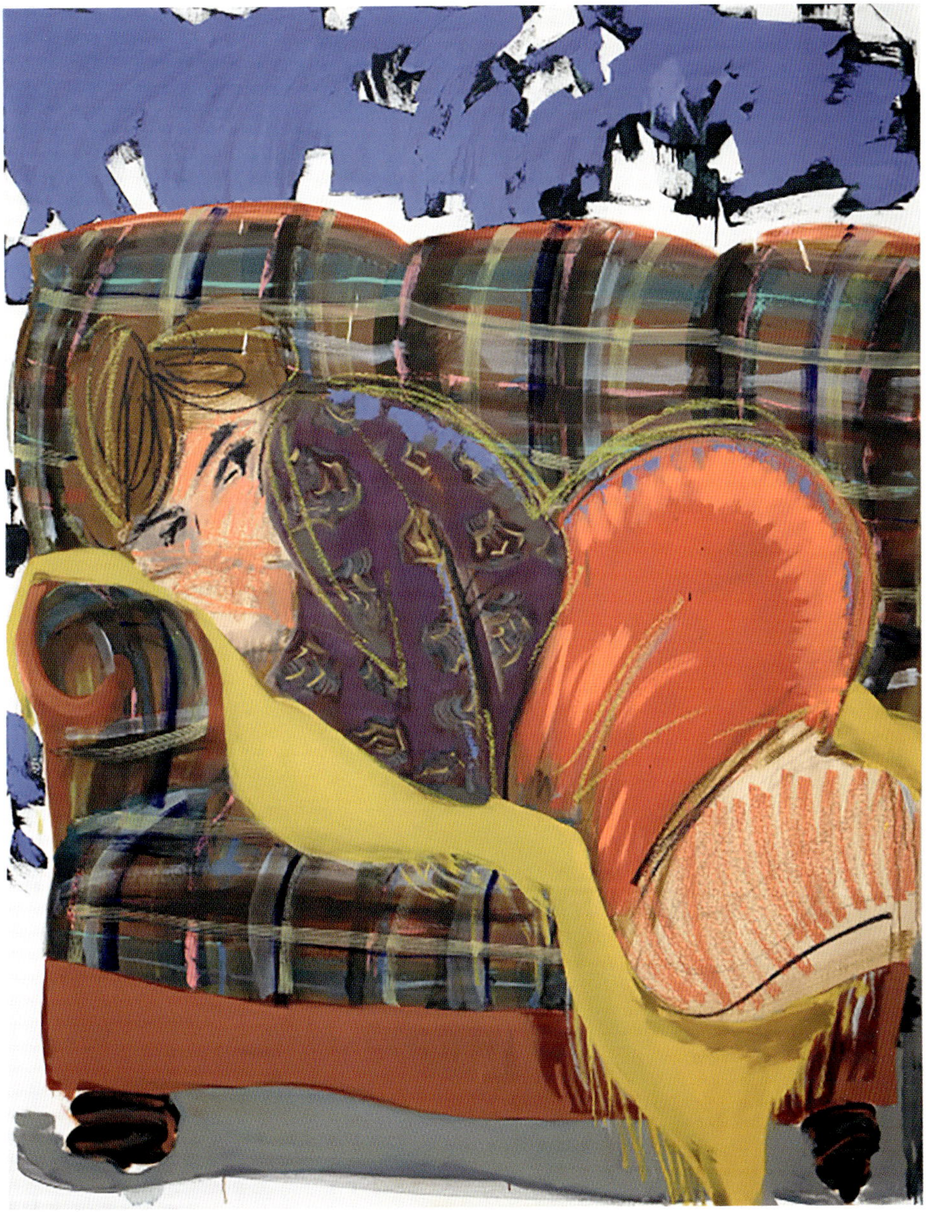

The Nap, 2021
Oil on linen, 208 × 163 cm

Daiga Grantiņa

Daiga Grantiņa (b. 1985, Saldus, Latvia) lives and works in Paris. Grantiņa's sculptures investigate the encounters between materials and their consequent relationships of dissonance and consonance, inducing an exercise in expanded vision. Her material gestures resonate with the structural shifts of organisms and environments, navigating relations of volume and form at the point where microscopic and macroscopic overlap and intersect. Her abstract vocabulary borrows from bodies and landscapes to explore indescribable matter, a plastic investigation of the formless and misshapen. Intuitively concocted forms self-consume and self-produce, at once a continuous development of a shared idea and a space of tension where the hierarchies of perception find themselves rearranged. An exhibition of Grantiņa's work will be held at Kunstmuseum Bern in 2024.

Word-colour-notes, February 2023
Ink and pencil on paper, 22.5 x 15 cm

Photos: Daiga Grantiņa's Studio

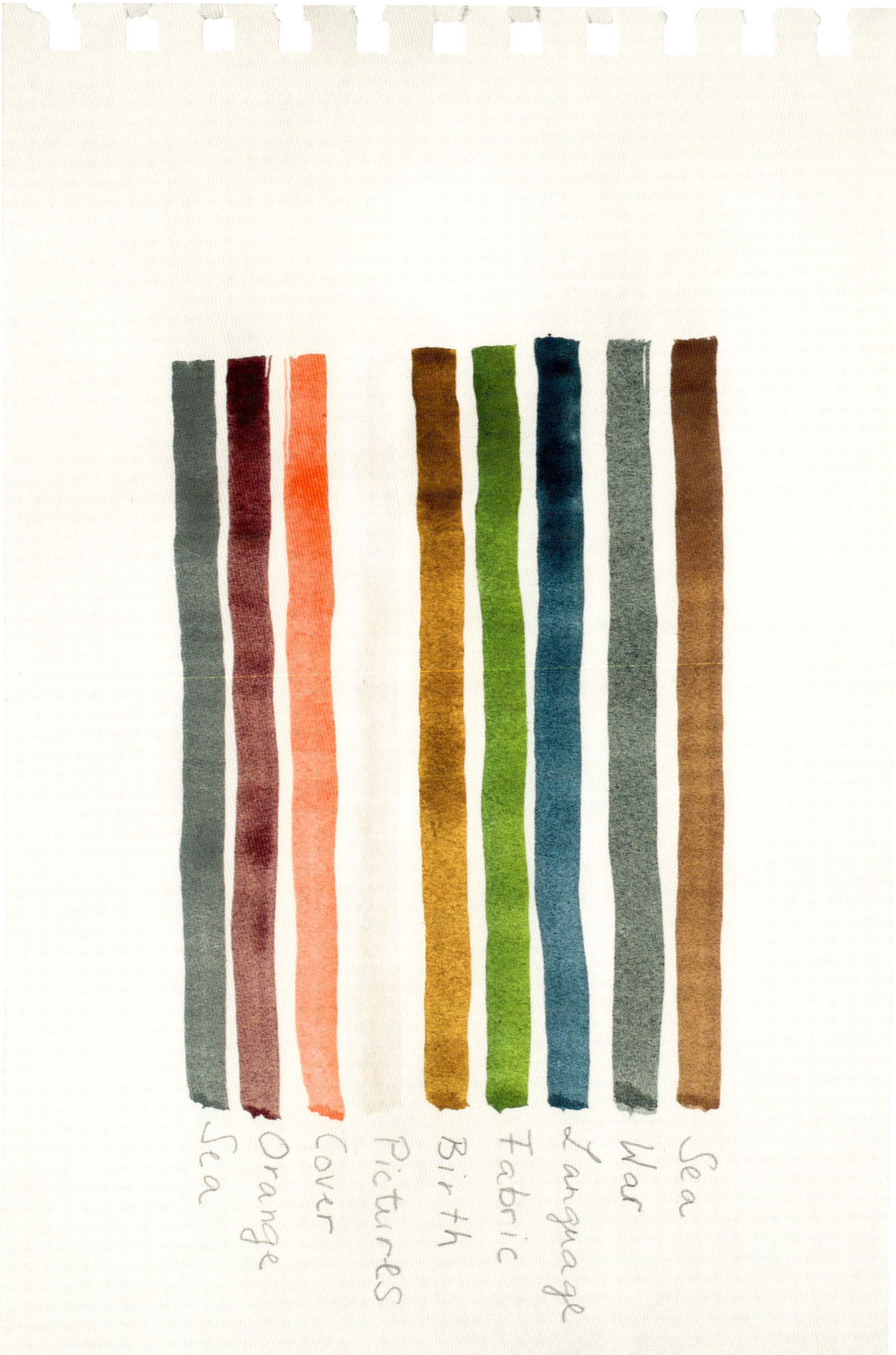
Sea
Orange
Cover
Pictures
Birth
Fabric
Language
War
Sea

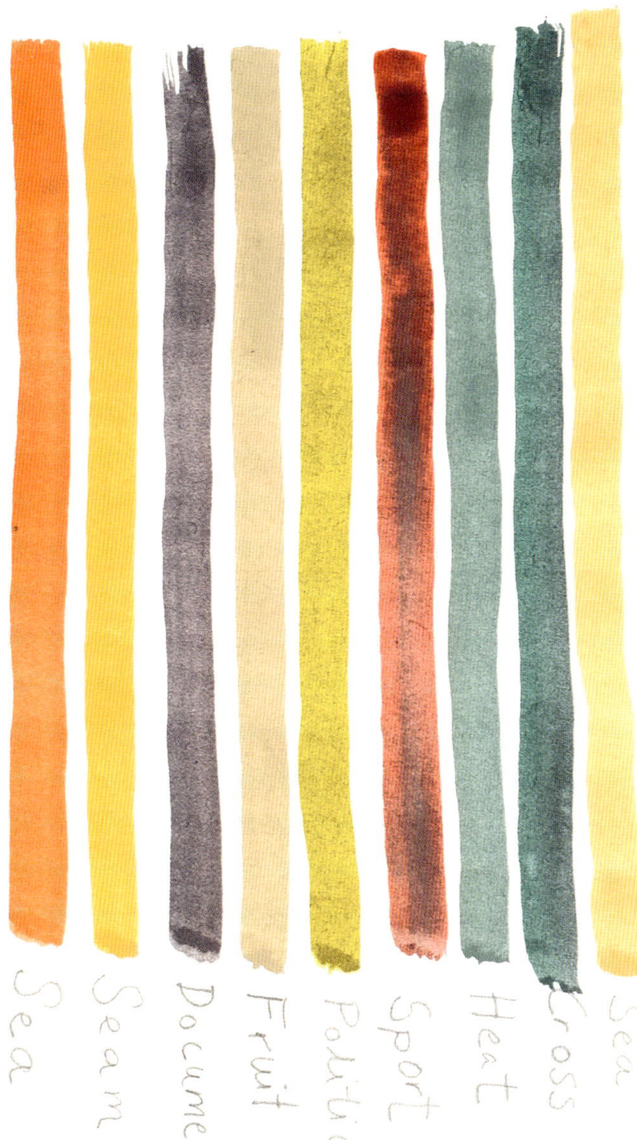
Sea
Seam
Document
Fruit
Politics
Sport
Heat
Cross
Sea

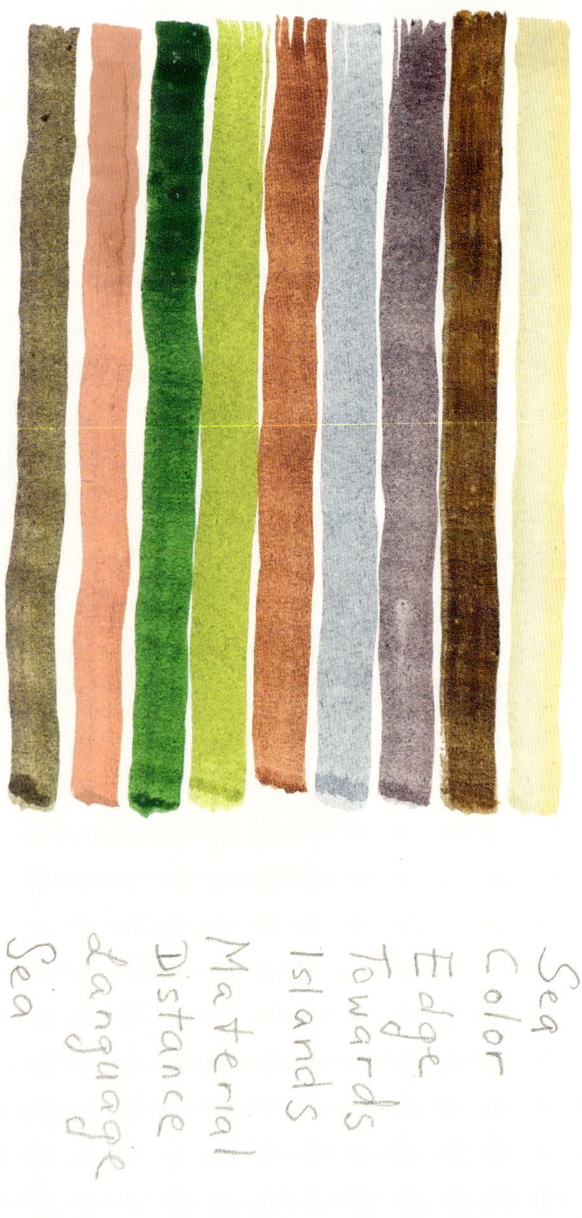
Sea
Color
Edge
Towards
Islands
Material
Distance
Language
Sea

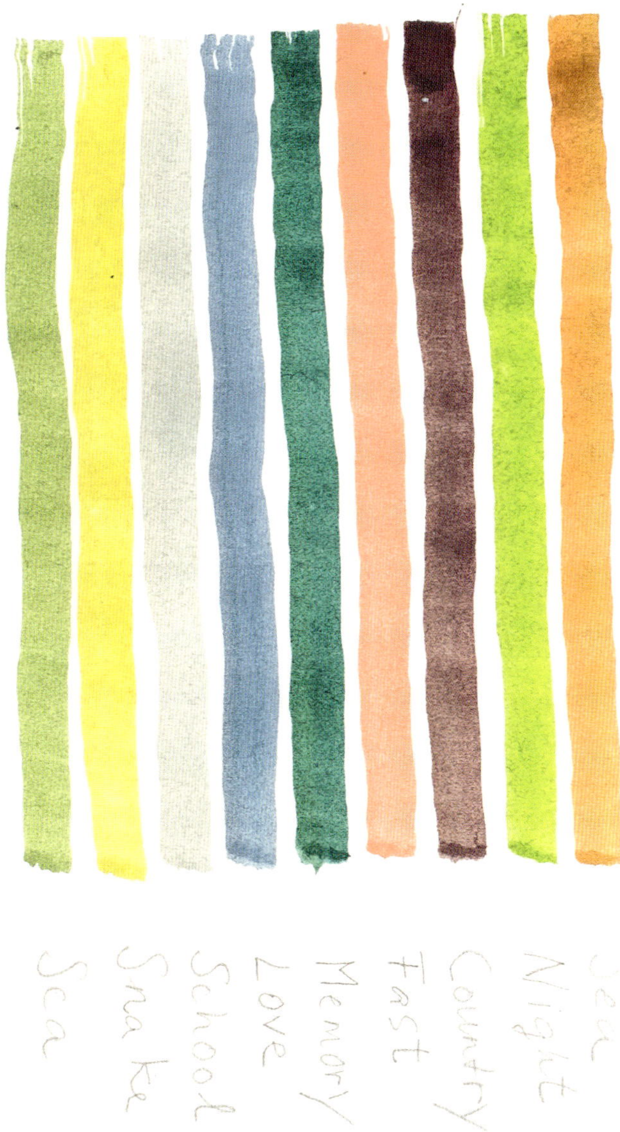
Sea
Night
Country
Fast
Memory
Love
School
Snake
Sea

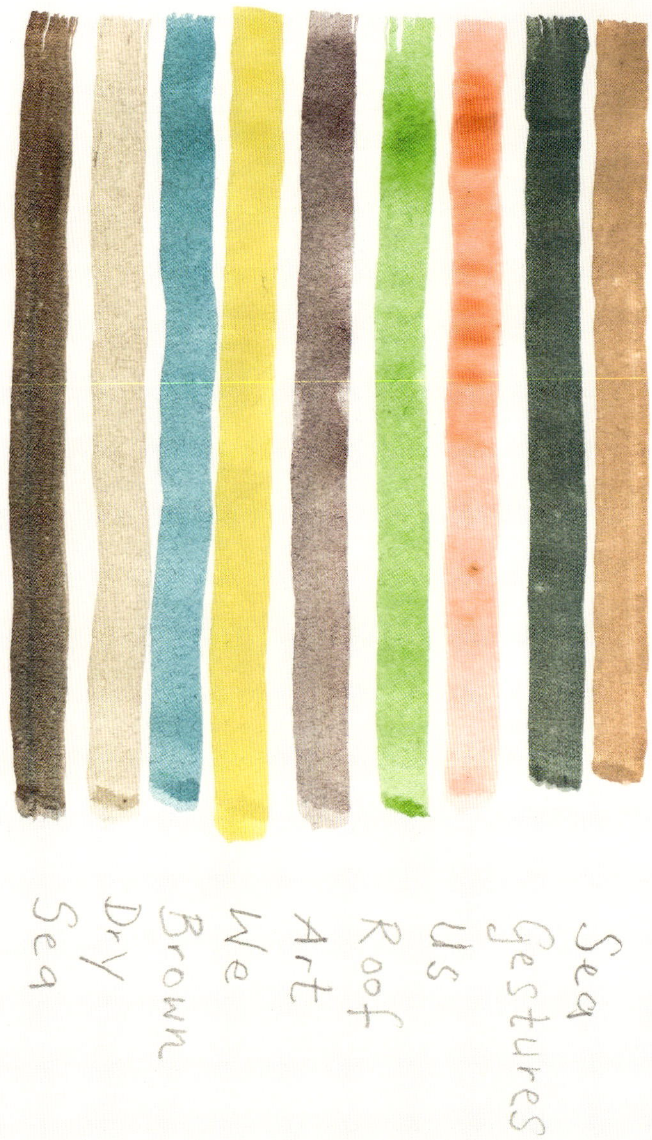
Sea
Gestures
Us
Roof
Art
We
Brown
Dry
Sea

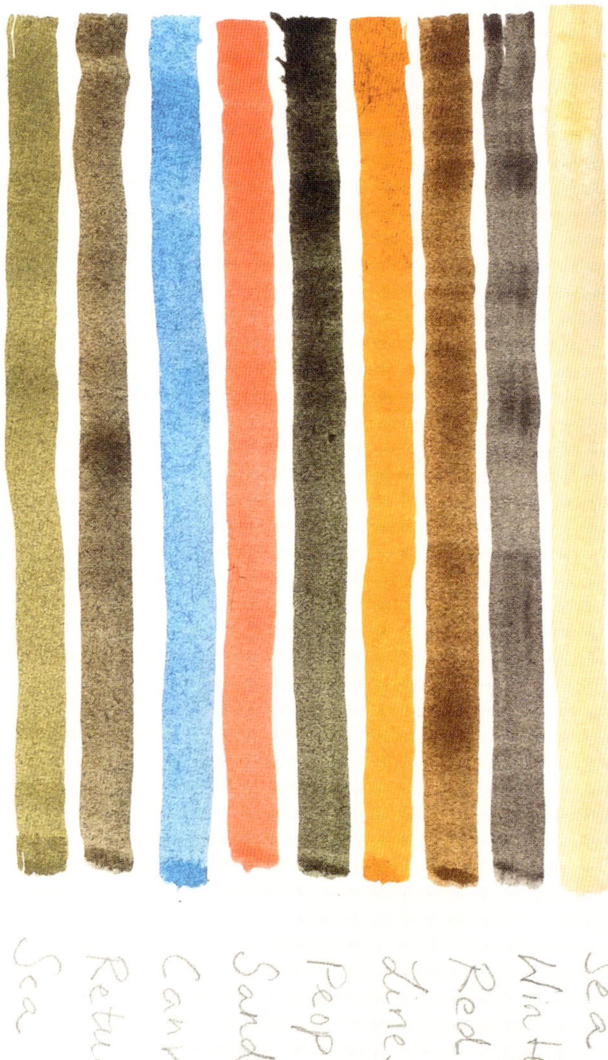
Sea
Winter
Red
Lines
People
Sand
Canvas
Return
Sea

Ingel Vaikla

Ingel Vaikla (b. 1992, Tallinn, Estonia) is a visual artist and a filmmaker based in Brussels who works primarily with video, 16 mm film, and found footage. Vaikla's artistic practice focuses on representation of architecture as a storyteller and on the relationship between urban space and its communities. She is on a constant search for visual language that would not simply observe architecture as an aesthetic sculptural form but would translate the existential, conceptual, and ideological qualities spaces manifest. She believes spaces do not only provide shelter but often become the concrete extension of our imagined identities and fluid bodies. Ingel is a former artist in residence at Higher Institute of Fine Arts (HISK), Ghent (2018–2019), Wiels Contemporary Art Centre, Brussels (2021), and is currently a PhD researcher at PXL-MAD School of Arts, Hasselt. Her works *Papagalo, what's the Time?* (2022), *EUR42* (2022), *Double Exposure* (2020), *Roosenberg* (2017), and *The House Guard* (2015), have been screened internationally at film festivals and art institutions such as International Documentary Film Festival, Amsterdam; Kunsthalle Wien; Contemporary Art Museum of Estonia (EKKM) (Tallinn); Beursschouwburg (Brussels); Manifesta 13 (Marseille); Videonale (Bonn); Tramway (Glasgow); European Media Art Festival (Osnabrück); and the Busan International Video Art Festival; among others.

Esposizione Universale Roma, EUR, Italy, 2020
Yugoslavia Pavilion Expo 1958, Wevelgem, Belgium, 2021
Slavutych, Ukraine, 2019

EUR

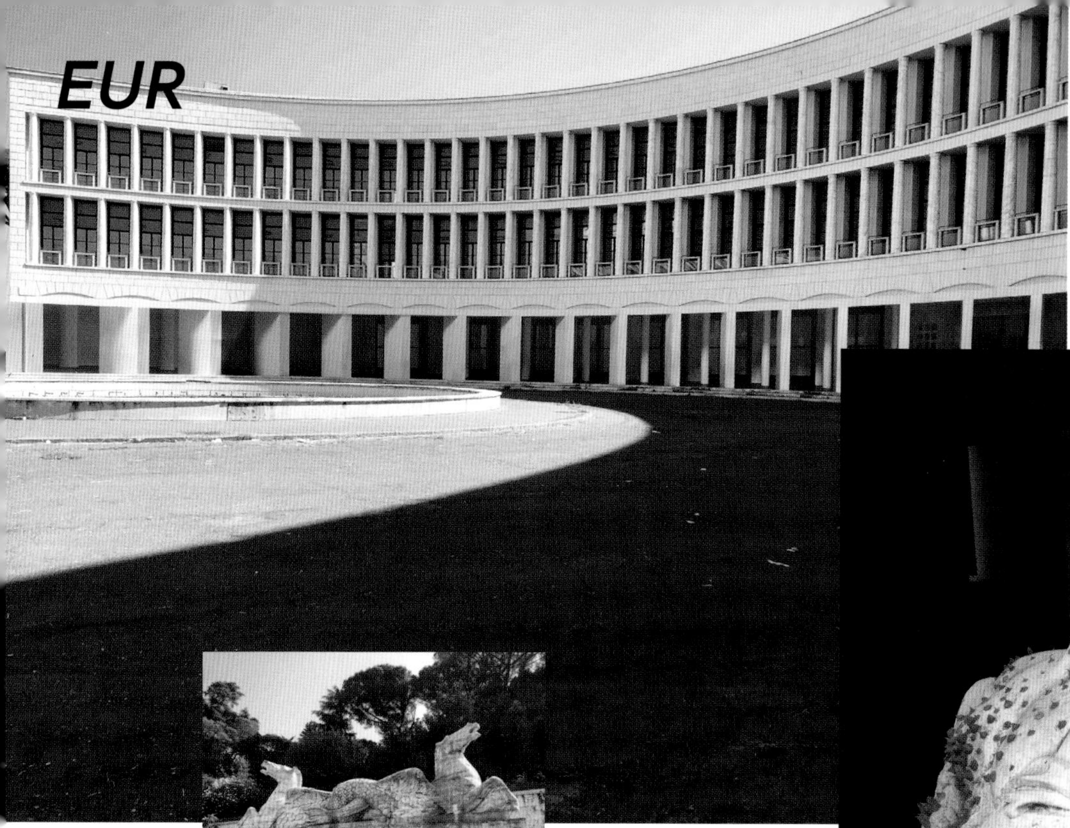

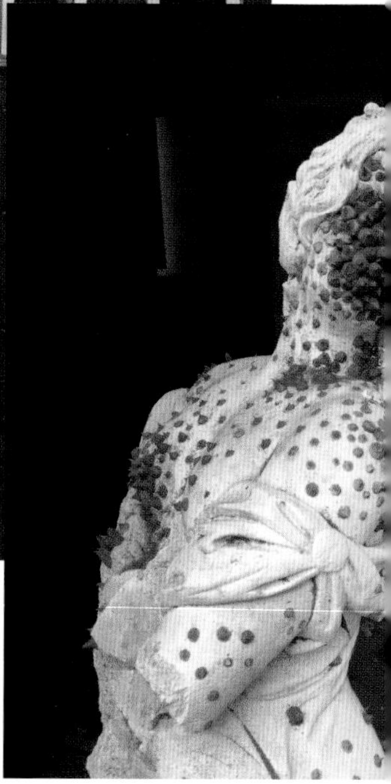

"Toute la mémoire du monde" Resnais
who is entitled to tell the history?
scream in space
Caro Diario, Moretti
Antonioni

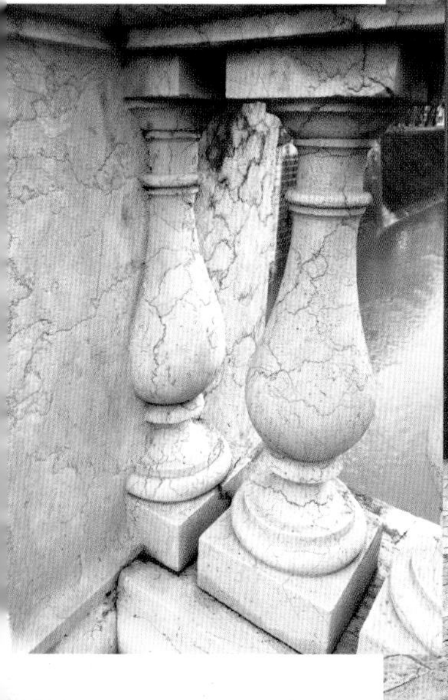

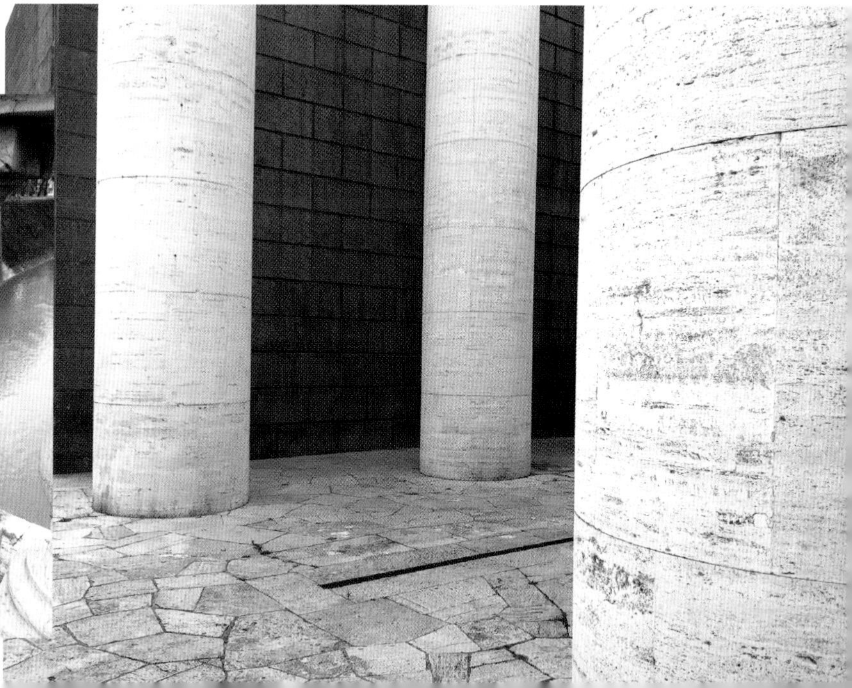

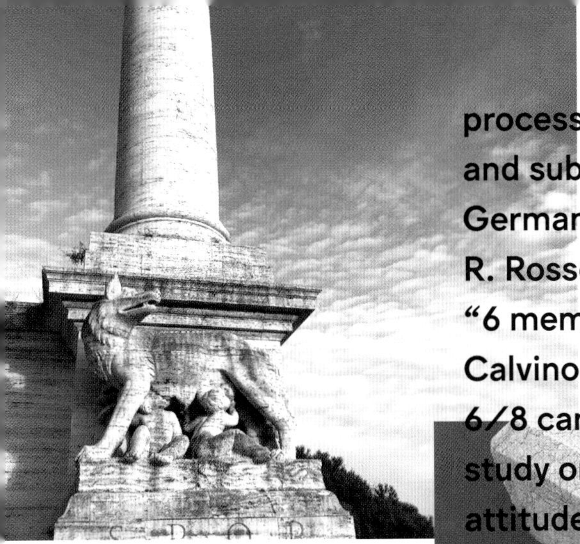

process and relations rather than object and subject
Germania anno zero
R. Rosselini (1945-46)
“6 memos for the next millennium”
Calvino
6/8 camera

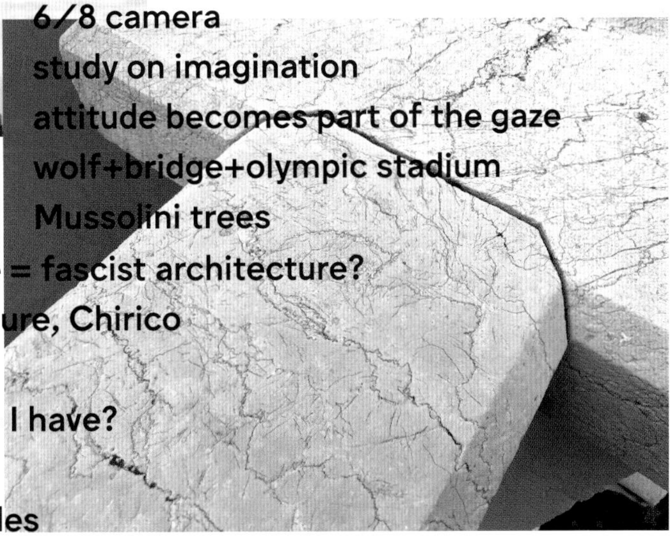

study on imagination
attitude becomes part of the gaze
wolf+bridge+olympic stadium
Mussolini trees

Aldo Rossi
Tresigallo
rationalist architecture = fascist architecture?
metaphysical architecture, Chirico
sogni
what do I see? what do I have?
Fellini; Roma
1. route with motorcycles
2. route from the motorcycles
3. details
4. shadows falling on buildings

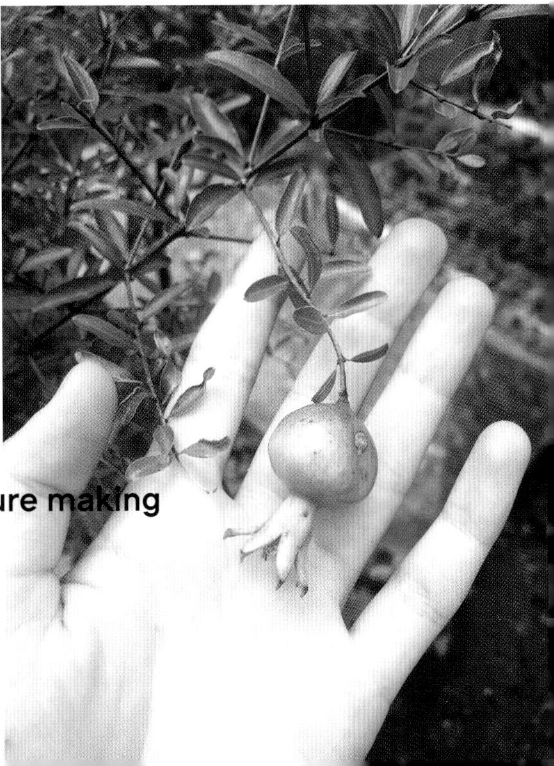

square Colosseum
erasure of histories
place as a character
Palazzo Congressi
transformation
coexistence
beyond
filmmaking as a proposal for a future making
Index Cards, Davey
roundabout
facade curve

expo58
BXL

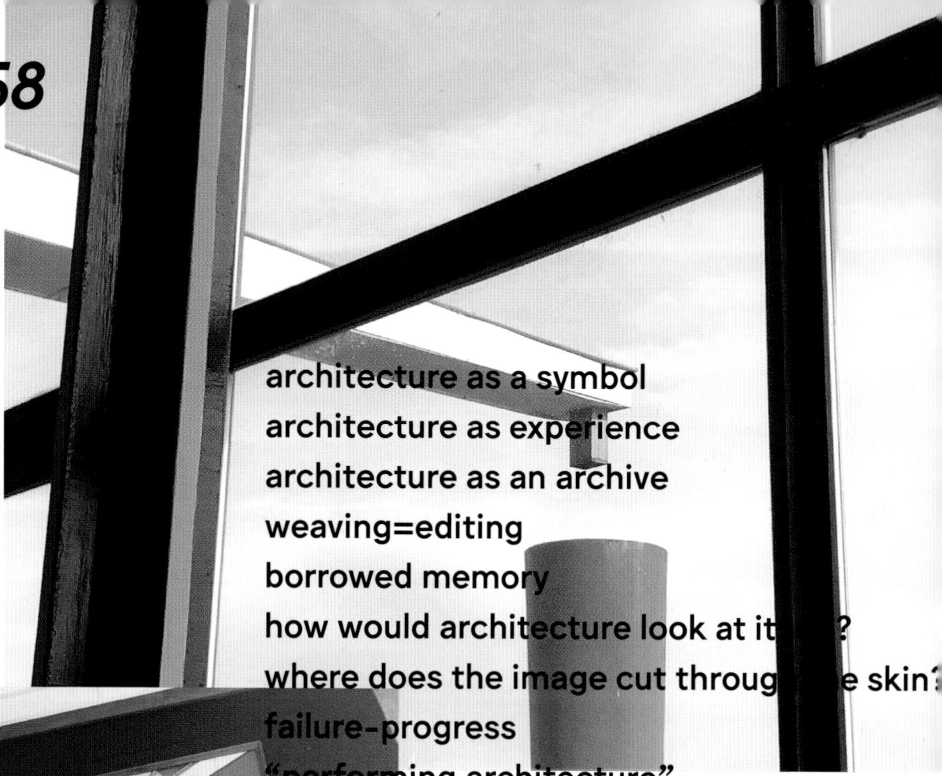

architecture as a symbol
architecture as experience
architecture as an archive
weaving=editing
borrowed memory
how would architecture look at it ?
where does the image cut throug e skin?
failure–progress
“performing architecture”
fetishism of architecture
expo=zoo
Vjenceslav Richter
children’s games, Alÿs
past–present
exterior–interior
moving body–solid wall
image–sound
hunting
closing door, swinging curtain
temporality

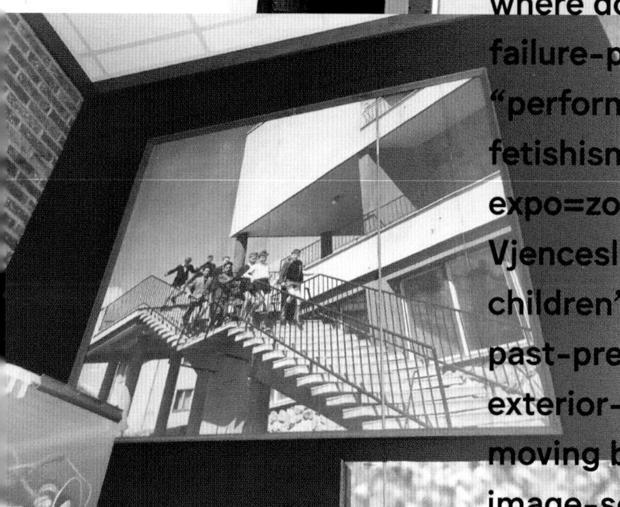

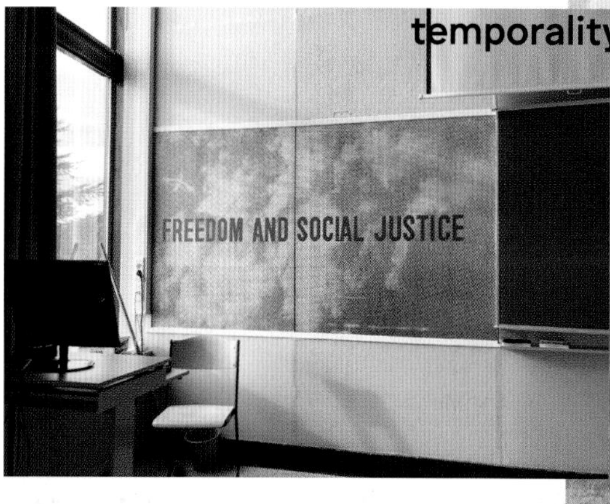

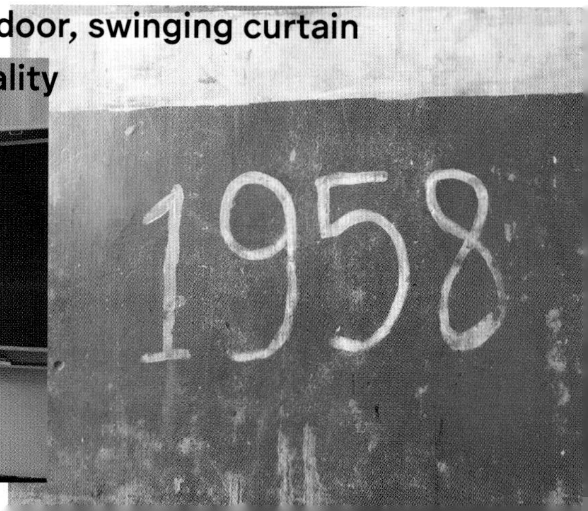

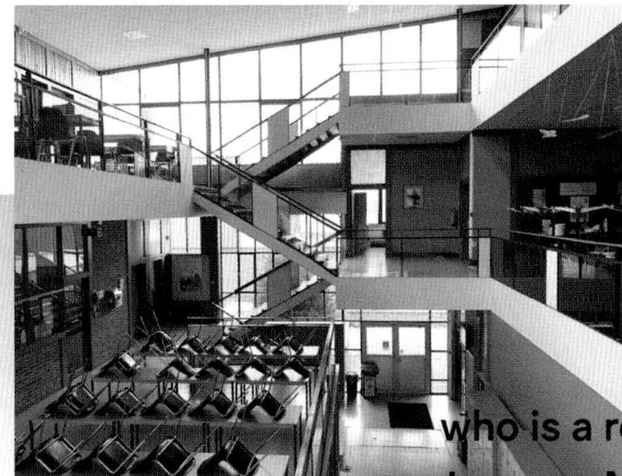

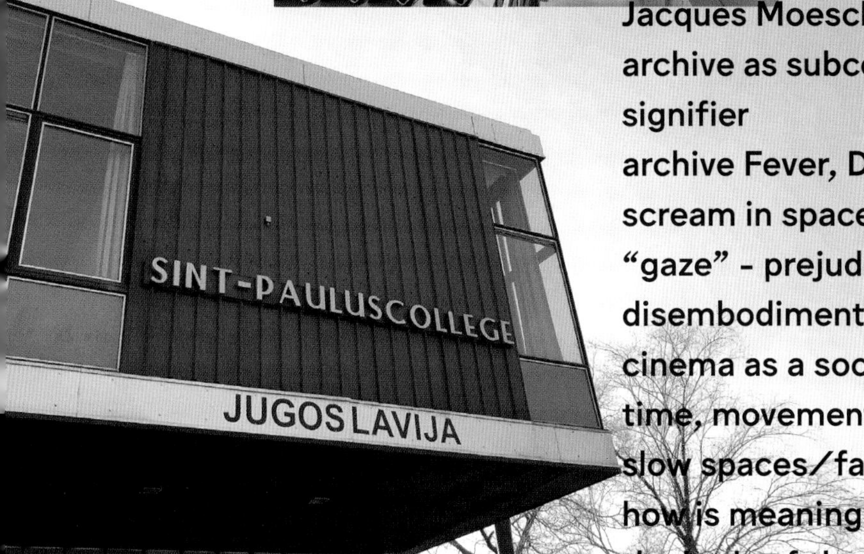

who is a reliable narrator?
Jacques Moeschal
archive as subconsciousness
signifier
archive Fever, Derrida
scream in space
"gaze" - prejudice
disembodiment of the camera
cinema as a social practice
time, movement, heat, death
slow spaces/fast spaces
how is meaning made?
the body of the spectator

rhythm
potential
Kulechov
grid, steel structure, light, glass reflection
archive as subconsciousness

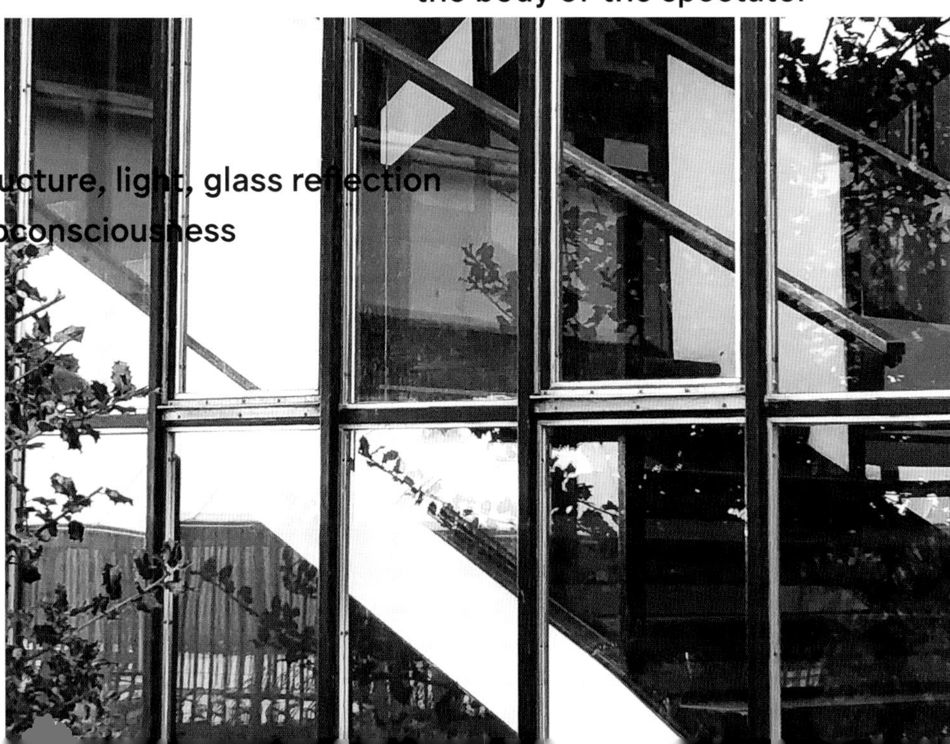

Slavutych

Riga district

Yerevanski eagle

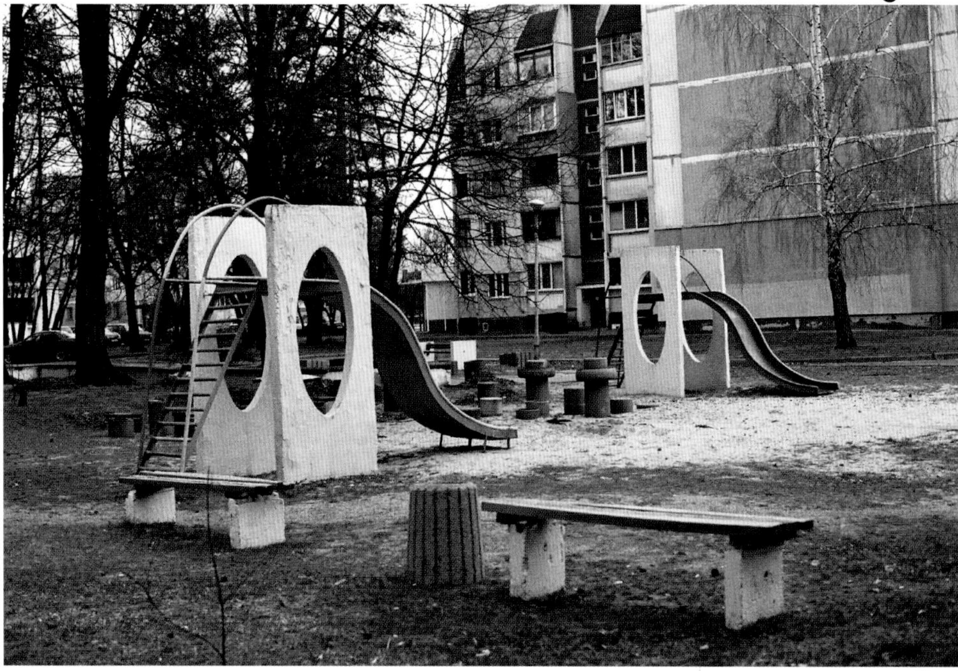

Baku, Tbiliski shelters

Moskowski playground

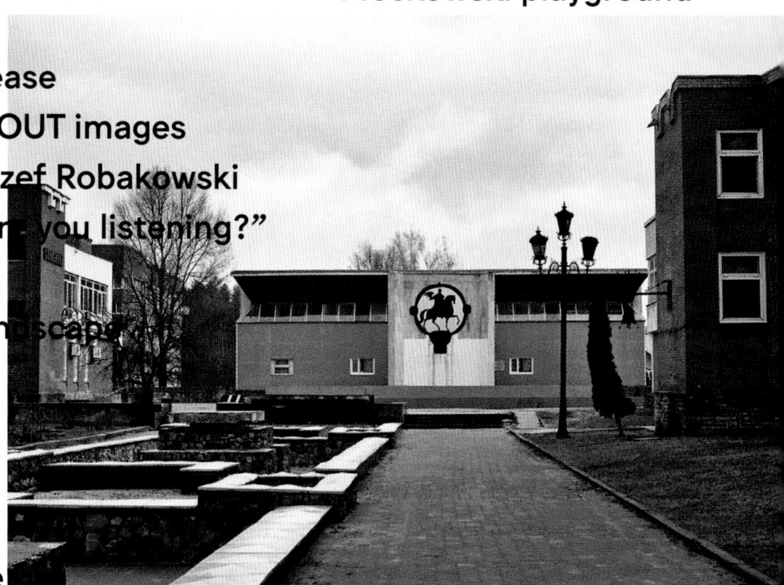

atomgrad
human scale
nostalgia as a disease
to think IN not ABOUT images
Z mojego okna, Jozef Robakowski
“spaces speak - are you listening?”
collective persona
body as a loose landscape
Svetlana Boym
Monograd
1986
city-dream space
fragmented frame
“death” as a structuring element of a city
not showing IS SHOWING
aesthetics of boredom
generation without memories

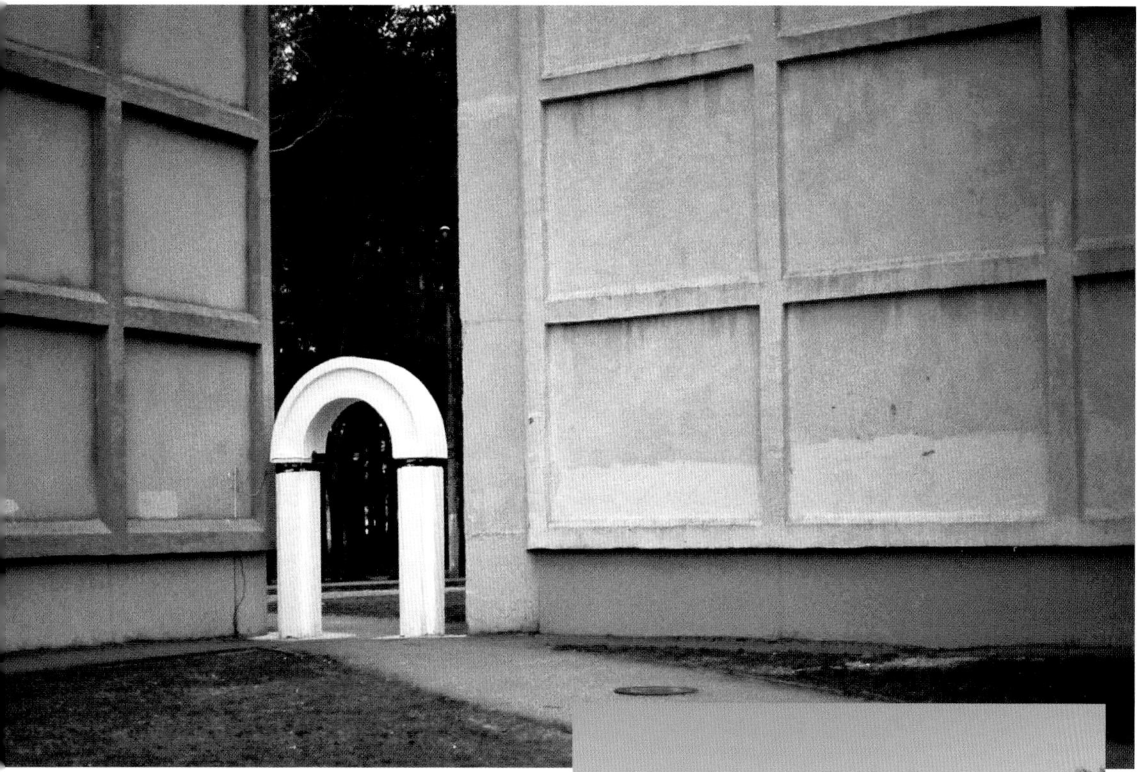

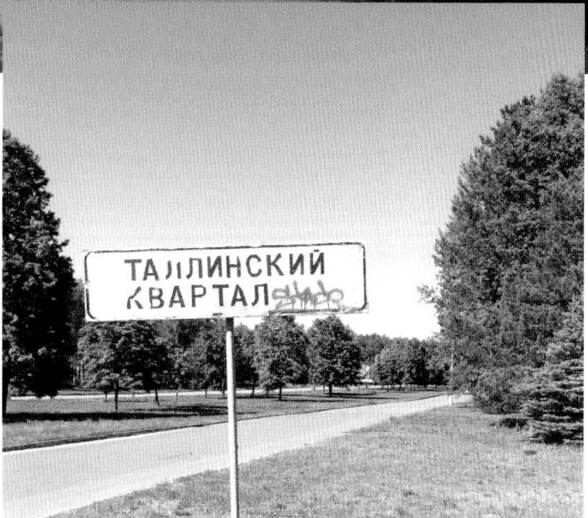

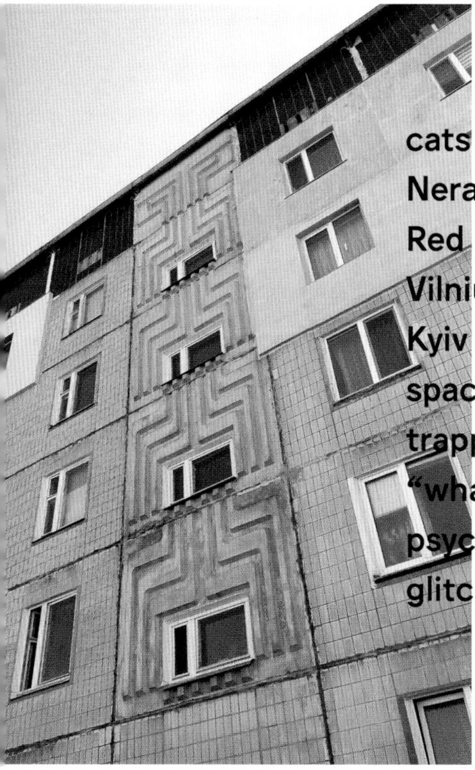

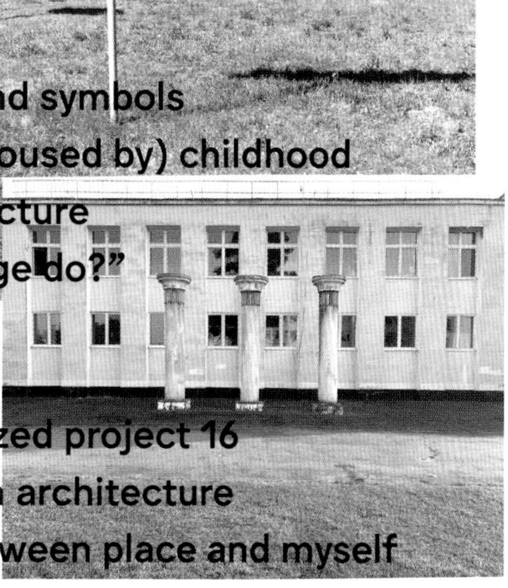

cats
Nerafa
Red brick
Vilnius district
Kyiv district - round symbols
space-memory (housed by) childhood
trapped in architecture
"what can an image do?"
psychogeography
glitch

standardized project 16
trapped in architecture
space between place and myself

II

Contemporary Nomadism

Artists' Geographies of Home and Belonging

Emma Duester

1 This essay provides a reflection on a longitudinal study of artists' careers as emerging and then as established professionals. It is a conclusion of what was found during interviews—with artists Laura Põld, Kriss Salmanis, Vineta Kaulača, Paulina Pukytė, Laura Toots, Liina Siib, Kristians Brekte, Zygimantas Augustinas, Arnas Anskaitis, Simona Žemaitytė, Kristi Kongi, Margus Tamm, Vytautas Viržbickas, Kaido Ole, and Edith Karlson—in 2013 and what has happened to them up until 2021. The artists I interviewed are originally from Estonia, Latvia, and Lithuania. However, many of them are now based across the EU. I interviewed these artists in 2013 in order to find out how they travel, migrate, and work across multiple borders. I wanted to find out how this affected their feelings of home and belonging. I then interviewed the same artists again in 2021 in order to find out how their careers had changed or developed as well as their feelings about this highly mobile lifestyle today. The artists I interviewed are of a particular generation of post-Soviet children, aged between thirty and fifty-five years old.

Introduction

This essay explores how contemporary visual artists from the Baltic states take part in regular cross-border mobilities throughout the European Union (EU) for work. The essay charts how artists travel and make homes in various regions of the EU. Many have transnational practices, which include particular ways of moving and placing homes. They often have unique combinations of onward migrations and regular mobilities. As a result of always being on the move, the meaning of home and belonging can encompass a broad spatiality and geographic area. For instance, they may feel their home is Europe overall or they may feel at home in Vienna, Tallinn, or Frankfurt. This is due to how artists develop multiple attachments not only to places across the EU, but also to the global art network.

Through this investigation,[1] I have found a "culture of mobility" among artists from the Baltic states of Lithuania, Latvia, and Estonia, as regular mobilities and migrations are necessary to gain international recognition and to progress their career. Many find that there is a "glass ceiling" in the Baltic states for their careers as artists. This has to do with a lack of local art markets, few dealers buying art, and governments cutting back on funding. Art scenes in Tallinn, Riga, and Vilnius had to be rebuilt during the 1990s due to the collapse of the Soviet Union, which means there has been relatively little time for them to develop as independent capitalist art scenes. This, of course, is only the case when we compare with the established art markets in Western or Northern Europe. These differences therefore lead to the "push factors"[2] that encourage artists to move out of their homeland, temporarily or otherwise, to locate career opportunities elsewhere. Furthermore, this "culture of mobility"[3] among artists is also germane to the historical moment. As Magdalena Moskalewicz writes, there is a particular generation of people from Eastern Europe whose current identity has been formed between two extreme conditions: the restricted mobility of the Soviet past and the accelerated mobility of today.[4] I argue that these artists have certain feelings towards mobility and home due to having the particular experience of both a closed and open EU.

The Connection between Mobility and Home in Artists' Lives

Mobility is a suitable term to illustrate the way artists travel and migrate, as it encompasses varying scales of movement. It can be used to refer to frenzied travel patterns, whereby movements are made every couple of days, which I refer to as "hyper-mobility," as well as to

2 P. Krishnakumar and T. Indumathi, "Push and Pull Factors of Migration," *Global Management Review* 8, no. 4 (2014): 8–13.

3 Emma Duester, *The Politics of Migration and Mobility in the Art World: Transnational Baltic Artistic Practices Across Europe* (Bristol: Intellect, 2021).

4 Magdalena Moskalewicz, *The Travellers: Voyage and Migration in New Art from Central and Eastern Europe* (Tallinn: Lugemik, 2017).

5 Duester, *The Politics of Migration and Mobility in the Art World.*

that of regular onward migrations, whereby movements evolve over time. The term mobility, rather than travel or movement, is relevant as travel relates more to travelling cultures and people exploring new places, while movement is too open-ended and is not restricted in terms of distance or time.

Artists have a particular type and style of movement. There are also distinct reasons and motives for their movements. The politics of the art world, which is highly mobile, and the nature of EU politics and economics, have impacts on the patterns and pace of artists' mobilities. This in turn affects these artists' feelings of home and belonging. This is not to say that being constantly mobile means that these artists are dislocated. In some cases, the opposite can happen whereby they find home in mobility. In this way, the concept of mobility can be seen as something more to do with routes as well as roots, while the concept of home can be developed to show it can be more mobile, multi-sited, and pan-geographic. This goes beyond a traditional sense of national belonging or having attachments to only a "homeland."

Analysing artists' mobilities provides a way to more deeply understand the meaning of being "at home." With this, we can also take the discussion of home away from its connection with a singular physical place.[5] For example, Petra Andits argues that the concept of home is neither solely fixed nor fluctuating, and states that people struggle between wanting order as well as flexibility in regard to feelings of belonging. The meaning of home can be more fluid—it can mean more than only

6 Petra Andits, "Rethinking Home, Belonging, and the Potentials of Transnationalism: Australian Hungarians after the Fall of the Berlin Wall," *Ethos* 43, no. 4 (December 2015): 313–331.

7 Linda Nochlin, "Art and the Conditions of Exile: Men/Women, Emigration/Expatriation," in *Exile and Creativity: Signposts, Travelers, Outsiders, Backward Glances*, ed. Susan Rubin Suleiman (Durham, NC: Duke University Press, 1998), 37.

a homeland, not something fixed, and not necessarily something that is singular.[6] I argue that regular mobilities means artists have to make several homes, both immediately and throughout their career. This often means their understanding of home becomes more mobile and spatial; it can be simultaneously attached to several places as well as people and practice. This helps to show the notion of home is not fixed, and conversely that the notion of mobility is not only about being uprooted. These individuals still have "homing desires," even after multiple cross-border mobilities, that are not necessarily connected only to their homeland.

The EU, the Art World, and Artists' Careers

The fact that artists migrate and travel regularly for work is not a new phenomenon. Visual artists have had transnational practices and have travelled across borders for work throughout history. As Linda Nochlin notes: "Artists traditionally have been obliged to travel, to leave their native land, in order to learn their trade. At one time, the trip to Rome was required, or a study-voyage to Italy; at other times it might be Munich or Spain or Holland or even North Africa; more recently, Paris was where one went to learn how to be an artist… and afterwards New York stole the heart of the art world from Paris."[7]

However, visual artists' mobilities across the EU have changed dramatically since the end of the Soviet Union in 1991 and the EU-27 accession in 2004, which included Lithuania, Latvia, and Estonia. The removal of hard borders across Europe has facilitated an intensification of mobility throughout EU nations. The existence of the EU and the Schengen Area mean that

8 European Commission, Directorate-General for Communication, *Borders and security: building an open and safe Europe* (Luxembourg: Publications Office of the European Union, 2014), https://data.europa.eu/doi/10.2775/25135.

9 Duester, *The Politics of Migration and Mobility in the Art World.*

there are no physical borders, checkpoints, or document checks for EU citizens. As the European Commission states, "one of the fundamental objectives of the European Union is to create an area without internal borders where people may move, live and work freely, knowing that their rights are fully respected and their security ensured."[8]

Artists from this region have since taken part in mobilities and migrations in multiple different directions across the EU, including to Western Europe, Northern Europe, and Southern Europe. An EU national or resident is entitled to work in any EU member state without needing a work permit. They have the same rights as a national of that country, notably with regards to access to employment, pay, and benefits.

The EU member states have varying economic, political, or cultural circumstances, which makes it necessary for some artists, as is the case with artists from the Baltic states, to leave their homeland. This is what I call a politics of mobility, whereby the juxtaposition of EU member states with economic, political, or cultural disparities creates new reasons for travel and a politics of mobility where there is pressure to go to certain places and where flows are centred in some places yet bypass others.[9] For these artists, this politics of mobility is felt through a pressure to leave homeland for career progression and to go to certain places that are "centres." In addition, for artists there is also pressure to be highly mobile, to be international, and to follow the global art market that is itself mobile, multi-sited, and has a particular global circuit of flows. The artist profession is innately precarious, because it is self-made and self-sustaining, so they have to take part in compulsory mobility across the EU for work and to make and maintain their networks.

There is the added precariousness for artists from Lithuania, Latvia, and Estonia, which pertains to politico-economic geographies determined by the global art market. This results in relatively less flow of art traffic, including artists, curators, and dealers, coming into contact with art scenes in Tallinn, Riga, and Vilnius. There are fewer collectors or dealers who are buying artworks, relatively fewer international curators to see exhibitions and take part in studio visits, and less support funding available due to the fact that government budgets and the market pricing of artworks are significantly lower than in Western Europe. However, there are initiatives such as the Estonian Contemporary Art Development Center, which was established to help develop the commercial gallery scene in Tallinn and initiate international collaborations.

One of the main trends of these artists' routes from Tallinn, Riga, and Vilnius is that they are not limited to only one destination and do not only follow one main, well-trodden route. They are not only going in the direction of established art centres, like London or Berlin. Instead, each artist has their own spatialities created through unique, multi-cross-cultural connections across the EU. In fact, these artists present myriad ways of travelling and dwelling, whereby each artist has different kinds, speeds, directions, rhythms, and amounts of roots and routes. Some live and move between two cities, while others have one main base and travel in multiple directions from there. For example, one artist lives in Vienna but also has mobilities across France, Germany, and the Baltic states; another lives in Bucharest but is mobile across Germany, Austria, and Belgium. Some have their main base (i.e., their studio) in the Baltic states but spend more than half their time away. As a result of having such mobile lifestyles, these artists form attachments to multiple places as well as connections to a network of curators, collectors, and other artists who are also always on the move.

As well as the nature and workings of the EU art world that affect their work practices, there are also broader EU realities that determine these artists' mobilities, migrations, and subsequent feelings of home and belonging. In interviews in 2013 with a number of emerging and established artists originally from Estonia, Latvia, and Lithuania, it became clear that work practices were affected by external EU political and economic factors in three respects. The first was the increased protectionist, anti-immigration policies within the EU that were at odds with transnational practices. The second was the extent to which mobilities and migrations were orchestrated through digital transnational networks, facilitated by new technologies, that enabled connections to continue during and after travel so that artists could be "present" simultaneously across multiple locations and maintain multiple homes and transnational networks, which helped them feel a sense of belonging to a community and practice rather than a physical place. The third was the increasing barriers for Eastern European nationals who are often misrepresented as post-Soviet artists or as economic migrants who long to "go home."

These artists' work practices continued to be affected by external EU political and economic factors when I interviewed them again in 2021—namely, Brexit and far-right politics; the COVID-19 pandemic; and the onset of the Russian war in Ukraine. For instance, some of the artists I spoke with left the UK due to it being too expensive or because of Brexit as it made them feel unwelcome. Some artists I spoke with said they would not choose to work in the UK because of the extra bureaucracy and costs needed. The artists also mentioned increasing far-right politics in the Baltic states as well as other places across the EU as having affected their transnational practices, for instance due to a lack of mobility funding. Brexit and other far-right politics go against transnational working practices and are slowly changing the open nature of the EU. In addition, the COVID-19 pandemic has also affected the nature of transnational art practices over the past three years. It meant that these artists had to be settled in one place, which some enjoyed because they had more time to be in their studio while others found it unsettling because they could no longer be mobile. Most scheduled exhibitions were cancelled or postponed at the start of the pandemic, though some resumed later and were then pushed together, happening all at the same time. The COVID-19 pandemic has also exacerbated inequalities in funding and opportunities across the EU, and many artists noted how there are more available funding opportunities in Western Europe but that they are often ineligible to apply. The Russian war in Ukraine has led to an increase in prices of materials and resources for all, including artists. Also, many artists have cancelled work in Ukraine and Russia or have had to postpone collaborative projects with Ukrainian artists. This combination of factors has once again pushed this region to the periphery. This is especially the case when looking from a Western gaze because of the political geography and proximity to the current war zone.

Feelings of Home and Belonging in Mobility

This particular type of highly mobile work affects the geographies and feelings of home and belonging, leaving artists with (physical and psychological) attachments in several places. For some, these attachments are to multiple cities, although, for others these attachments are more specifically tied to people, studios, or even materials. Those who have attachments across multiple places must find ways of renegotiating their feelings

10 See Duester, *The Politics of Migration and Mobility in the Art World* and Emma Duester, "For necessity or pleasure? Towards a politics of artists' mobilities," *Crossings: Journal of Migration and Culture* 6, no. 2 (October 2015): 131–142.

of home. In order to do this, they locate, or root, themselves across these spaces and places through social relations and by creating a synthesis of all these attachments. This means that both the geographies of and feelings towards home and belonging become multi-sited. In other words, home spans a wide psychogeographic area.

As well as this, while artists belong in a certain way to their career, they also belong to their art network. Many told me that in hyper-mobility you must find things that are equally mobile to attach your feelings of home. For instance, some say they "live in" travel. This means that, for them, travel itself provides a sense of home and belonging. For others, they say they form attachments to their materials or to their network who are also always on the move.

Some artists keep a studio in one place in order to have an anchor point for their multi-directional mobilities, even for those who are always away or con-stantly on the move. This relates to my previous work that states that artists need an anchor point in order to be comfortable in hyper-mobility.[10] For instance, one artist uses their base in Vienna in order to be more mobile across France, Austria, and Germany. Another artist uses their base in Frankfurt in order to be mobile across Scandinavia, the Baltic states, Germany, Austria, and Belgium. Some feel they need one base to always "come back to" as well as to help "propel" them to go on their next trip in order to sustain these mobilities in multiple directions and for very short but regular periods. Hence, mobilities are sustained through the use of a strategically located anchor or pivot point at the centre of their multi-directional mobilities.

11 Avatar Brah, *Cartographies of Diaspora: Contesting Identities* (New York: Routledge, 1996).

For some artists, their thoughts and feelings about home and belonging are always in question. There may be a tension because they have a family but want to do more travelling or are now tired of their hyper-mobile lifestyle and long to be more settled. Some want to be more settled in one place as established artists, and so they are now more selective and do shows remotely and become more efficient in making types of art that they do not have to install themselves. Some do not go to all their exhibitions. Instead, they ensure that their artworks can be installed without them physically being present.

Travelling and having transnational bases can heighten considerations about the meaning of home and belonging. Some artists must also make home in mobility, whereby home becomes attached to aspects of their lives that are also mobile, such as artworks, materials, and their transnational networks (also always on the move). Home is a broad geography or spatiality. In this sense, their feelings of home are not only about their homeland but a feeling of home and belonging to their art practice and community. This can be felt wherever they are physically located as well as when they are on the move.

While some feel more connected to their homeland, others realise that they do not need to be living in their homeland in order to keep their connections there. Alternatively, they can feel more "like themselves" in another city. Birthplace is not necessarily where someone feels most at home. This means that a homing desire, as Avtar Brah describes, can be applied to additional homes or to multiple residences (past and present) as well as to their ancestral homeland. Artists are not necessarily displaced through travel as, in fact, their understandings of home and belonging can be heightened.[11]

Discussion and Conclusion

In this investigation, I found that all of those I spoke with want to feel at home, either in one or several places, even with hyper-mobile lives. They all have a "homing desire," but not necessarily to only their ancestral homeland. Many feel they can keep their roots in their homeland through maintaining connections and participating in the local art scene; they do not feel they must choose or give up their roots when living outside of the Baltic states or when moving onto the next place. They enjoy the fact that they are not required to have just one base or home. This age group also seems to appreciate and make the most of this hyper-mobility because they know how it was before, with closed borders and no opportunity to travel and work in multiple places. However, with the growing popularity of far-right movements in governments across the EU, and considering events like Brexit, we may see less and less of this kind of transnational work in the future, especially if governments make it more difficult to be mobile across member-state borders. The Russian war in Ukraine has also divided Europe once again between East and West. In addition, while the COVID-19 pandemic halted all travel and some work, it has also had a lasting effect on artists' feelings towards mobility and home.

Artists lead transnational lives. This means that their understanding of home and belonging is geographically and spatially broad. Their homes are multiple and in various locations across the EU. Their idea of "home" therefore includes all these locations, often in different aspects or to different degrees—one may signify friends while another may signify the location of their main gallery representative. Another distinction about their homes is that it is not singular—their spatiality of home and belonging is EU-wide. They see and share their moves as being to-and-from cities, even not recognizing different countries. They view and use the EU as one space and feel at home in Europe and identify themselves as Europeans or global natives. Moving multiple times, with intense travelling, has provided these artists today with a clearer perspective on what home means.

These artists' right to access this type of multi-directional mobilities and multi-sited homes across the EU—without passports or working visas and not agonising over citizenship rights—determines how they form attachments to places across multiple borders and, hence, how they think about home and belonging. Their understandings of home and belonging are determined and germane to the political structure of the EU, the Schengen Agreement, and other everyday practicalities. They are able to make multiple homes and subsequently plant many roots because they have the right to remain in and work for as long as they wish in any EU member state and because they are free to return to their homeland whenever they wish. Being able to go "back home" to Tallinn, Riga, or Vilnius has been made easier with cheaper transportation and faster technology that allows them to travel back or communicate with family and friends regularly. This affects their feelings of home elsewhere as well as their feelings towards homeland.

A Love Letter to the Non-Belonger

Neringa Černiauskaitė

1 Pakui Hardware is the name coined by curator Alex Ross for the collaborative artist duo of Neringa Černiauskaitė and Ugnius Gelguda, which began in 2014. The title Pakui Hardware refers to Pakui, special attendant to a Hawaiian Goddess, who could circle Oahu island six times in a day. Thus Pakui Hardware is high-speed and brand politics as mythic semio-commodity as well as the desire to transcend material limitations. Semio-capital meets materiality.

Had you asked me some years ago "What is belonging?" I would have given you a very different answer. "Networked community, not bound to a specific land or culture," would have been my reply. At least this is where Pakui Hardware[1] was born—in that semiotic, digital and communal cloud, all while dreaming of obtaining a body of flesh and bones. It is a collective "creature" made of a long history of thought, speculations, and aspirations. Even if conceived in New York around 2014, it felt best in the embrace of like-minded agents—artists, thinkers, writers—spread widely around the Web. New York was all precarity and culture. A narcissistic beast, spellbinding and crushing. A temporary home that transforms you for good.

What is "belonging" three years into the pandemic and a year in the war in Europe? The shared enthusiasm of a global online community seems like a distant dream. Borders are tightened, new walls erected. The words "digital nomad" makes me shudder: the pandemic clearly revealed the hypocrisy of this term and lifestyle. Try to be a nomad coming from 106th place in the list of most powerful passports in the world. Nomadism became gentrified, a luxury choice for the privileged few. It feels obscene to reflect nomadism when my own country plays ping-pong with Belarus, pushing refugees,

2 Belarus (illegitimate) president Alexander Lukashenko's regime has orchestrated a refugee crisis on the borders with Lithuania, Poland, and Latvia, which "could be considered an act of hybrid warfare using migration strategically to put pressure on the EU and create discord within the bloc. This amounts to state-sponsored human trafficking aimed at creating a humanitarian crisis to force the EU and its member states to accede to Belarus's demands, namely ending their sanctions." Sascha-Dominik (Dov) Bachmann, "Is the Belarus migrant crisis a 'new type of war'? A conflict expert explains," *The Conversation*, November 16, 2021, https://theconversation.com/is-the-belarus-migrant-crisis-a-new-type-of-war-a-conflict-expert-explains-171739. This crisis, however, unmasked a grim reality of racist border politics of Lithuania, Poland, and Latvia, that have employed a violent strategy of physically pushing the refugees back to Belarus from the frontier zones.

including those with small children, back and forth across borders.[2]

These last three transformative years also provided some answers to a number of uncomfortable yet nagging thoughts. I wouldn't necessarily even call them "thoughts"; it's more like an ungraspable sense of awareness that acquired unique tones depending on a situation. It was a sense of "non-belonging" that filled and pressed my guts, making me cower inside while facing the external world. This feeling and I grew together—through a brief encounter with the bleakness of life in the Soviet Union during my very early years, through a rough ride in the wild capitalism of the 1990s, and, finally, through the long years of "cultivation," of putting forward our best efforts to become fully Western. To no avail. How many of us there are, these cultural Frankensteins, disguising the too-visible seams in our "personalities" with most inventive techniques and make-ups? Too many to be left unnoticed.

It was in Czech curator's Michal Novotný's travelling project, provocatively titled *Orient*, that I understood that feeling of non-belonging translated into words (and selected artworks). It is a suppressed inferiority complex that we carry, which was born out of a set of faulty (and

3 Valentinas Klimašauskas and Michal Novotný, "Meditation on the Eastern European Identity: A Conversation with Czech curator Michal Novotný," *Arterritory*, November 5, 2018, https://arterritory.com/en/visual_arts/interviews/21838-meditation_on_the_eastern_european_identity/. *Orient* was presented at three art institutions: Kim? Contemporary Art Centre, Riga, Latvia (April 20 to May 20, 2018); BOZAR Centre for Fine Arts, Brussels, Belgium (June 20 to August 19, 2018); and Bunkier Sztuki Gallery of Contemporary Art, Krakow, Poland (September 21 to December 16, 2018).

failed) projections that we had towards the West and vice versa. As Novotný reflects in a conversation with the curator and writer Valentinas Klimašauskas: "Orient is a reference towards Edward Said's 'Orientalism', in the sense that Eastern Europe as much as the Orient never really existed, but was, or is, more a series of projections. However, it also has to do with a lack of information, certain ignorance, not only of people, but also western media, schools and other institutions. But we must not forget the projection is double sided, we have also had our West, our 'occident', that was very different from what we imagined, or what the exotic image was, which was given to us via the cultural dominance that still persists."[3] In order to avoid aggressive nationalism that might grow out of the disappointment with those failed projections towards the world, Novotný proposes to look for a sense of belonging to a place, rather than a nation.

Nation-state is a recent concept, as we all know. It is a naturalised fiction of imagined communities, if we follow the thought of Benedict Anderson, a fiction that defines material reality and lives of each of us. No wonder the calls to go post-nation, to shake off this powerful dream of the nation-state, have become louder and clearly reasoned. Universal statelessness is a brighter and more symmetrical vision on the other end of the spectrum of fiction. Yet there was some kind of stutter in my mind when I tried to make this elegant leap from nation-state to post-nation to a stateless world. The full Russian invasion of Ukraine revealed the ugly face of that stutter: to go post-nation one needs to accept that on equal terms.

In their sensitive conversation for *Errant Journal*, Ukrainian art historian Asia Bazdyrieva and Ukrainian artist Alevtina Kakhidze slowly peel away the hardened layers of a critique of nation-state and imperialism. The Russian war against Ukraine unveiled an invisible yet real division between the Left that only sees the injustice and suffering brought by the Western imperialism, while failing to ever analyse other forms of imperial agenda employed by non-Western countries and powers, such as the Soviet Union or Russia. Having presented itself as a self-sacrificing fighter against the Western hegemony, Russia has created a hard-to-break image of a protector and an anti-imperialist "brother" that will come to the rescue. Another faulty projection gone wrong. When Russia invaded Ukraine in February 2022, the rift in reading this tragedy between those in the so-called former Soviet states and those who have no direct experience of occupation and later a permanent threat by Russia, grew even deeper. The sense of non-belonging acquired a new shape—you have been met with suspicion for all those years when trying to relate your stories of oppression by your "great" neighbour.

As Bazdyrieva, whose heart-breaking, poetic, and immediate accounts on Instagram have become essential to so many of us since the first days of the Russian invasion, patiently explains in the conversation with Kakhidze, the critique of a nation-state "emerged from a position of former empires and is not fully applicable to the places that have never been empires. When we start a conversation from the position of non-empire, we, in a

4 Asia Bazdyrieva and Alevtina Kakhidze, "Notes on a Revolution (or at least a hope)," *Errant Journal* 4 (2022): 19.

5 Bazdyrieva and Kakhidze, 20.

way, work to decolonize nation state critique."[4] Yet such decolonization could not fully take place, because the patronizing neighbour would not cede to implement its zombified imperial vision: "The tragedy is that we have to resist erasure all the time, before we even have time and capacity to find better words or to articulate different political models."[5]

As the pandemic swept us back to Lithuania from Berlin, this war, this inconceivable aggression, has been too close to home to bathe ourselves in bright utopian visions of a stateless world. The relation to this insignificant patch of land, the people around, the landscapes, and the mercury skies gained unfamiliar urgency. But the non-belonger has returned with(in) me, even if I call this country my home. And I learned to embrace it, to cultivate it. The non-belonger prevents one from becoming too comfortable with imposed narratives and given realities, from fully immersing oneself in the alluring fantasy of a unity based on nationality. Substituting the precariousness of metropolitan life with a slightly more stable, sustainable, and familiar environment can easily enwrap you within a blanket of oblivious comforts. Without much notice, one can quickly get entangled in the web of local matters, personalities, and gossip, while slowly drifting away from more "global" urgencies and the art scene itself. With limited or even in some cases prohibited travel, the threads connecting to the "outside" world were getting thinner by the day. Even the internet felt local at times. First came the pandemic, then the war pushed us harder to detect the "sores" and imagine future scenarios that would touch more than the nearest environment, expanding to a multitude of minds and bodies. Virtual and technological care, failures of "rational" thought, vulnerability and resilience in the shadow of bodily and global inflammation—these focus points have become the portals we were building towards the world outside of our studio walls in Vilnius. Like every artist, we were trying to construct a language that would not require deep and specific knowledge on the explored subject. A language that is visceral, tactile, contagious. A language from one non-belonger to another.

The non-belonger urges us to look for ways of being together as multitude, while having in mind the unique and unequal experiences of life. It invites us to listen to the voices of those who have been spoken for, to give them a chance to tell stories of their own.

Dear non-belonger, stay with me for a little while.
So much is left to learn.

Pakui Hardware

Pakui Hardware is an artistic duo of Neringa Černiauskaitė (b. 1984, Klaipėda, Lithuania) and Ugnius Gelguda (b. 1977, Vilnius, Lithuania) who live and work in Vilnius. The duo's work explores the plasticity of bodies. They trace how diverse technologies expand, test, and control bodily potential. The hybrid materials that the artists employ correspond to hybrid bodies that surround us. These questions are analysed through such examples as invasive and transformative relationship to bodies, automation, synthetic biology, and new materiality. Pakui Hardware has presented solo shows at BALTIC Centre for Contemporary Art, Gateshead (2021); Museum der bildenden Künste (MdbK) Leipzig (2019–2020); MUMOK, Vienna (2016); and Contemporary Art Centre, Vilnius (2014); among others. Pakui Hardware participated in group shows at 16th Istanbul Biennial (2019); MAXXI, Rome (2019); 13th Baltic Triennial (2018); and Kunsthalle Basel (2017). Pakui Hardware (with Marija Teresė Rožanskaitė) will represent Lithuania at the 60th Venice Biennale in 2024.

Creatures of Earth and Air, 2020

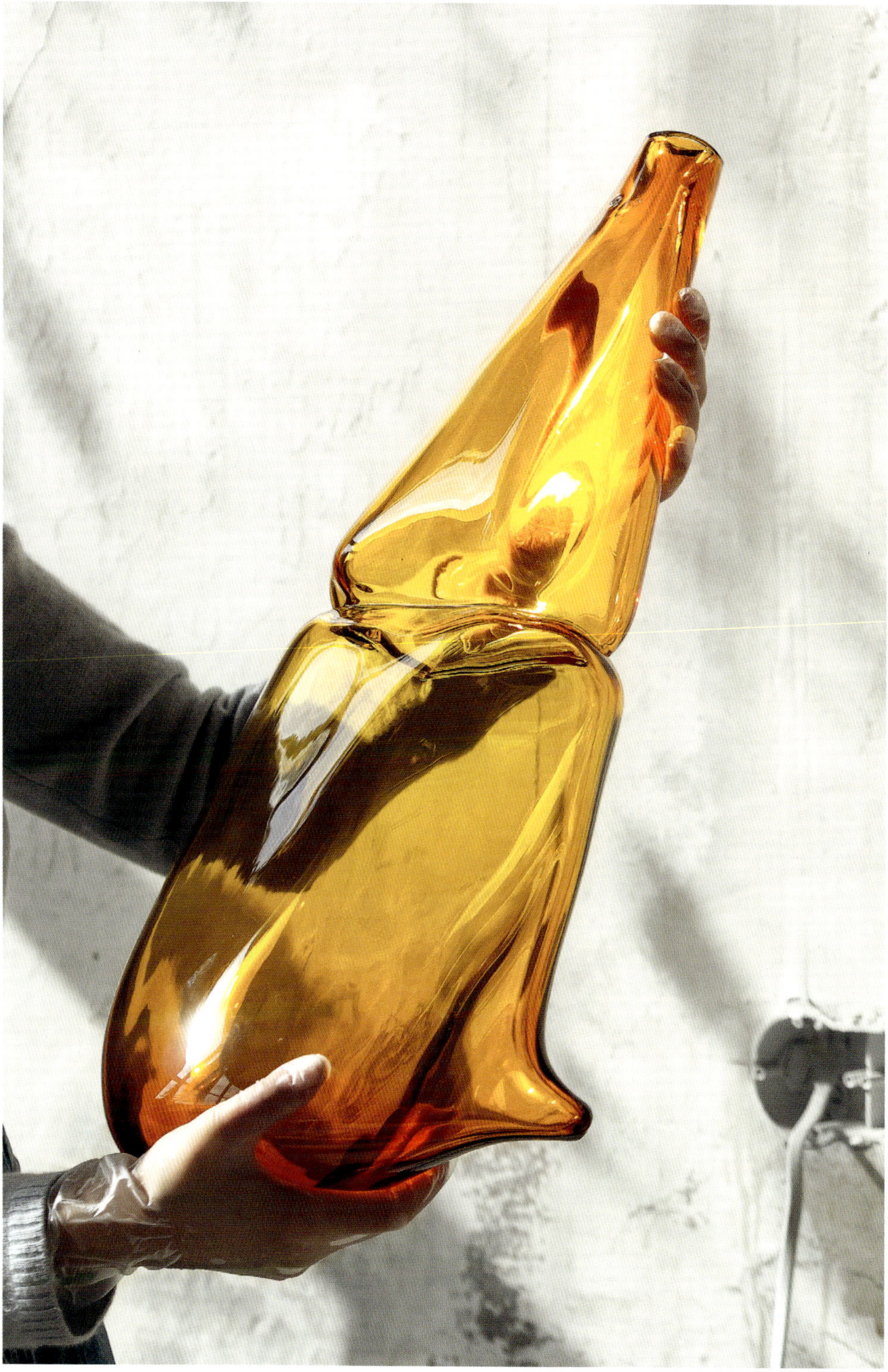

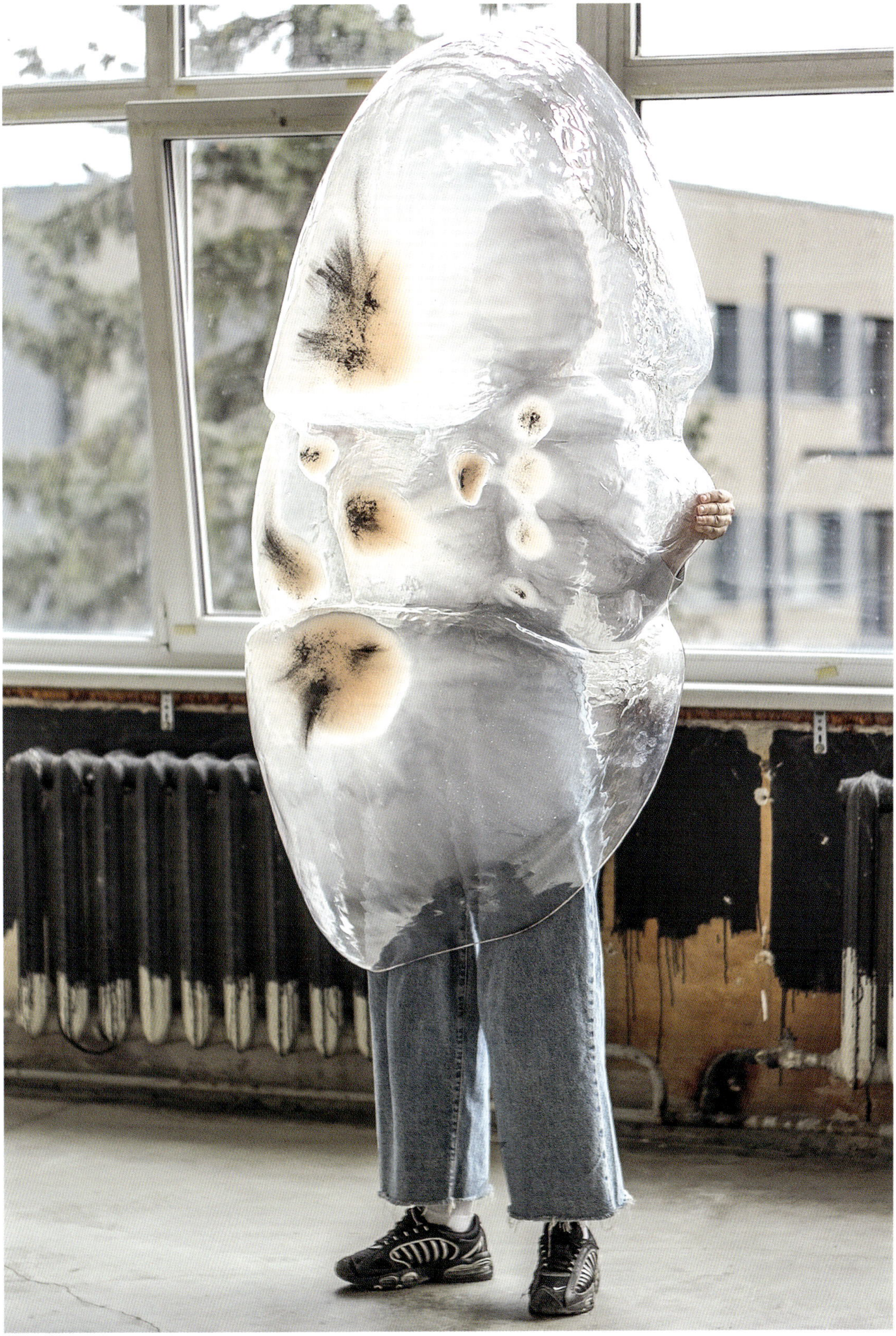

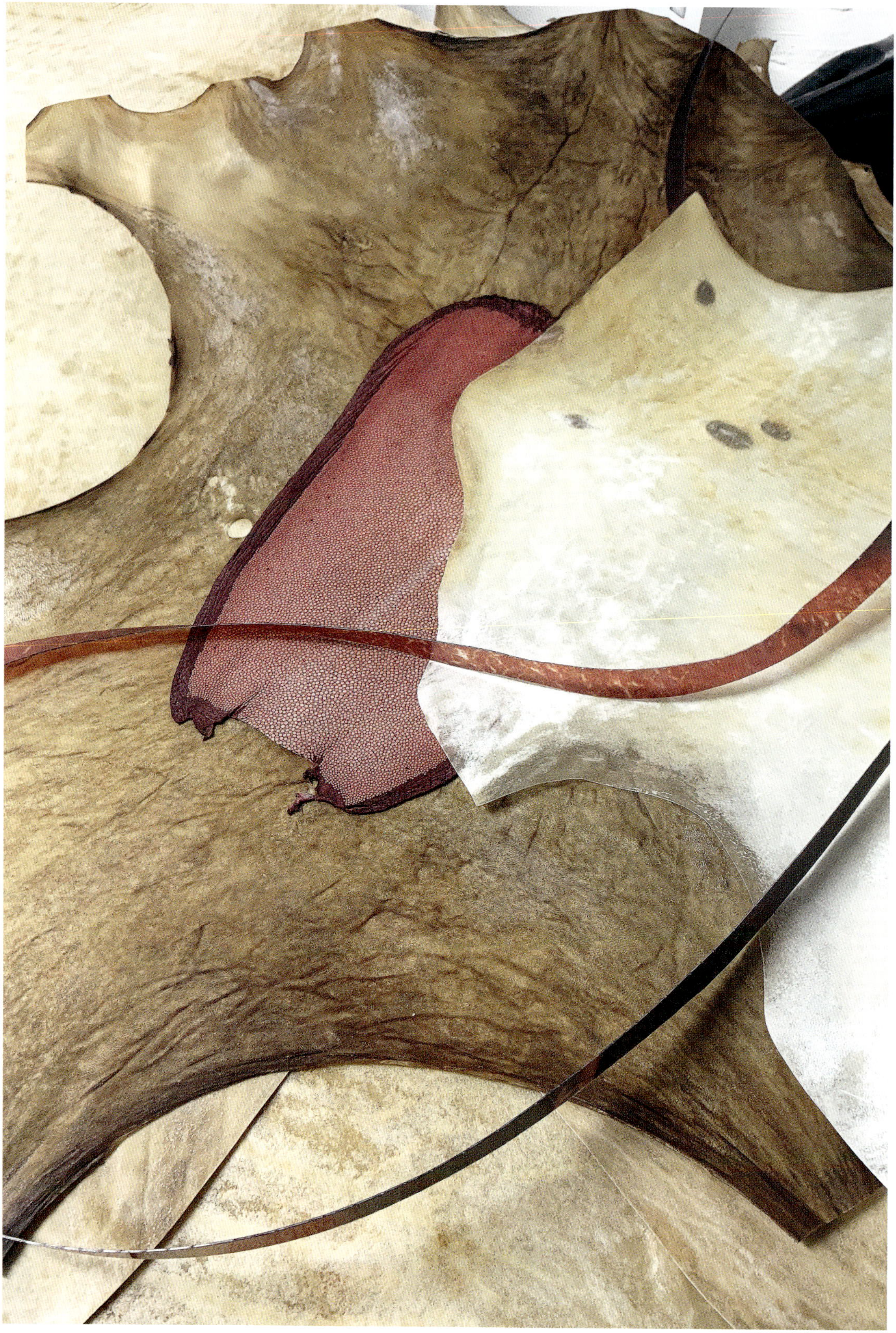

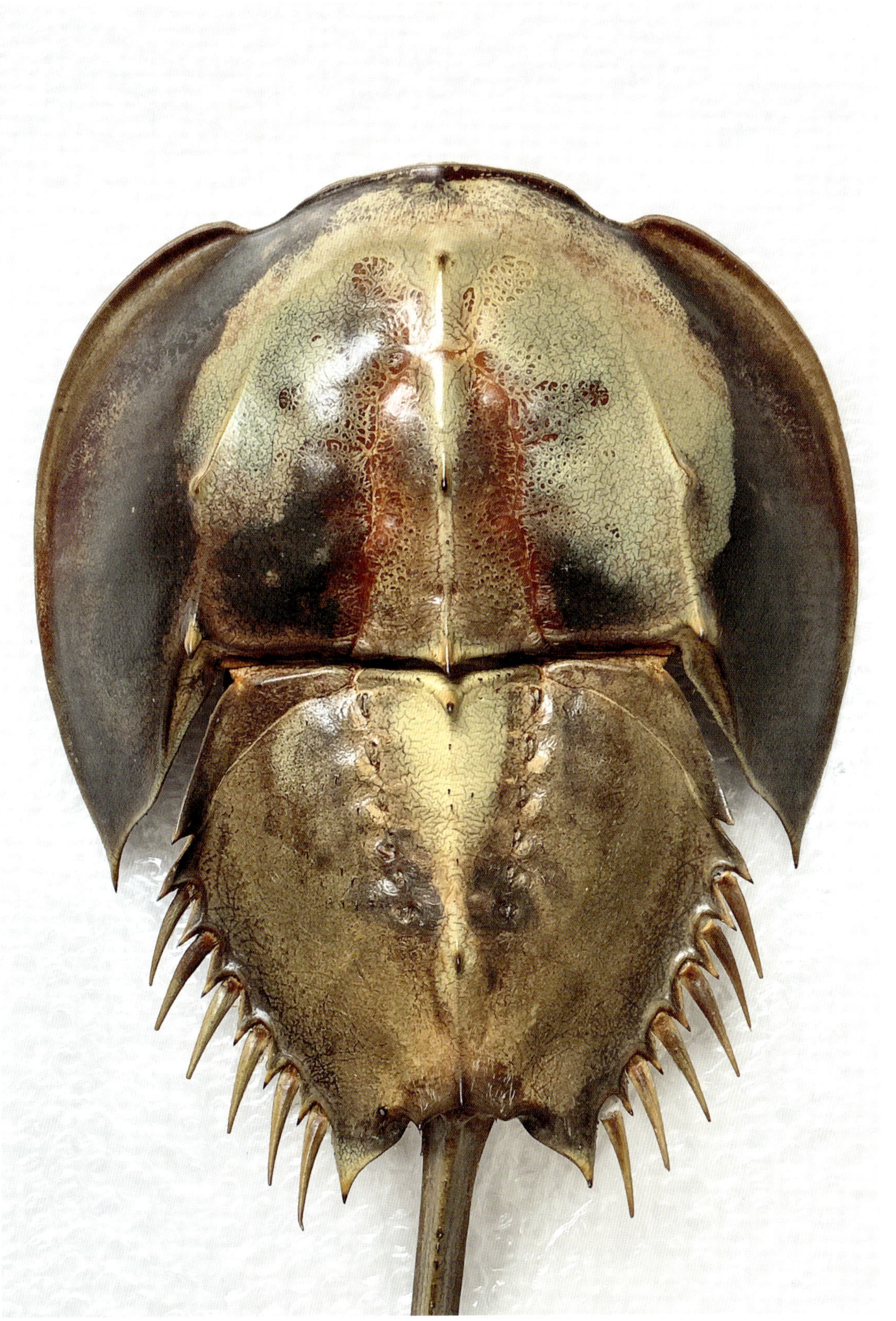

Our bodies
are not hard shells

They are porous
hosts of life

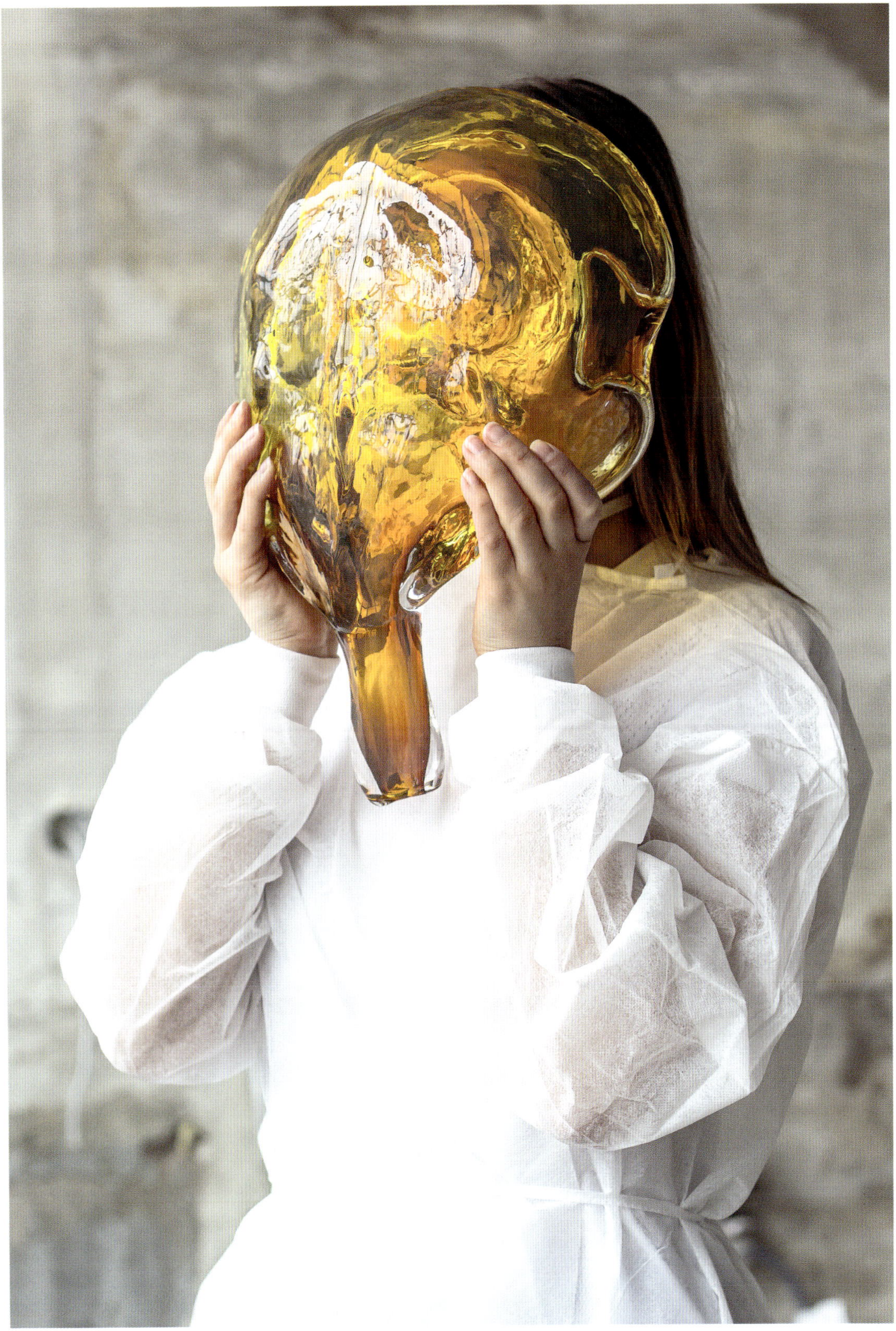

Merike Estna

Merike Estna (b. 1980, Tallinn, Estonia) lives and works in Tallinn and Mexico City. A participant in the performance art scene associated with Academia Non Grata alternative art school in the early 2000s, Estna later acquired formal art education at the Estonian Academy of Art where she attended painting (BA) and Interdisciplinary Arts (MA) classes. Estna relocated to London in 2007, where she completed an MFA Art Practice degree at Goldsmiths College in 2009. Estna's practice is primarily focused on the processes of painting, approaching the artwork as an integral part of life rather than it being about life. Borrowing patterns and colour combinations from applied arts and crafts, vocabularies which traditionally have not been accepted in the visual language of painting, her work challenges the masculine territory of painting and questions the strict separation between the two discourses. Initially applying patterns and treatments to canvases, Estna gradually progressed to cover clothes, objects, and entire spaces as her research into colour and acts of painting expanded. Estna's recent exhibitions include *Soil will not contain our love*, Kai Art Center, Tallinn (2022) and *Nightfall/Videvik*, Publics, Helsinki (2021), among others.

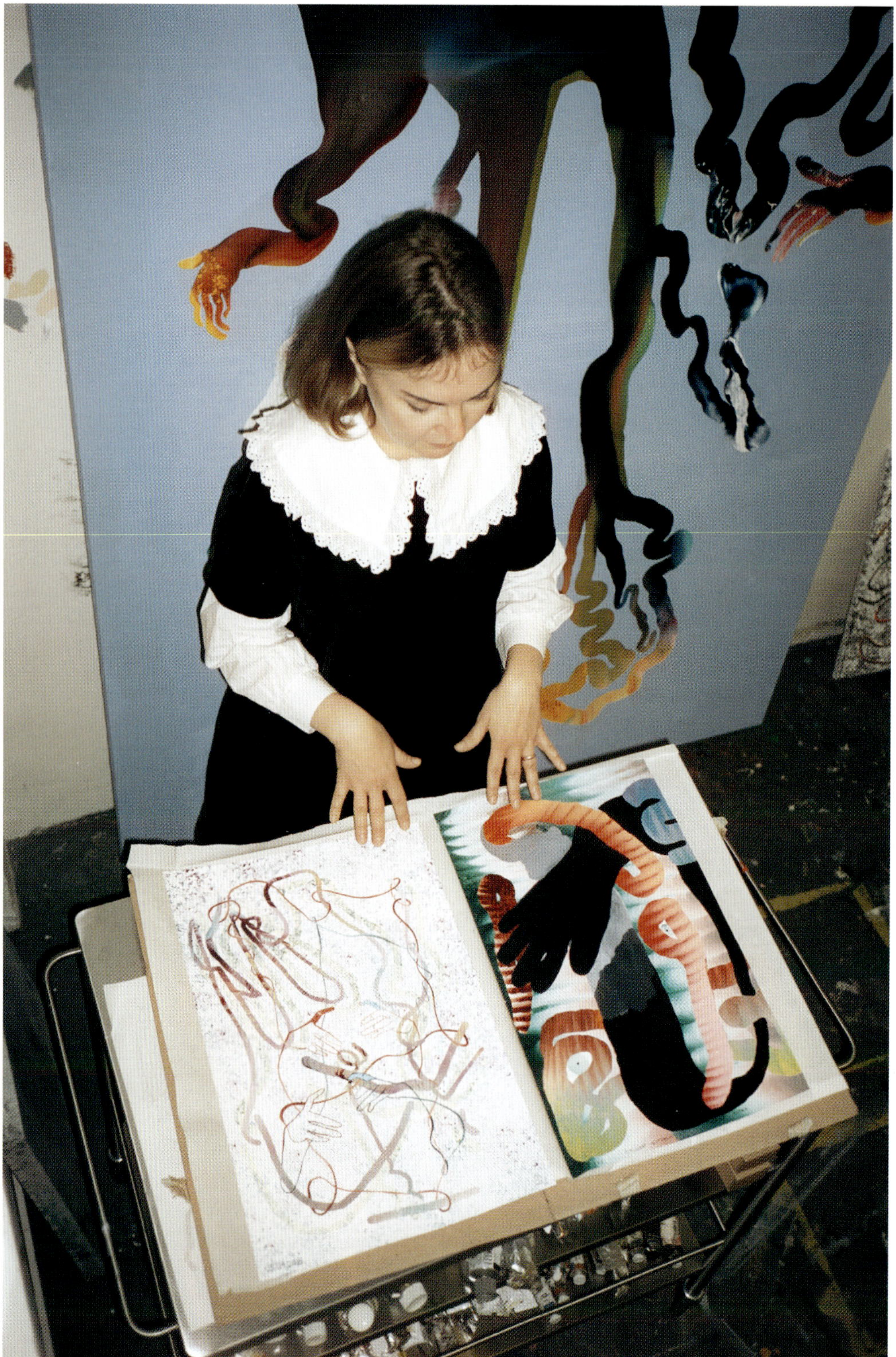

Merike Estna in her Tallinn studio, 2022
Photo: Marta Vaarik

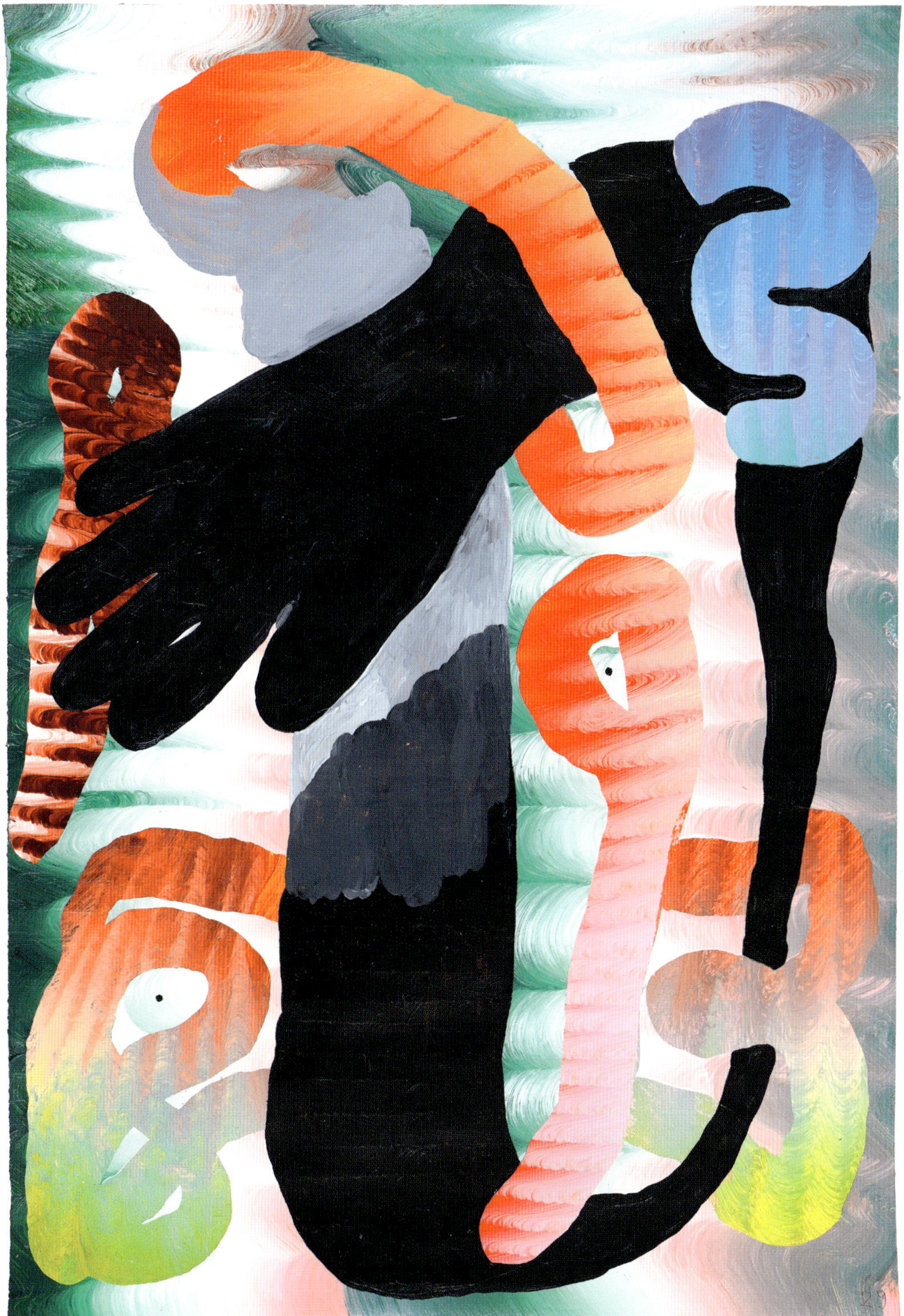

Daily painting no 29, 2018
From a series of 146 paintings on paper, mixed media, 52 x 36 cm each
Photo: Stanislav Stepaško

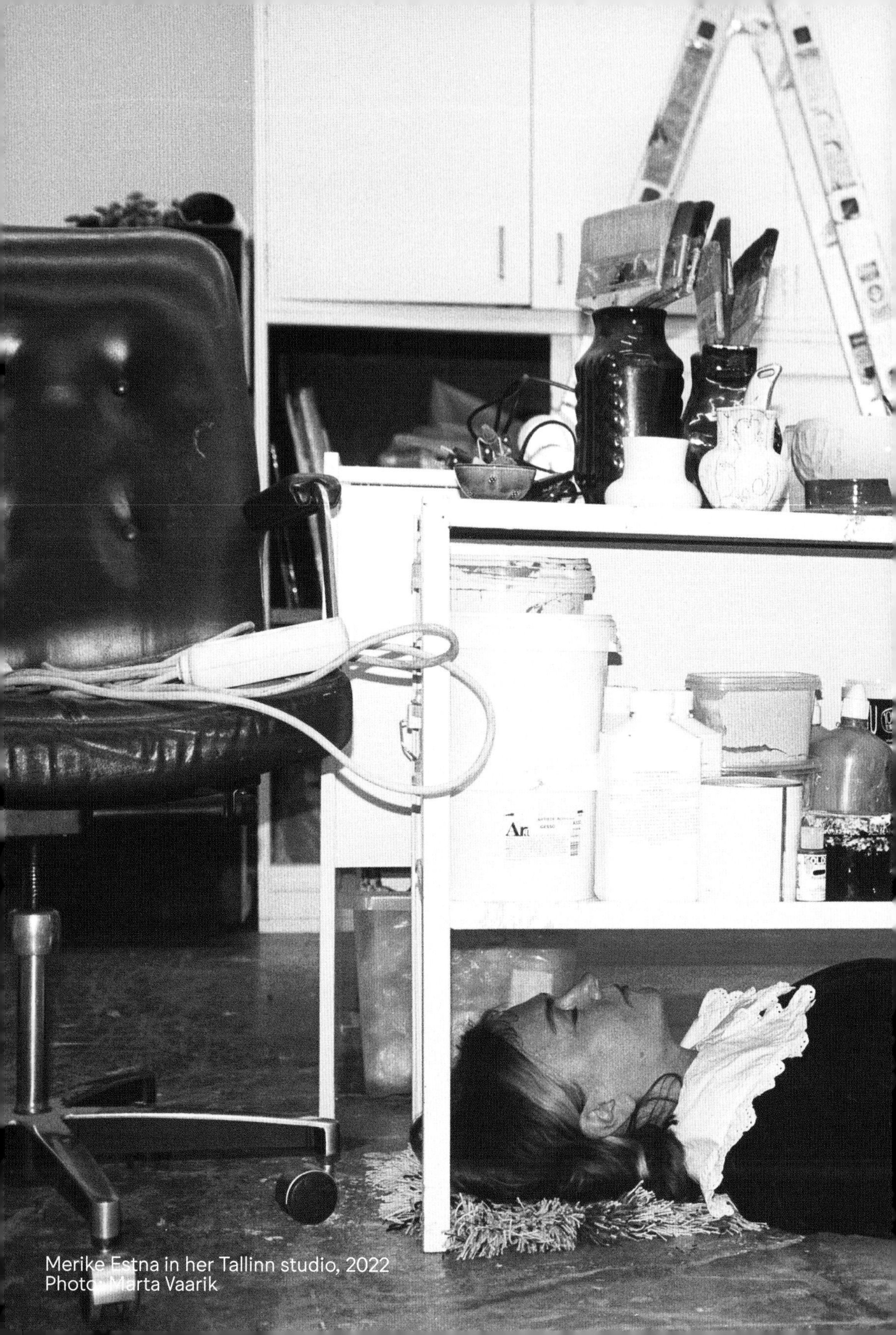

Merike Estna in her Tallinn studio, 2022
Photo: Marta Vaarik

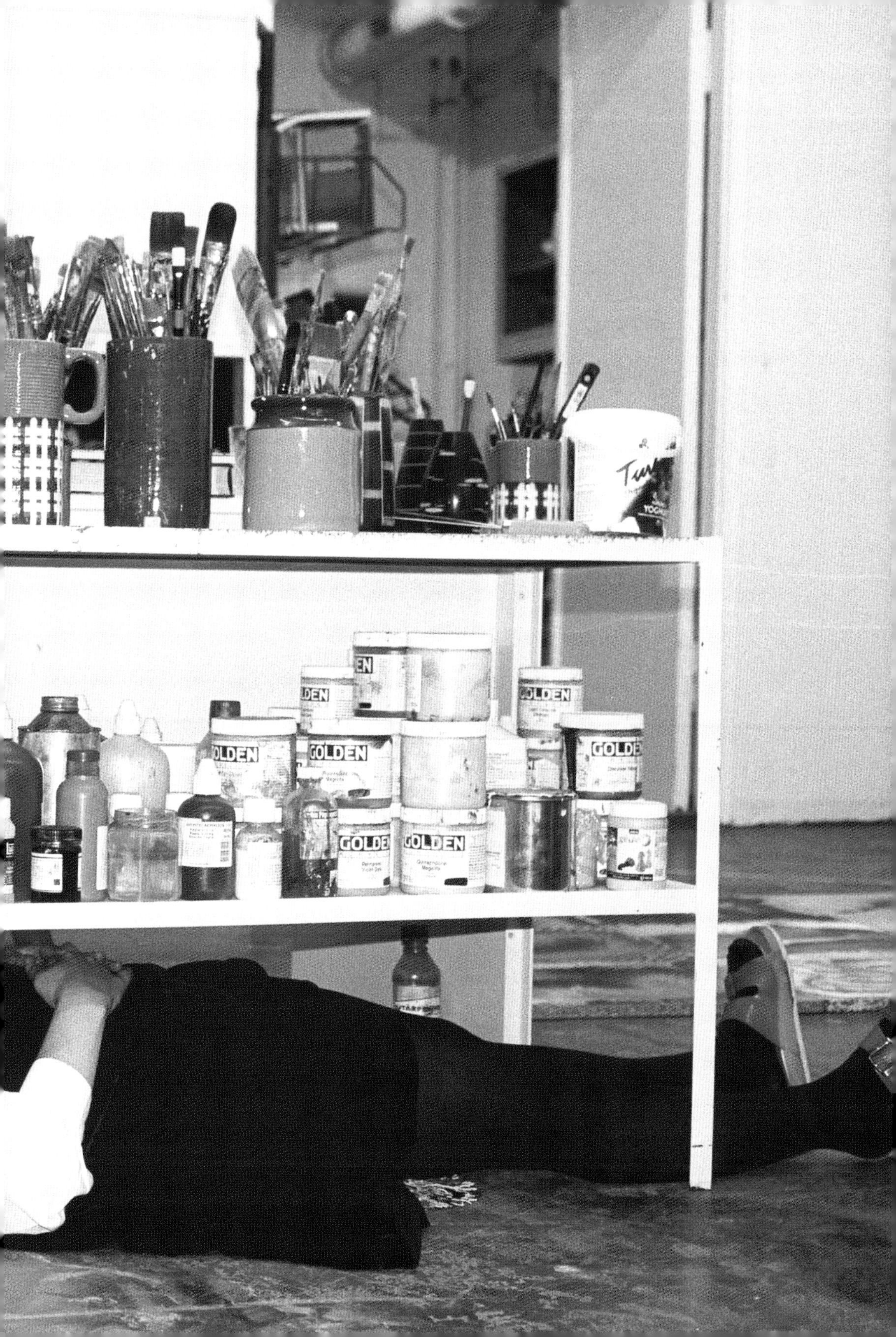
GOLDEN
GOLDEN
GOLDEN
GOLDEN
GOLDEN
GOLDEN
GOLDEN

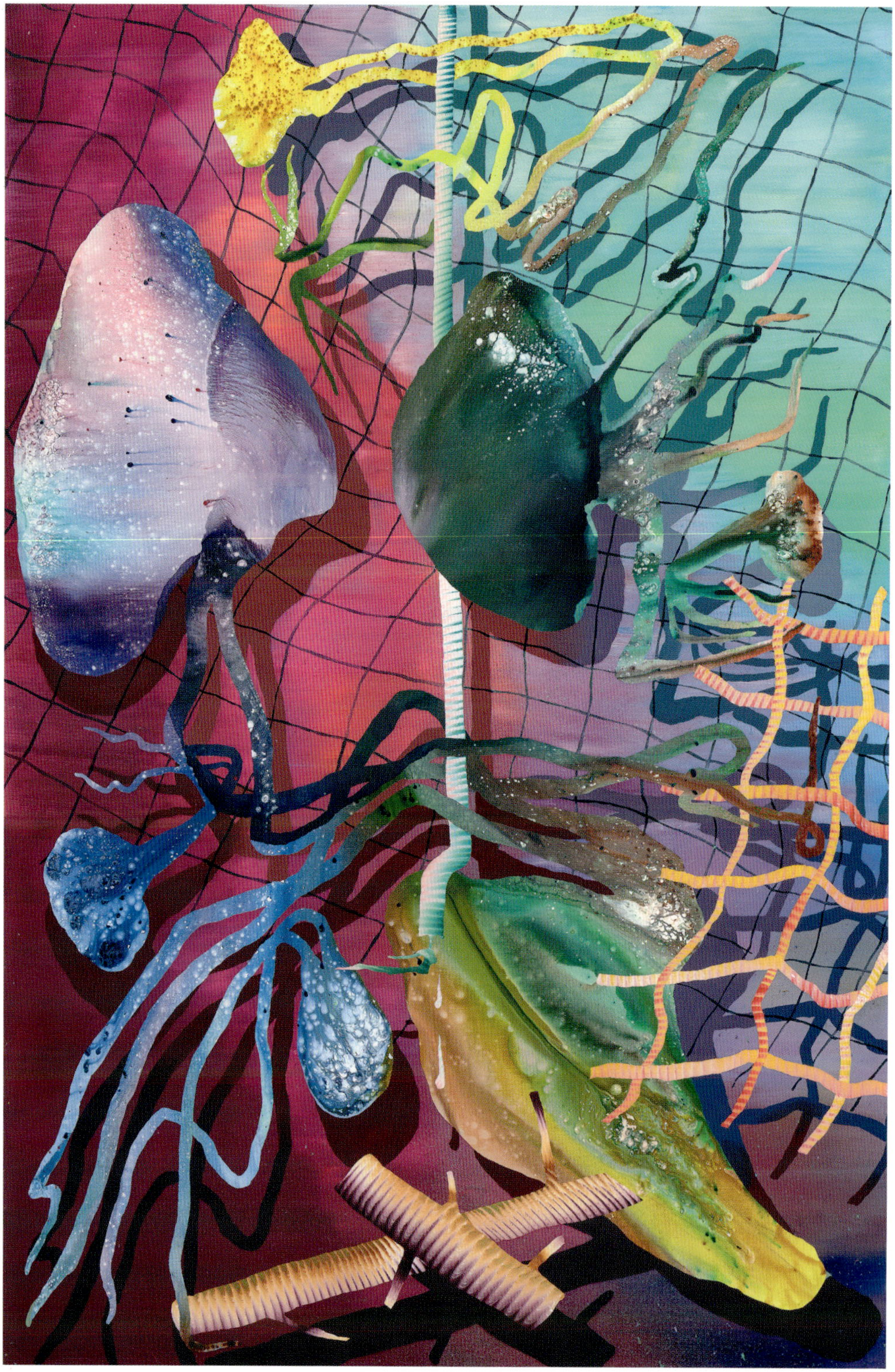

Detail from *Ocean of Endangered Times*, 2019
Acrylic and oil on canvas, 45 x 61 cm (detail); 6 x 4 m (original size)
Photo: Stanislav Stepaško

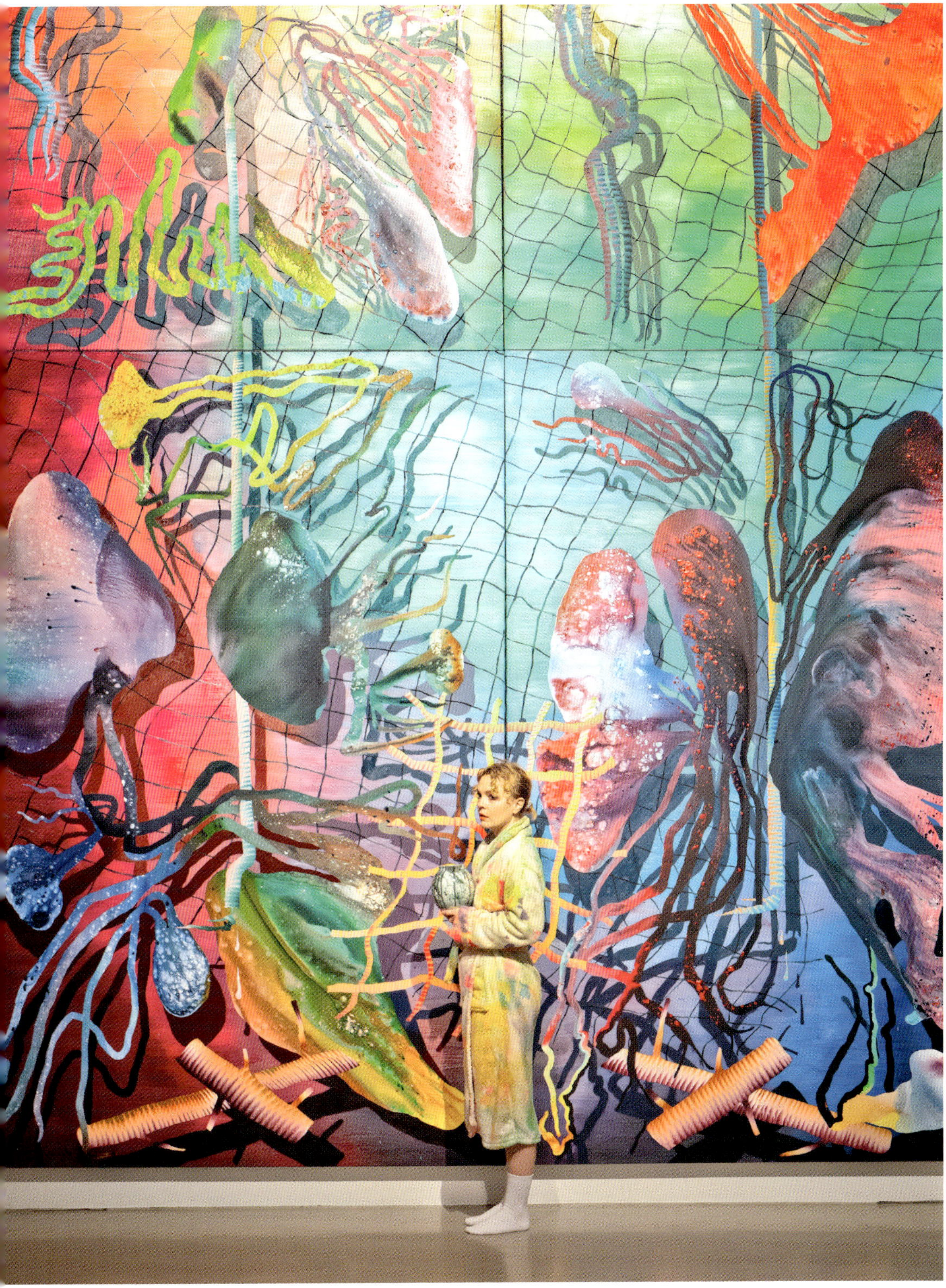

Ghost of the future, filled with memories of past, 2019
Exhibition view with performative presence by Merike Estna, Moderna Museet Malmö, Sweden
Courtesy Merike Estna Studio
Photo: Helene Toresdotter/Moderna Museet

Agnė Juodvalkytė

Agnė Juodvalkytė (b. 1987, Vilnius, Lithuania) is a visual artist currently living in Berlin and Vilnius. Her practice is largely focused on abstract painting and textiles. Juodvalkytė uses textiles as a framework to understand culture, history, and technology. She works with different materials, such as clothes, textiles, natural pigments, graphite dust, fabrics made by her grandmother, plants, and incorporates various mediums. Often presented in an anthropomorphic way, her works breathe their past into the present, becoming multidimensional artefacts extending not only into space but also into time. She received a BA in painting at the Vilnius Academy of Arts (2010) and studied visual arts in Spain at the Universidad de Castilla La Mancha (UCLM, Cuenca) (2009). Her recent shows include solo exhibitions *Tools for the Future (ANSKA)*, Galerie Bernau, Bernau bei Berlin (2022) and *ANSKA*, Blake & Vargas, Berlin (2021), as well as group exhibitions *Sweet Dreams Foundation*, Nida Art Colony, Lithuania (2022); *Gathering*, Atletika, Vilnius (2021); and *Audra*, Pamario Gallery, Juodkrantė (2021).

Tools for the Future, 2022

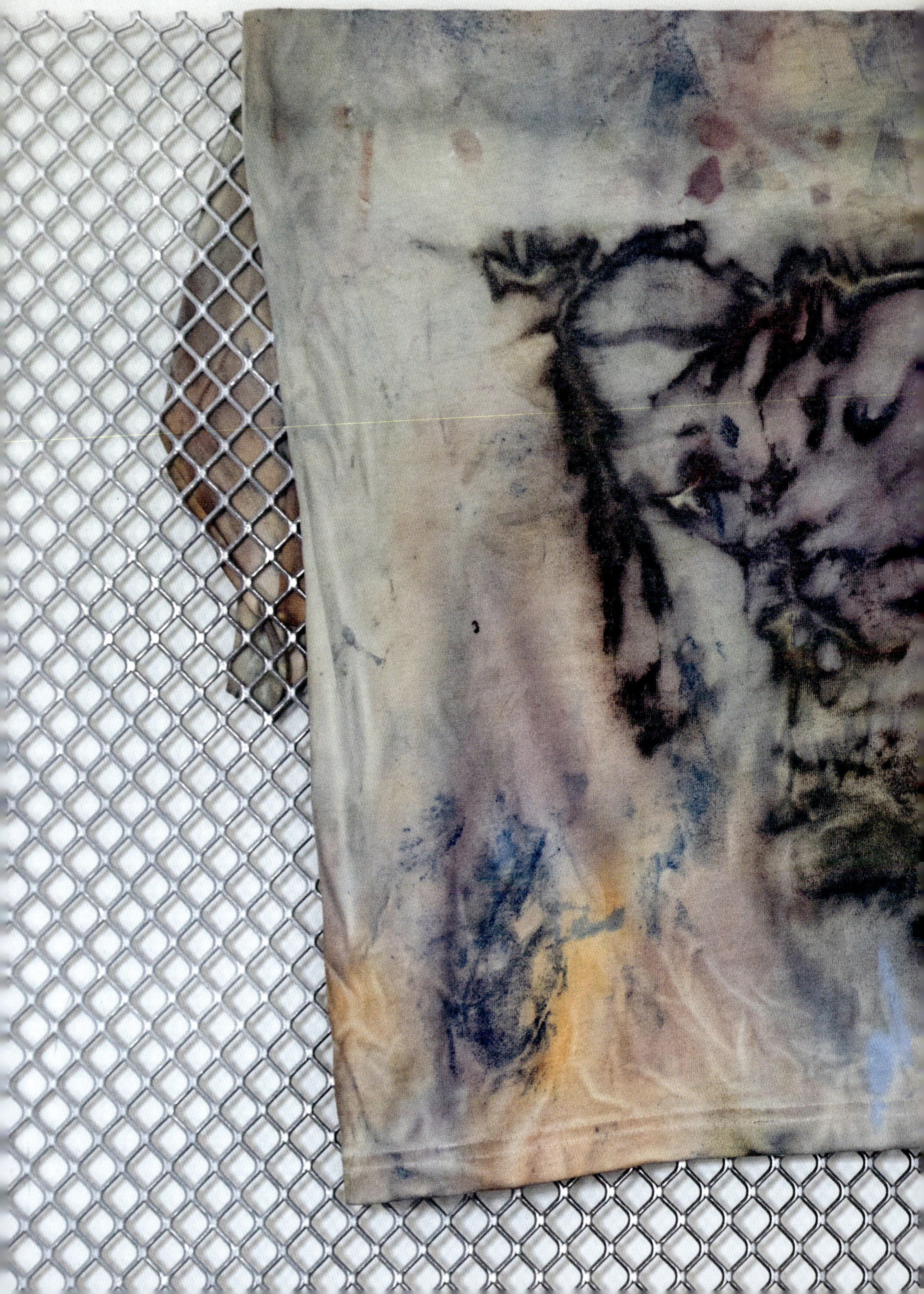

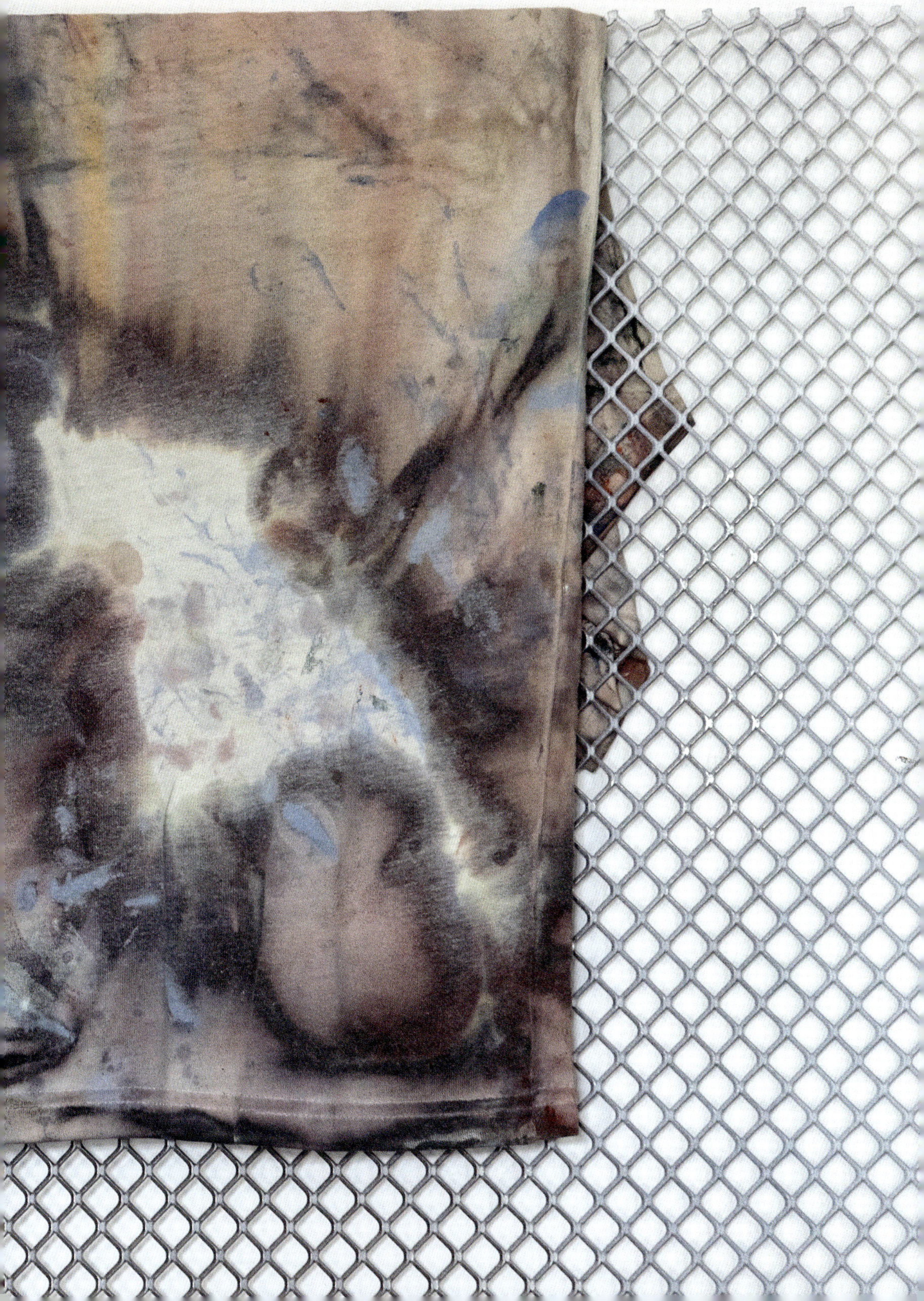

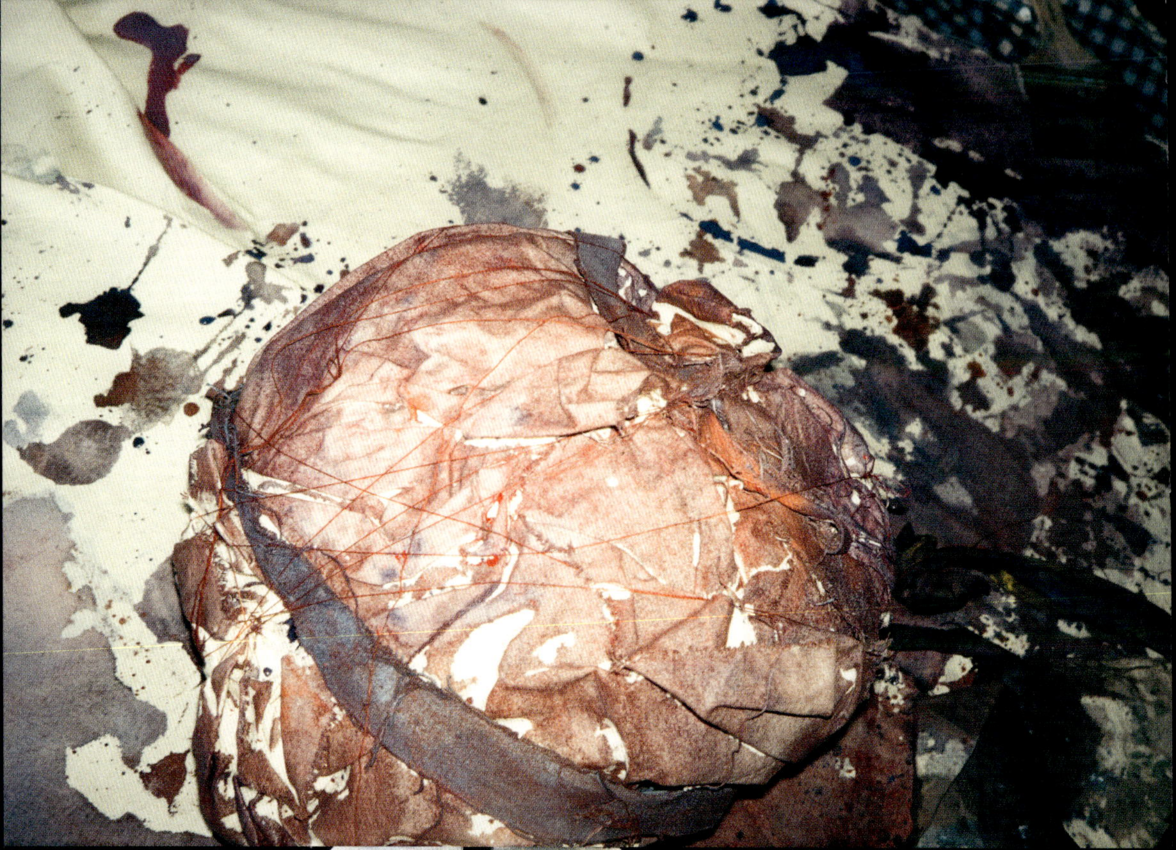
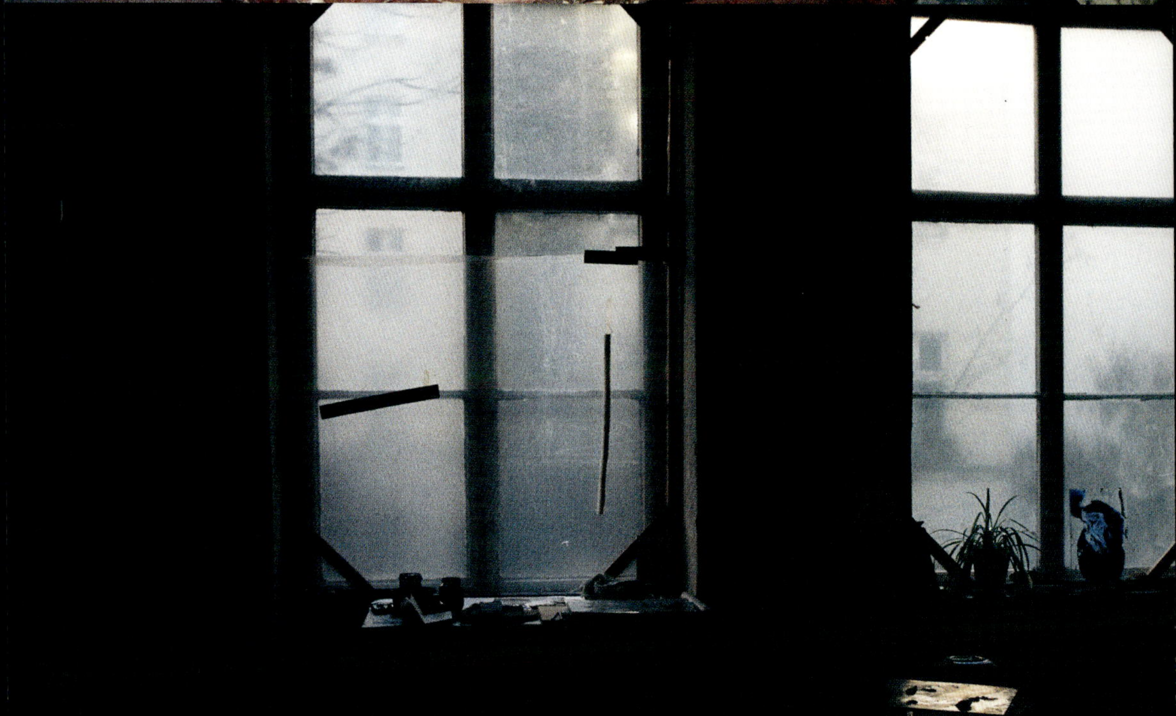

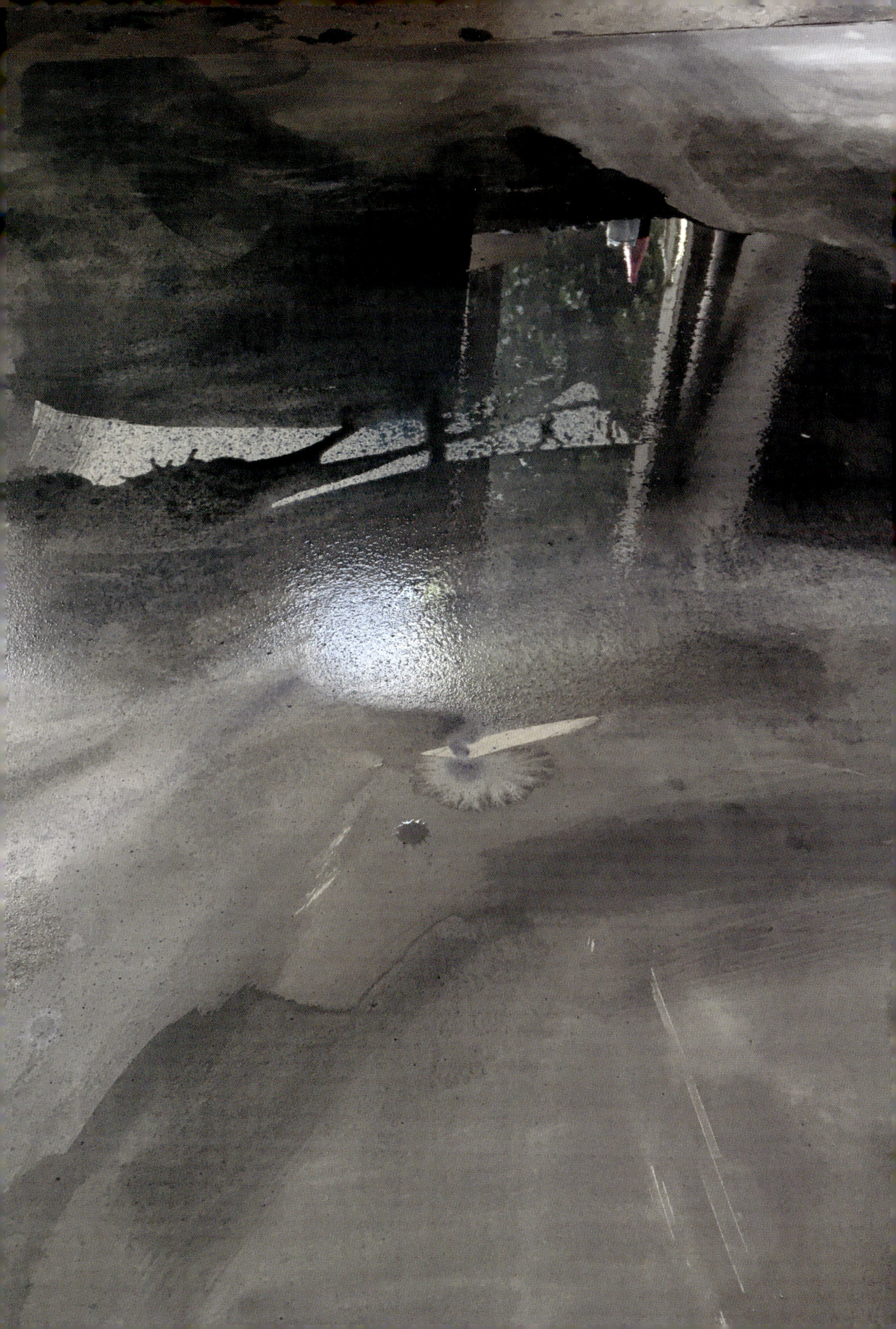

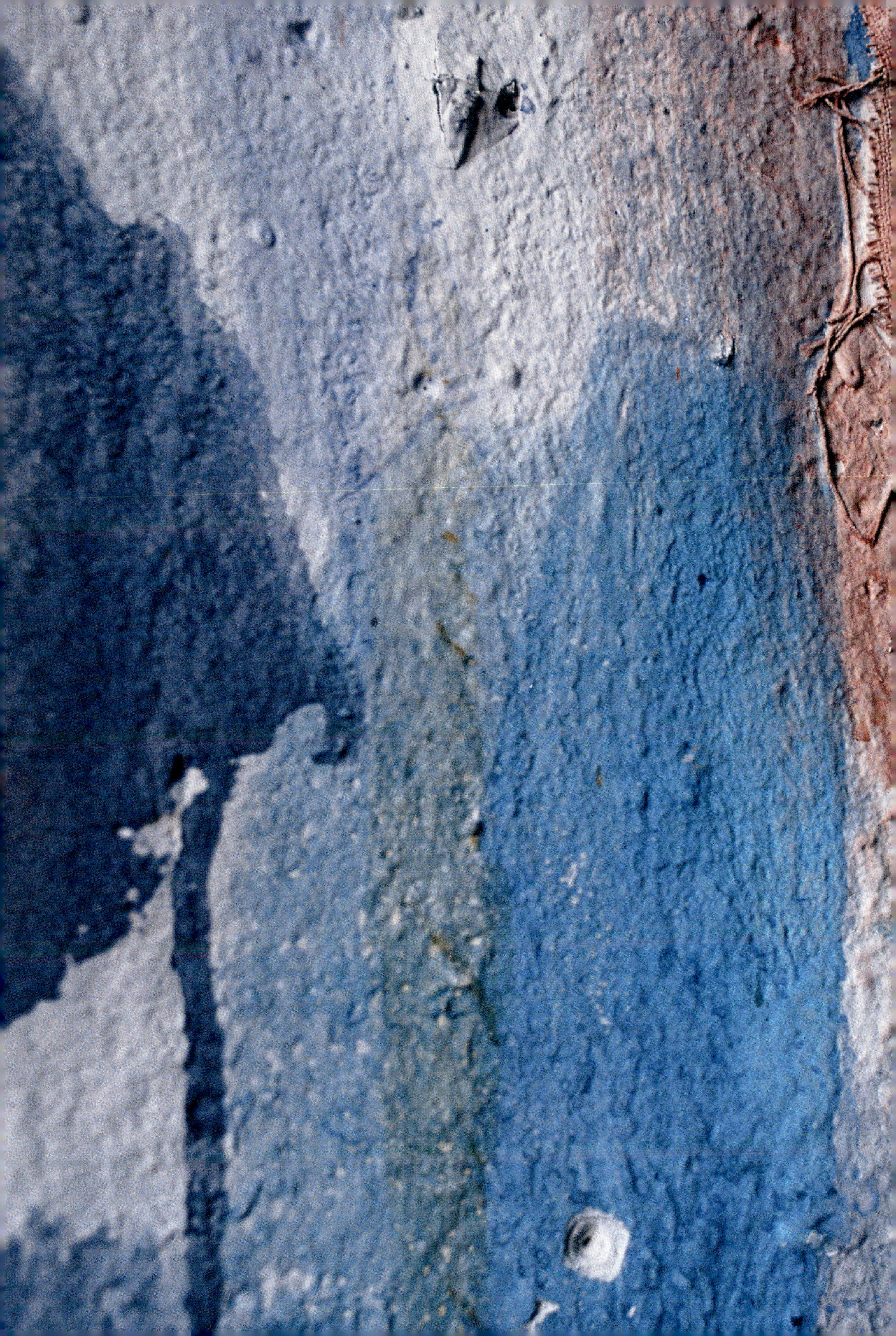

Katja Novitskova

Katja Novitskova (b. 1984, Tallinn, Estonia) lives and works in Amsterdam. Her work tackles the complexity of depicting the world through technological and cultural mechanisms. By uniting art and science on the level of nature, Novitskova brings awareness to the mediation and representation tools used to depict these realms. Through her use of visual materials found online, AI technologies, and installation she creates works which vacillate between physical and digital domains. Her work has been exhibited internationally in solo and group exhibitions, including Kraupa-Tuskany Zeidler, Berlin (2022); MUDAM Luxembourg (2021); Kunstfort bij Vijfhuizen (2021); Belgrade Biennal (2021); Migros Museum für Gegenwartskunst, Zürich (2020); Sharjah Art Foundation (2020); Hamburger Bahnhof, Berlin (2019); Marta Herford Museum, Herford (2018); Whitechapel Gallery, London (2018); Kumu Art Museum, Tallinn (2018); Baltic Triennial, Vilnius (2018); and the Estonian Pavilion at the 57th Venice Biennale (2017).

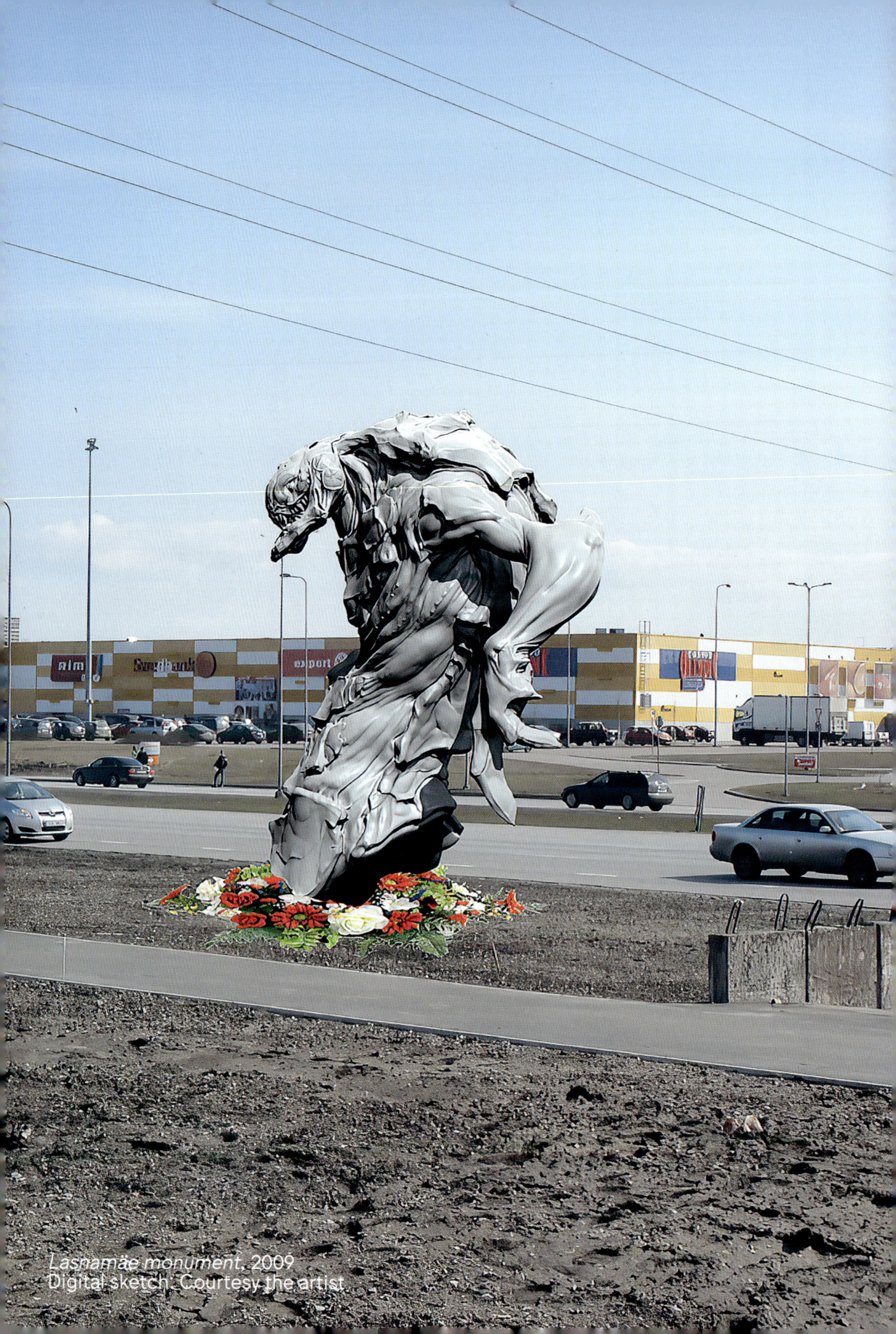

Lasnamäe monument, 2009
Digital sketch. Courtesy the artist

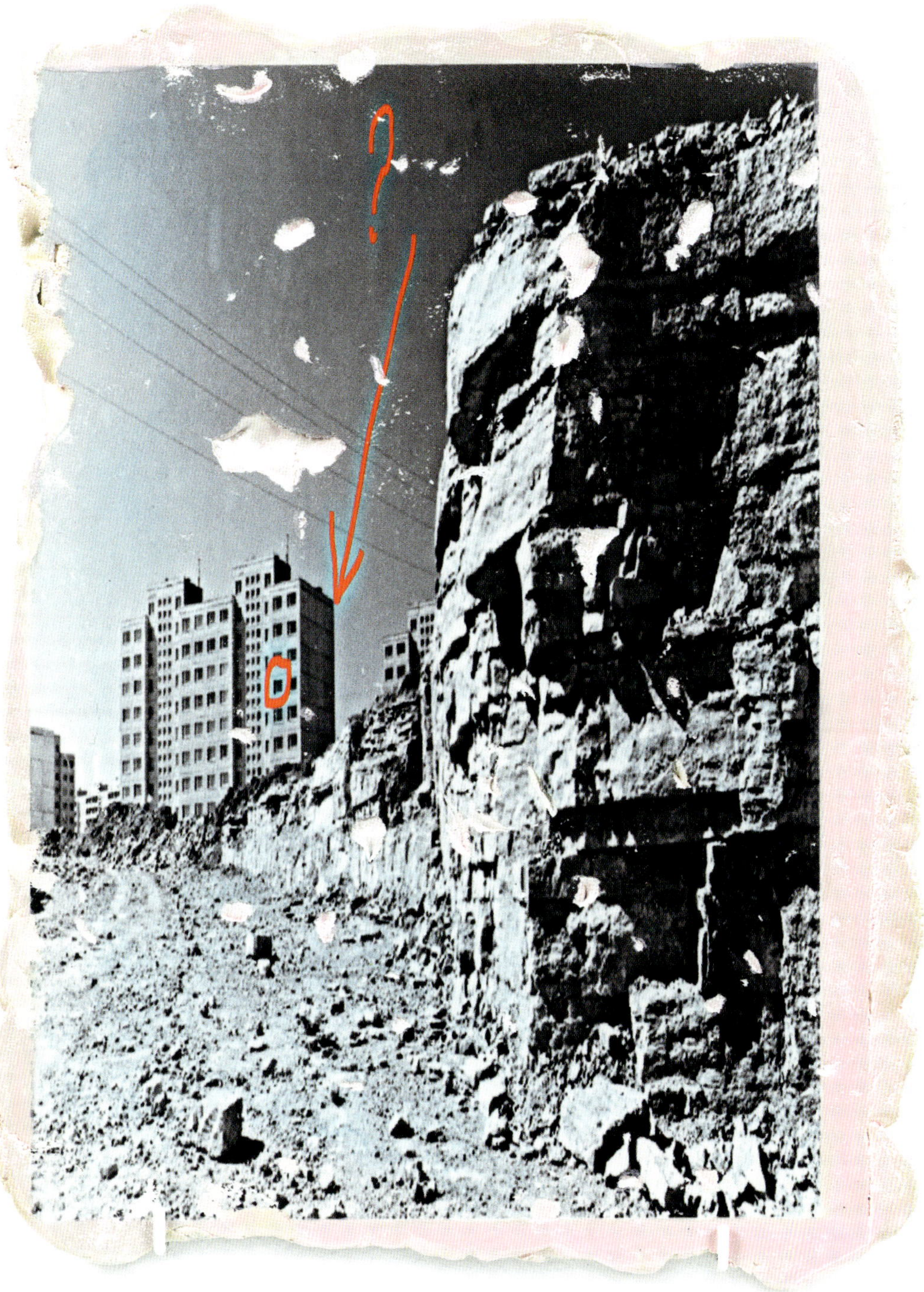

Annual Report, 2018
UV resistant ink, epoxy clay, and nail polish
Courtesy Kraupa-Tuskany Zeidler and the artist
Photo: def-image

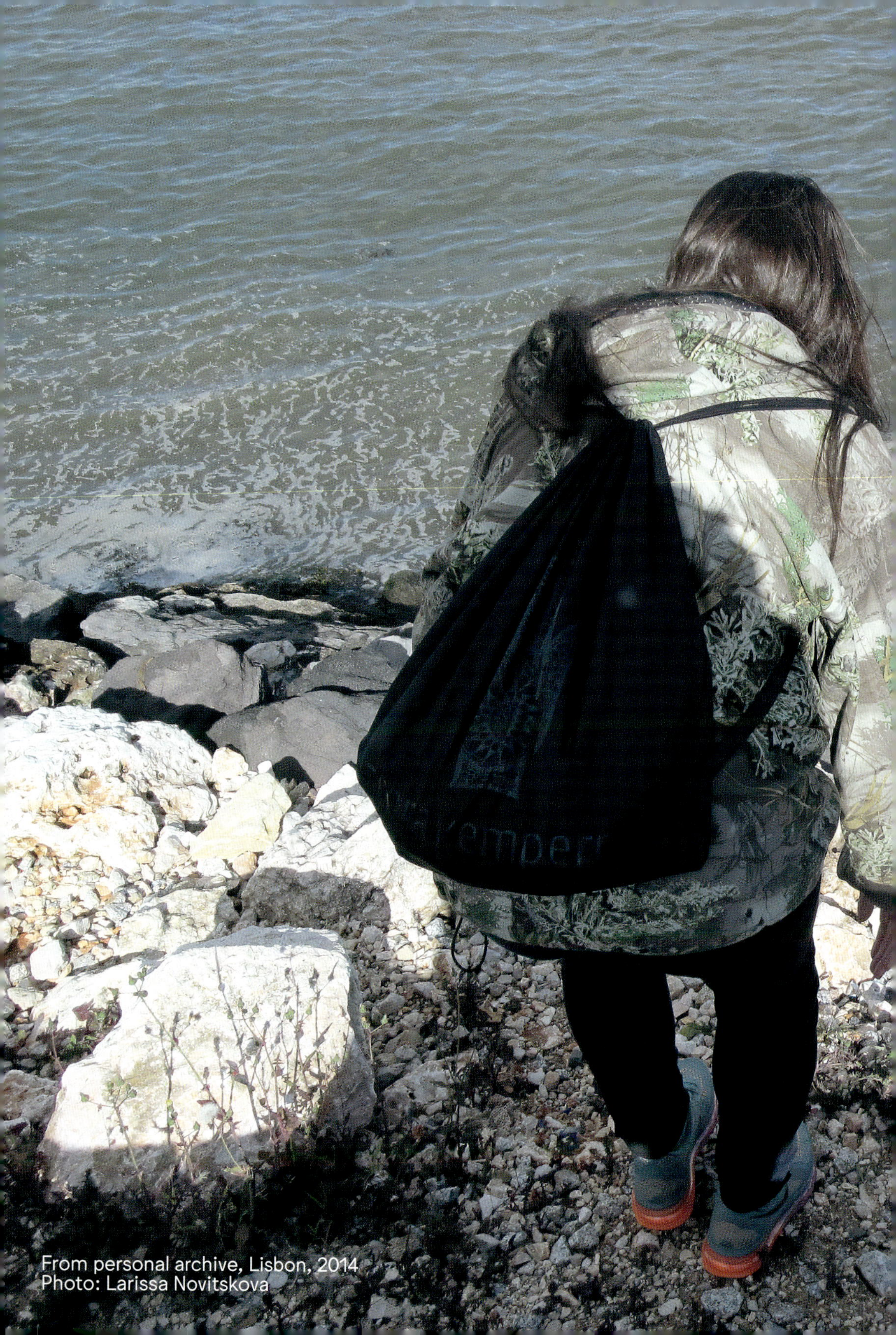

From personal archive, Lisbon, 2014
Photo: Larissa Novitskova

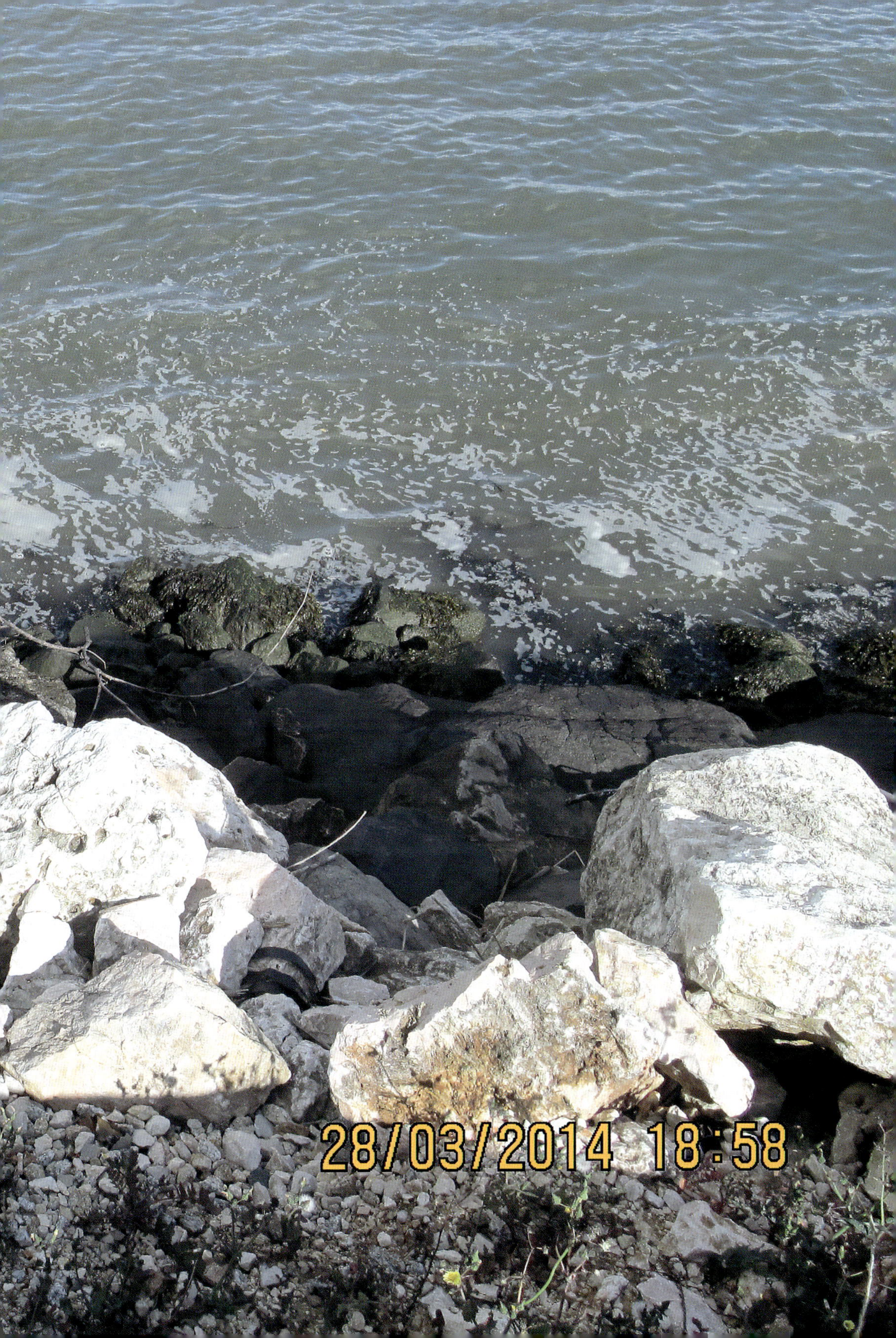
28/03/2014 18:58

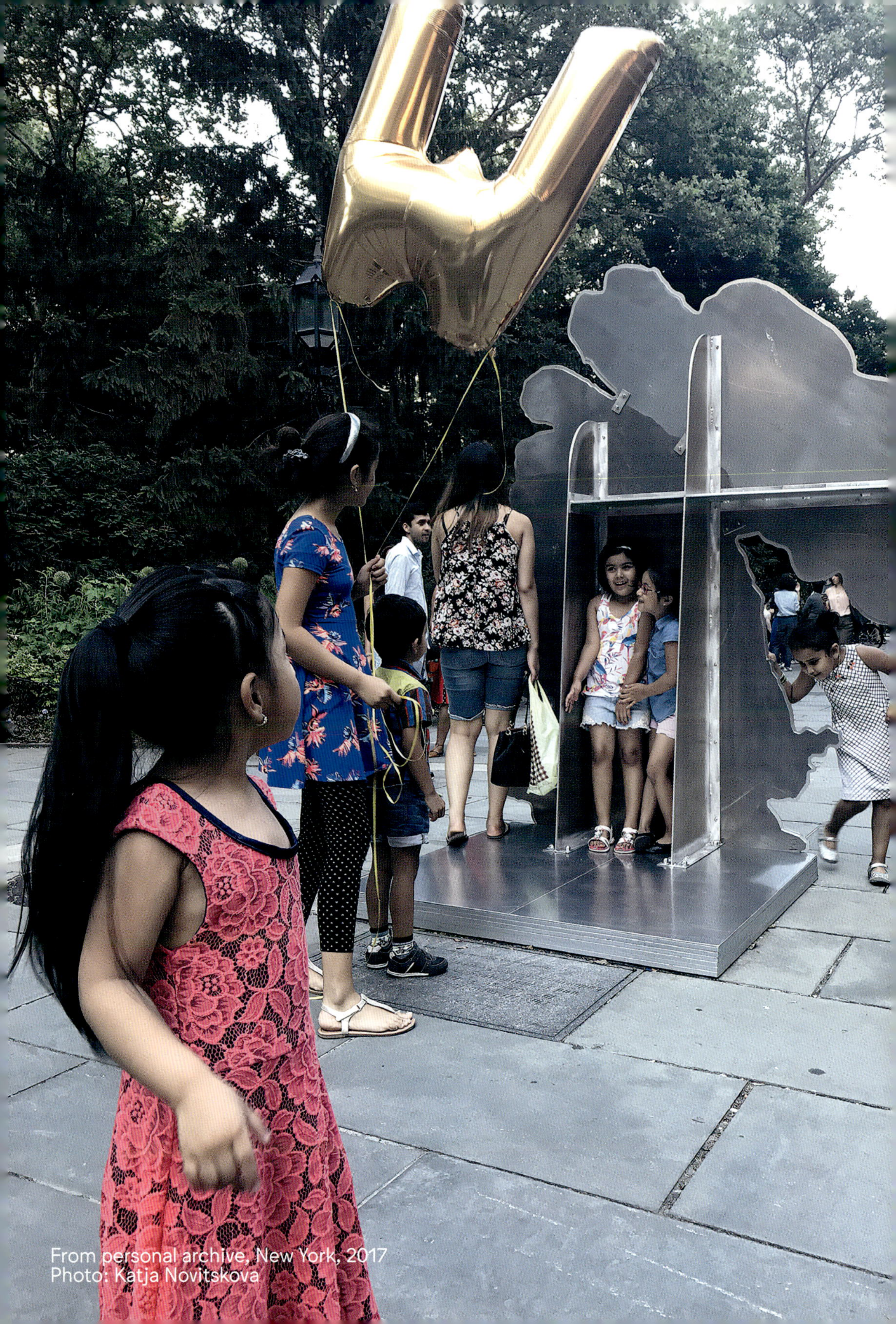

From personal archive, New York, 2017
Photo: Katja Novitskova

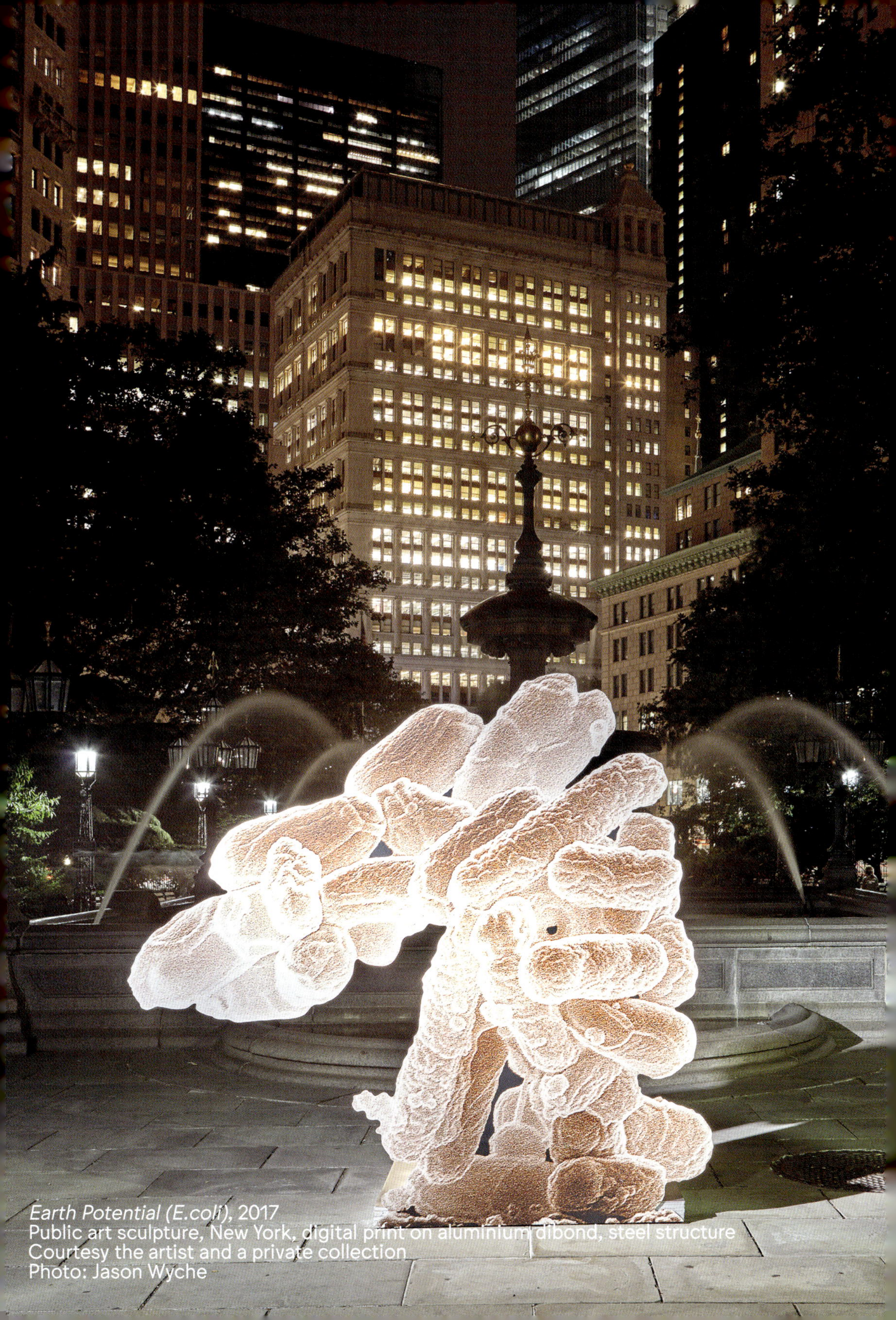

Earth Potential (E.coli), 2017
Public art sculpture, New York, digital print on aluminium dibond, steel structure
Courtesy the artist and a private collection
Photo: Jason Wyche

145

Dorota Gawęda & Eglė Kulbokaitė

Dorota Gawęda (b. 1986, Lublin, Poland) and Eglė Kulbokaitė (b. 1987, Kaunas, Lithuania) are an artist duo based in Basel. Both are graduates of the Royal College of Art in London and founders of the YOUNG GIRL READING GROUP (2013–2021). They work in multiples across performance, painting, sculpture, fragrance, and video installation—where language breaks down and one genre morphs into many. An interest in folklore runs through their work, weirding the relationship between the body and the landscape. The duo has exhibited internationally, including: Shedhalle, Zürich (2022); Kunstraum Niederoesterreich, Vienna (2022); Centre Culturel Suisse, Paris (2022); Kunstverein Hamburg (2021); Istituto Svizzero, Palermo/Milan (2021); Swiss Institute, New York (2020); Julia Stoschek Collection, Düsseldorf (2020); Kunsthalle Fribourg (2020); Futura, Prague (2019); Lafayette Anticipations, Paris (2019); Palais de Tokyo, Paris (2018); 6th Athens Biennale (2018); Kunsthalle Basel (2017); ICA, London (2017); MOMA, Warsaw (2016); Berlin Biennale 9 (2016), among others. They are the recipients of the Allegro Artist Prize (2022); CERN Collide Residency award (2022); and the Swiss Performance Art Award (2021).

Dorota Gawęda and Eglė Kulbokaitė's visual essay *Backstage (Separation Anxiety)* offers a brief glimpse into the production process for their *Mouthless* video series created between 2020 and 2023.

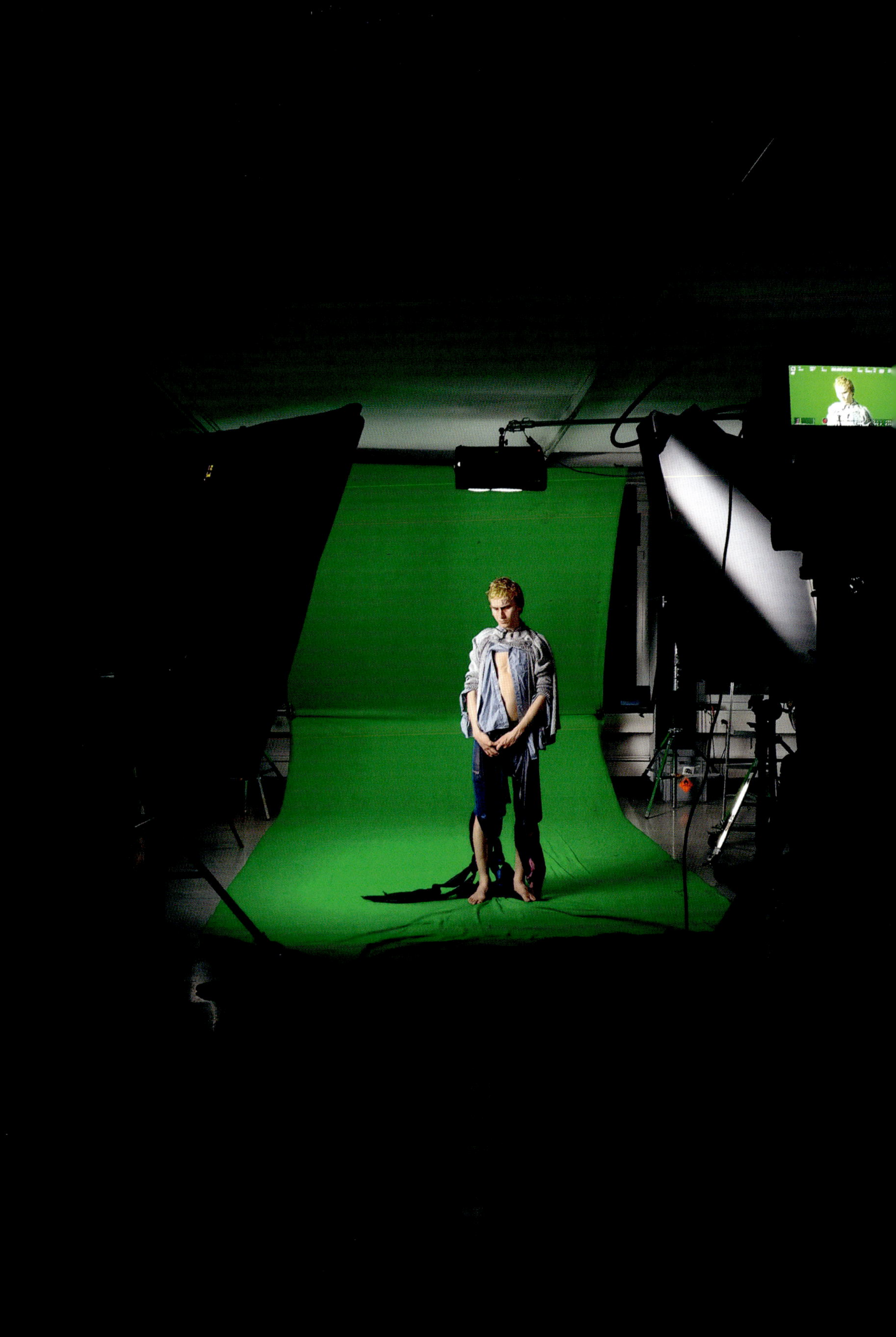

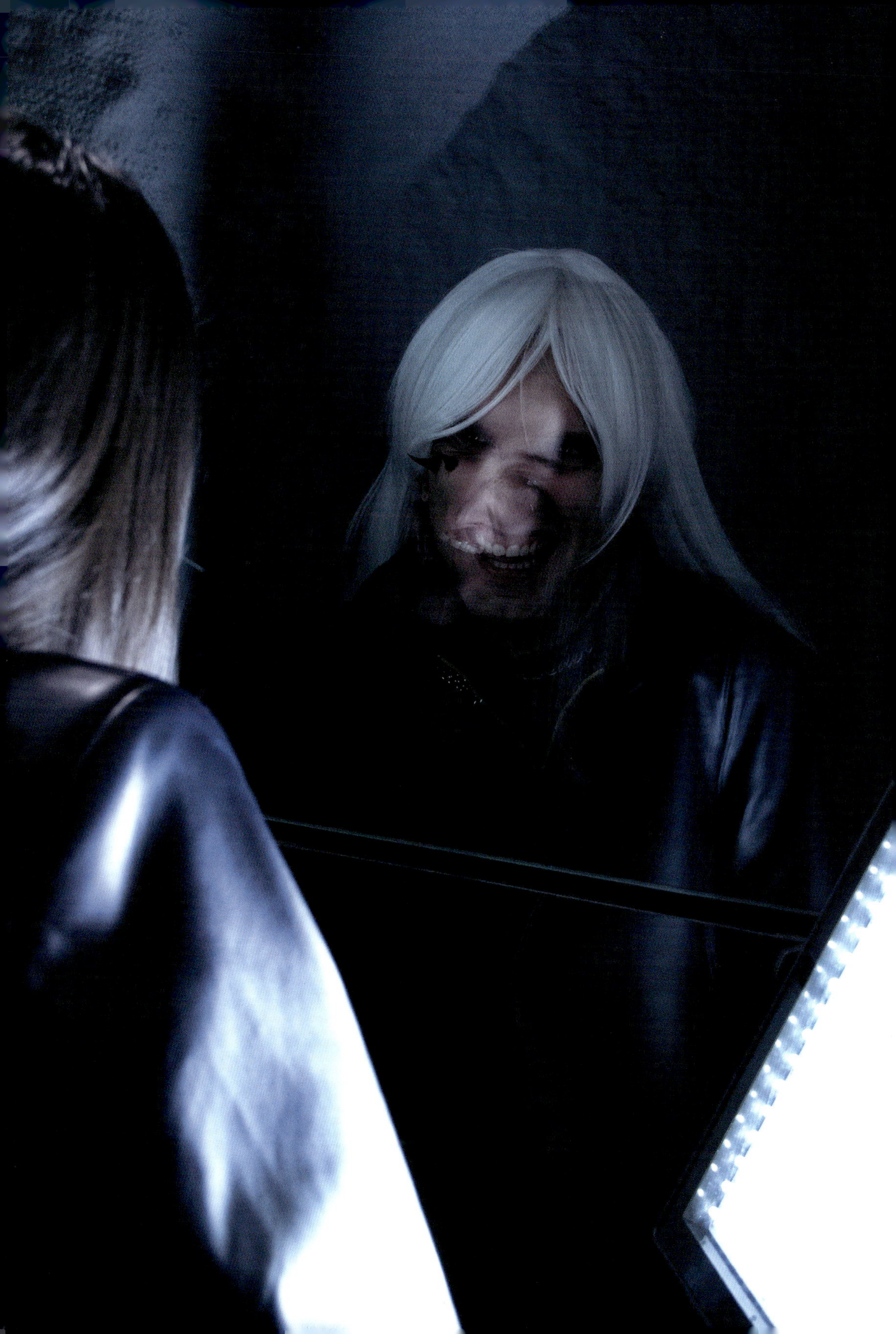

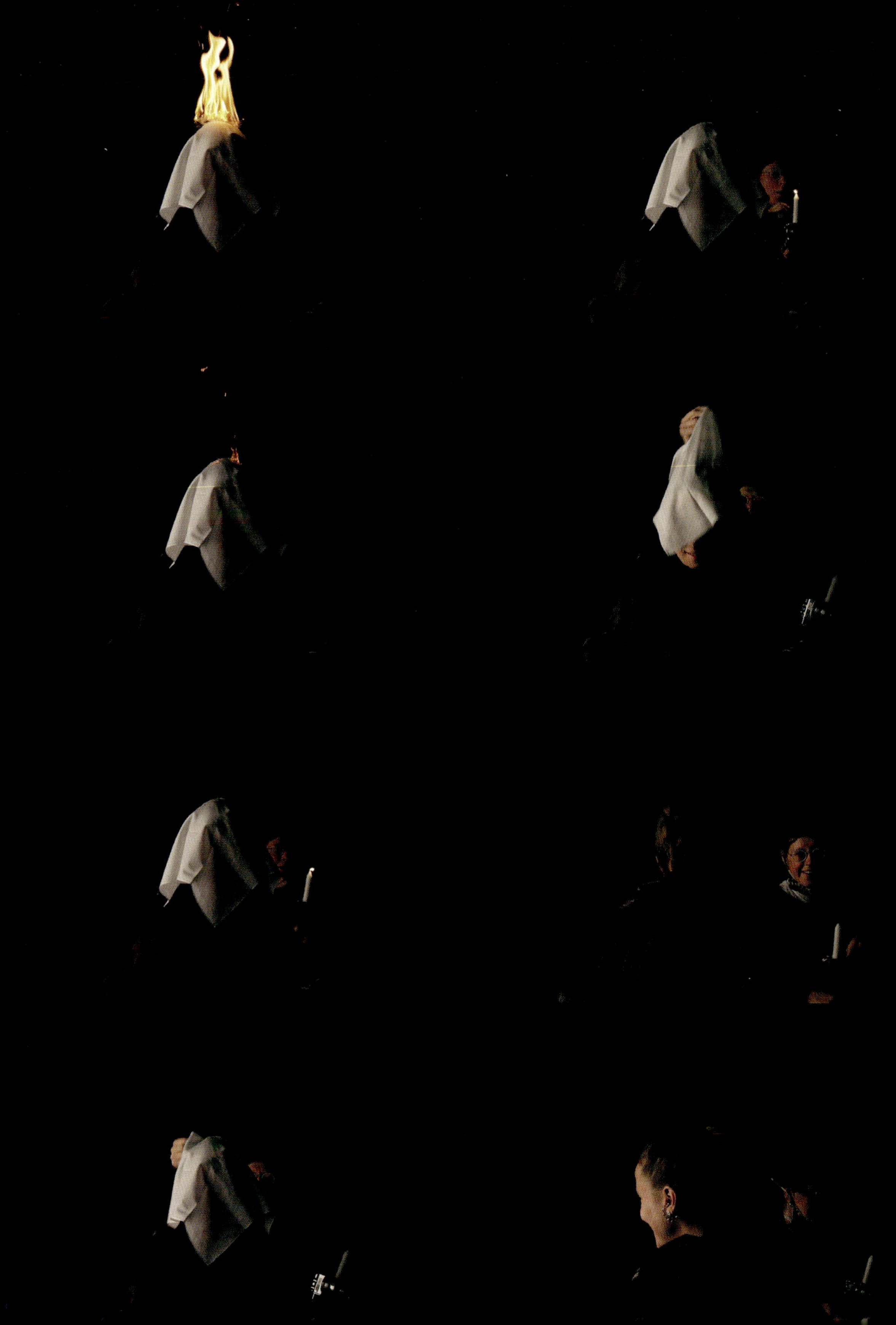

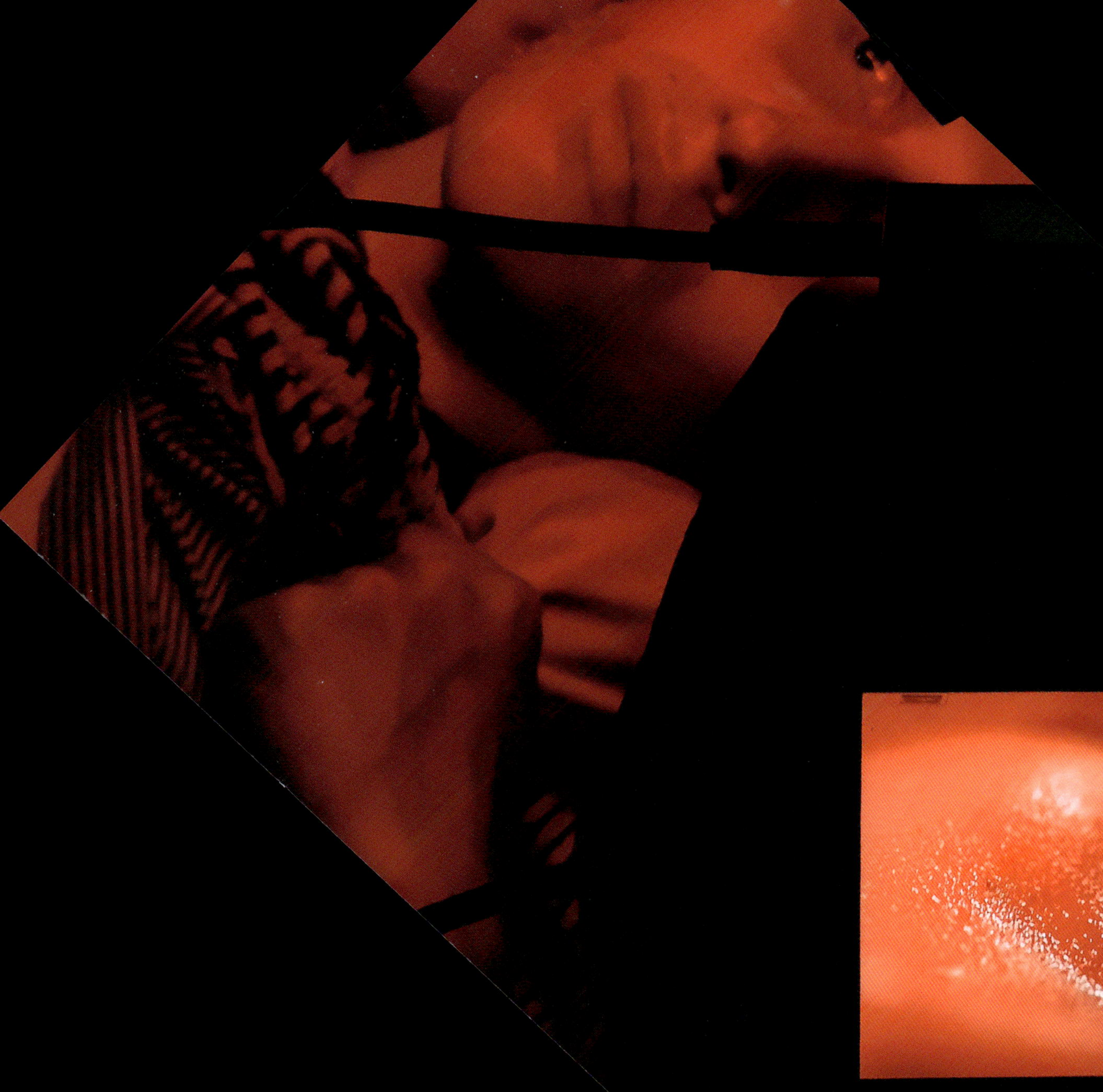
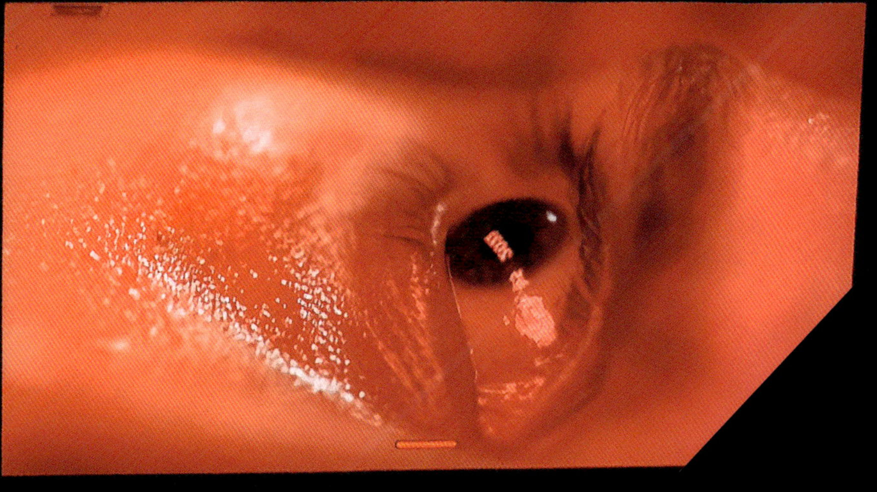

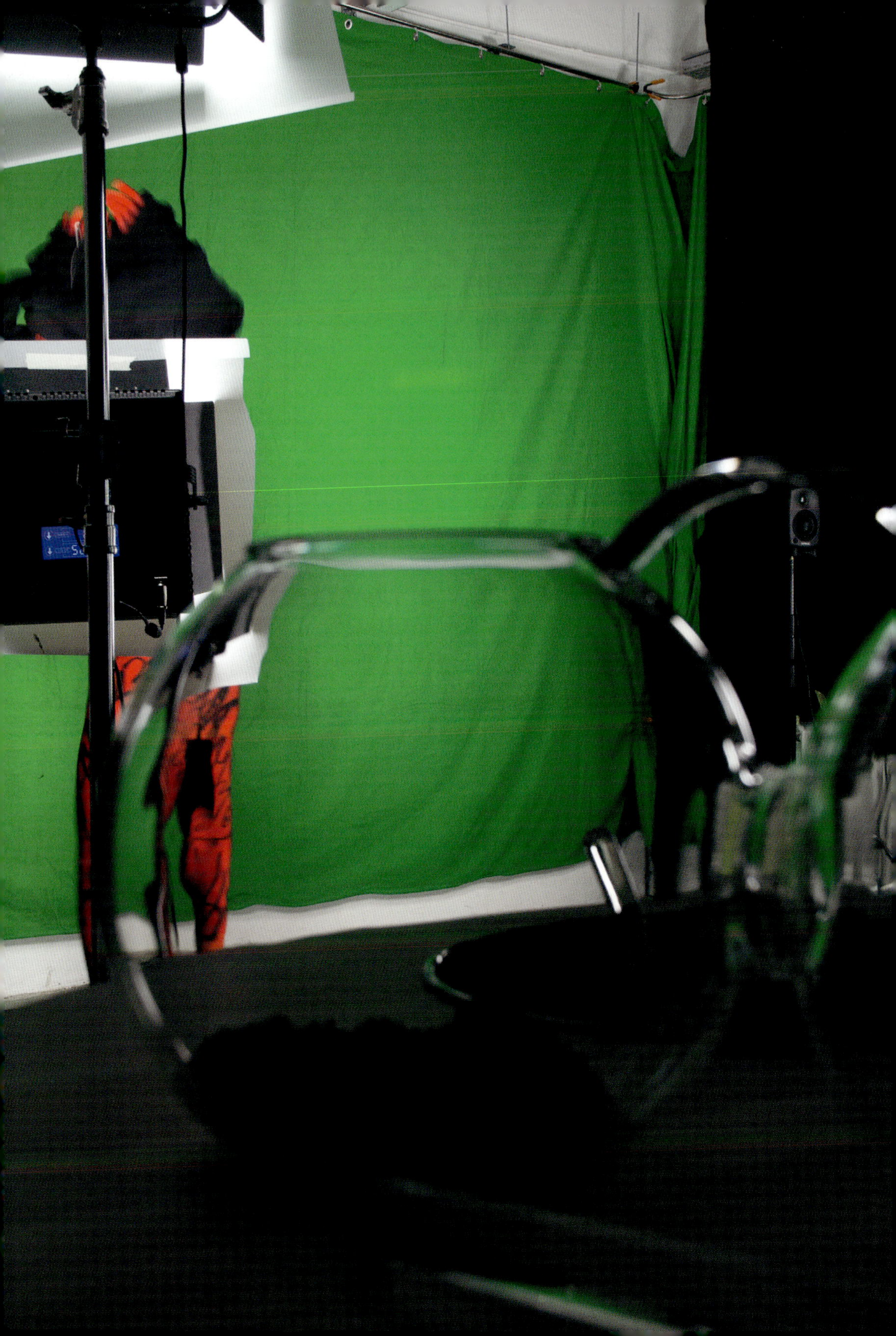

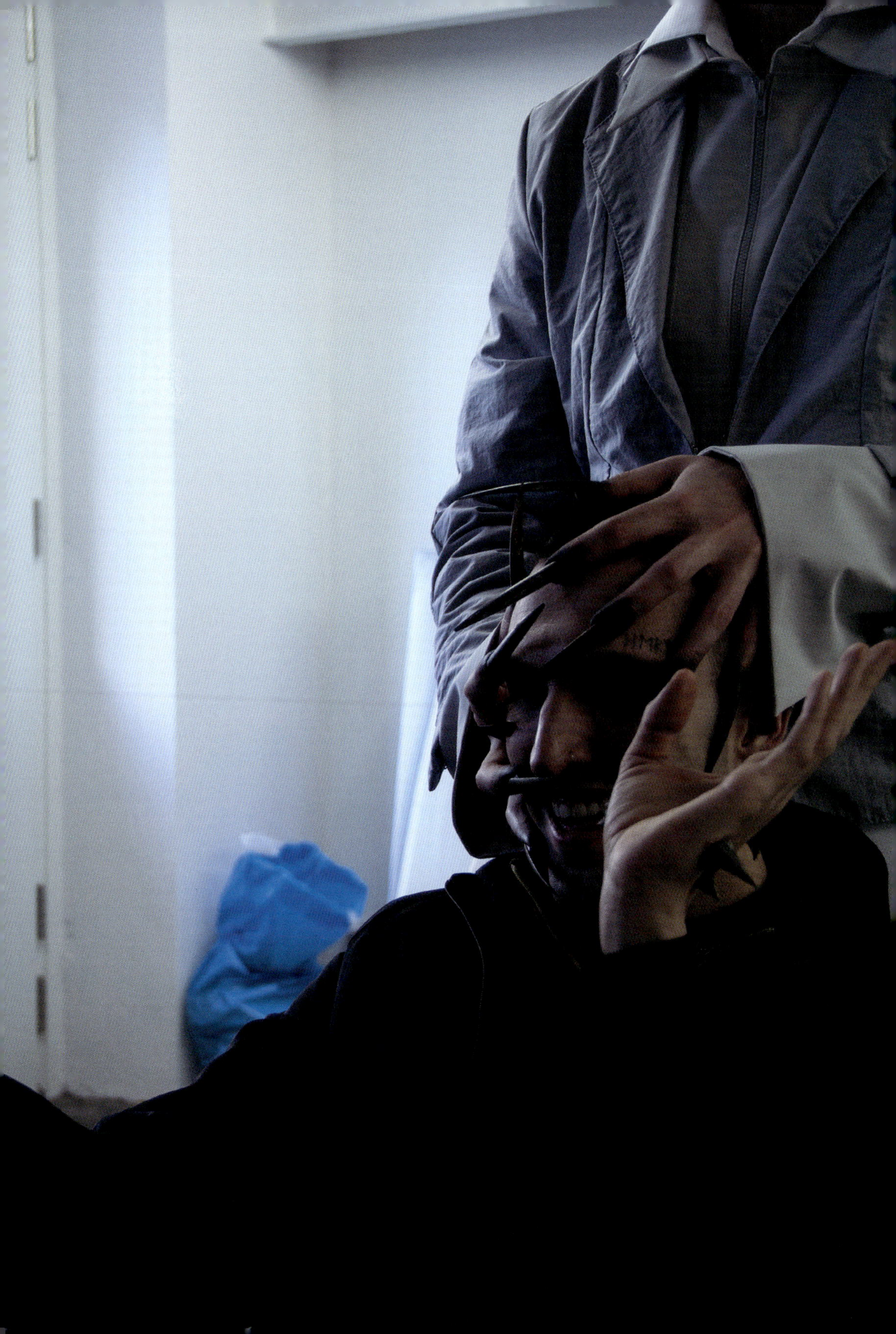

Lina Lapelytė

Lina Lapelytė (b. 1984, Kaunas, Lithuania) lives and works in London and Vilnius. Lapelytė's early work focused mainly on improvised and electronic music. Her more recent performance-based practice is rooted in music and flirts with pop culture, gender stereotypes, and nostalgia. Her works engage trained and untrained performers, often in an act of singing through a wide range of genres such as mainstream music and opera. The singing takes the form of a collective and affective event that questions vulnerability and silencing. In 2019, her collaborative work *Sun & Sea (Marina)*, co-produced with Vaiva Grainytė and Rugilė Barzdžiukaitė, and curated by Lucia Pietroiusti, won the Golden Lion award at the Venice Biennale. In 2020, Lapelytė received the national art and culture prize in Lithuania. Lapelytė holds degrees in classical violin and Sound Arts, and an MA in Sculpture from the Royal College of Art, London (2013). Her recent shows include: Frac des Pays de la Loire, Nantes (2023); Lafayette Anticipation, Paris (2022); Gherdeina Biennial (2022); Haus der Kunst, Munich (2021); BAM, New York (2021); Museum of Contemporary Art, Los Angeles (2021); Kunstenfestivaldesarts, Brussels (2021); Tai Kwun Contemporary, Hong Kong (2021); and the Glasgow International (2021).

Lina Lapelytė's home studio, Vilnius, 2020

Photos: Diāna Tamane

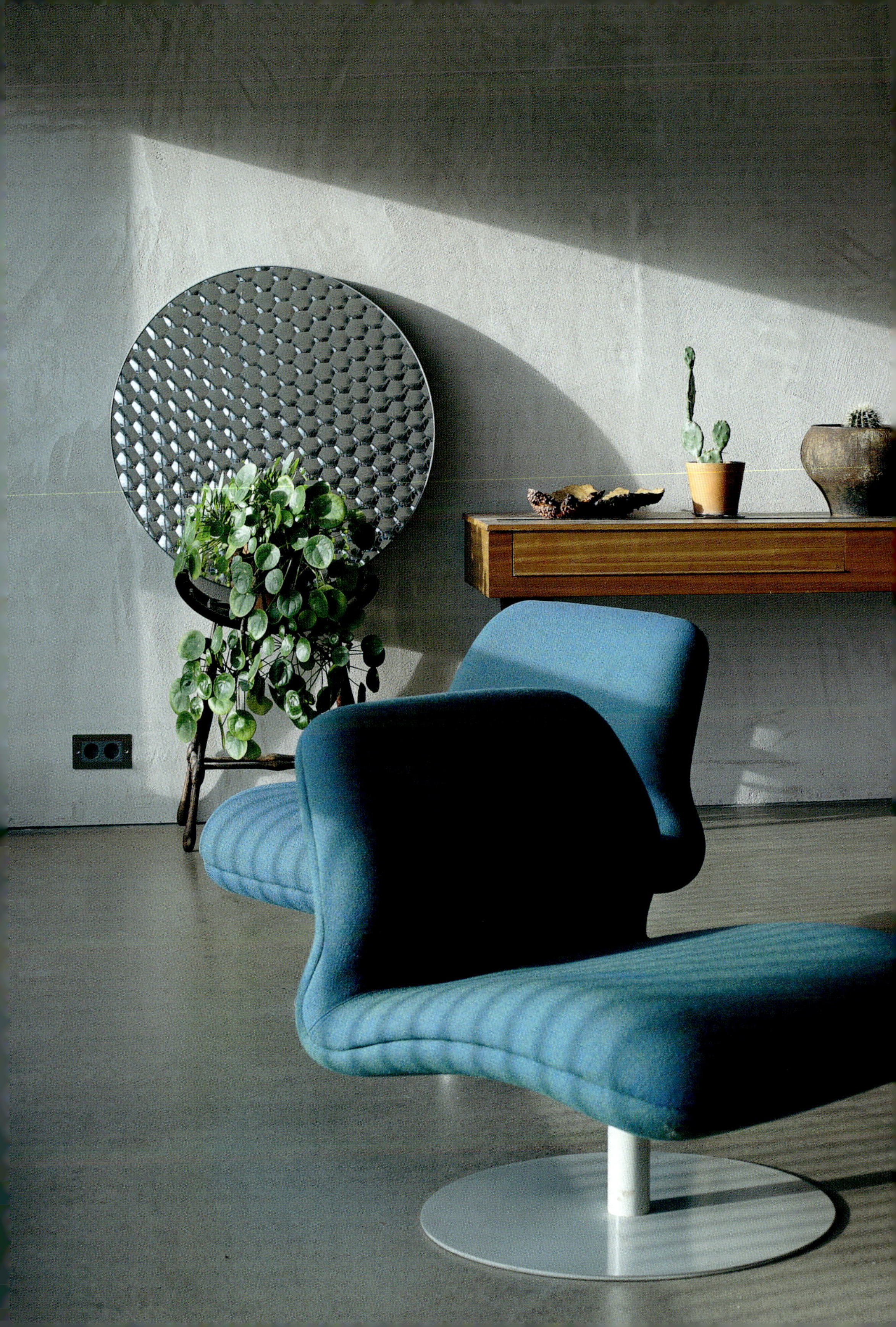

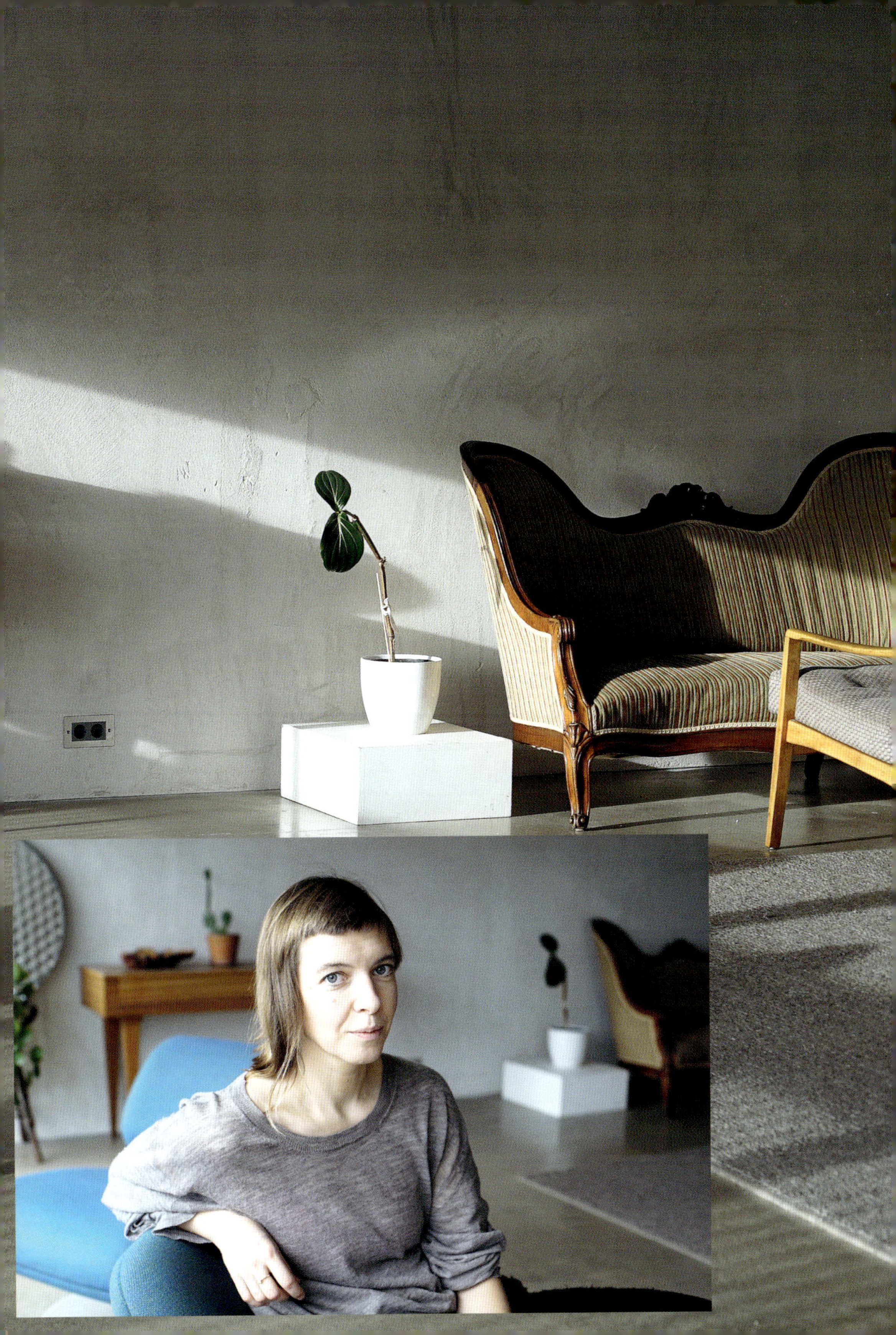

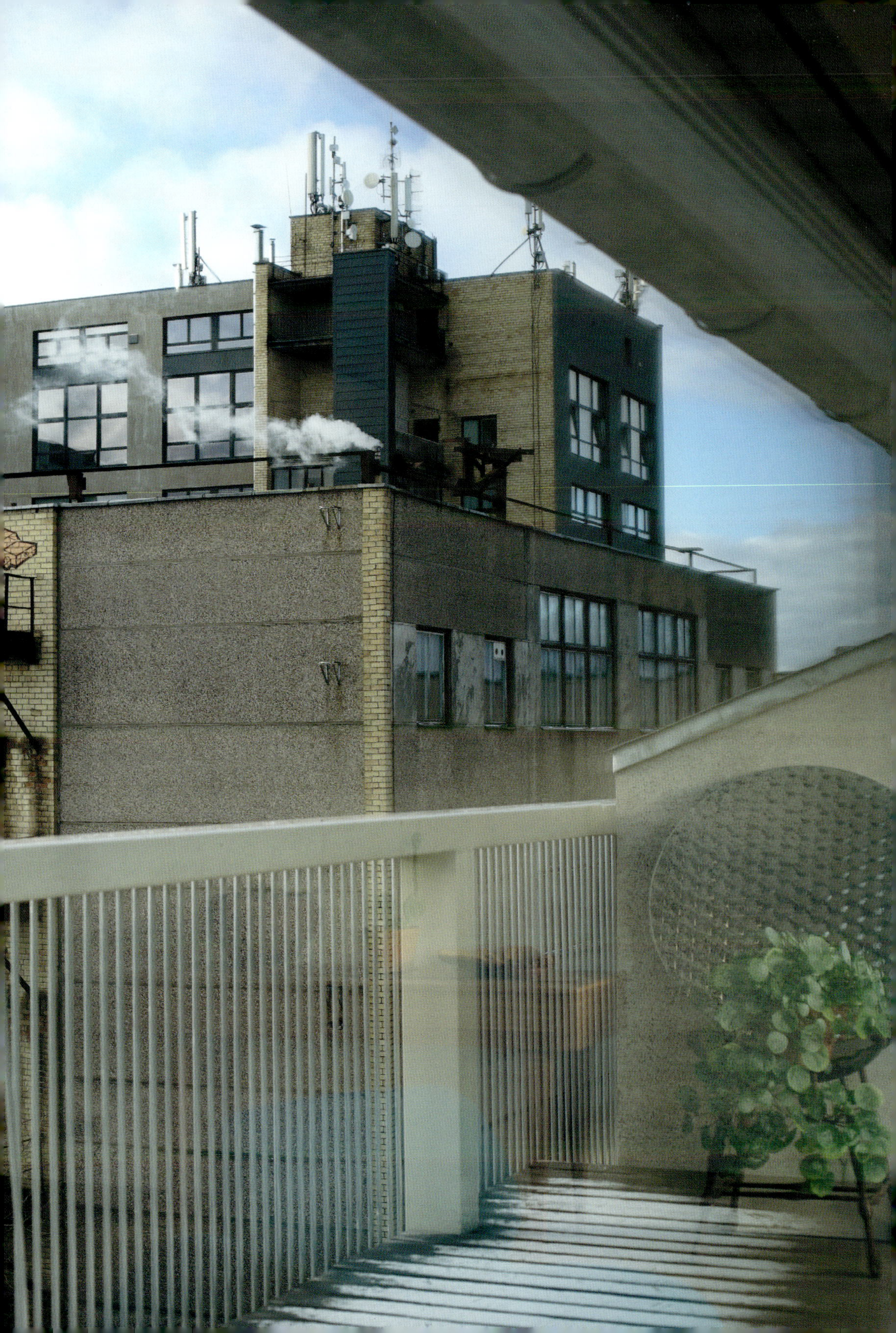

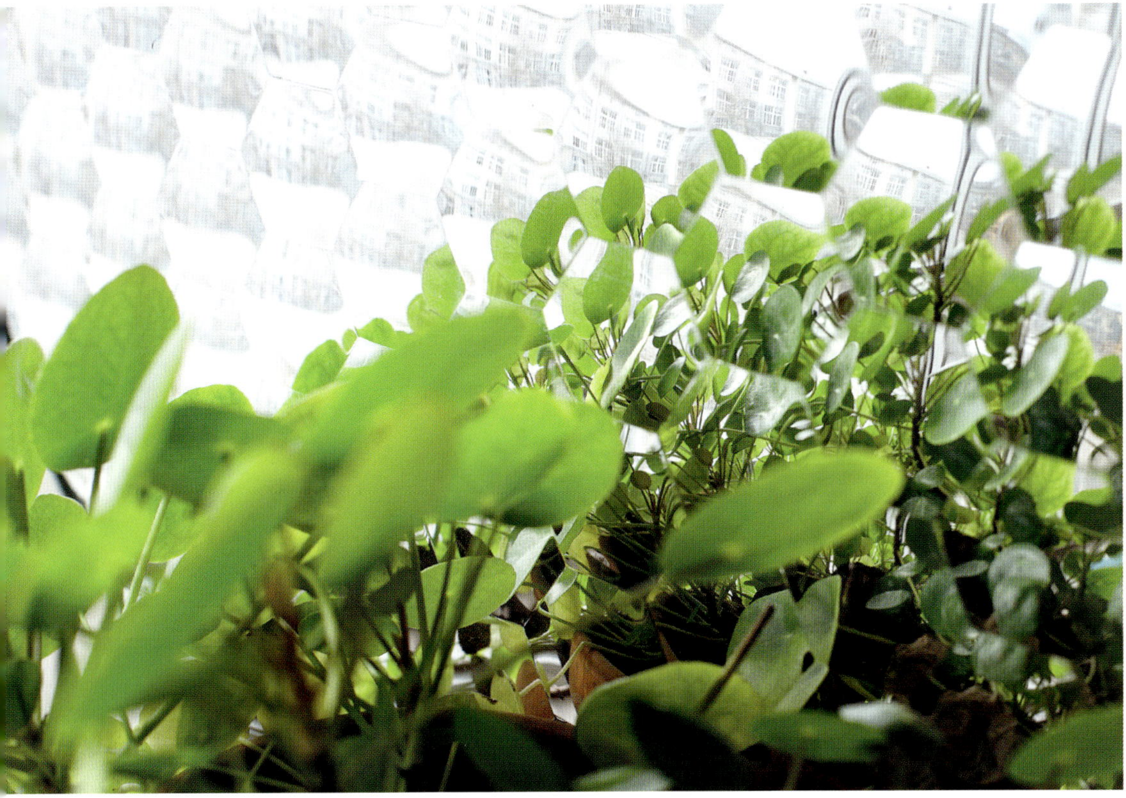

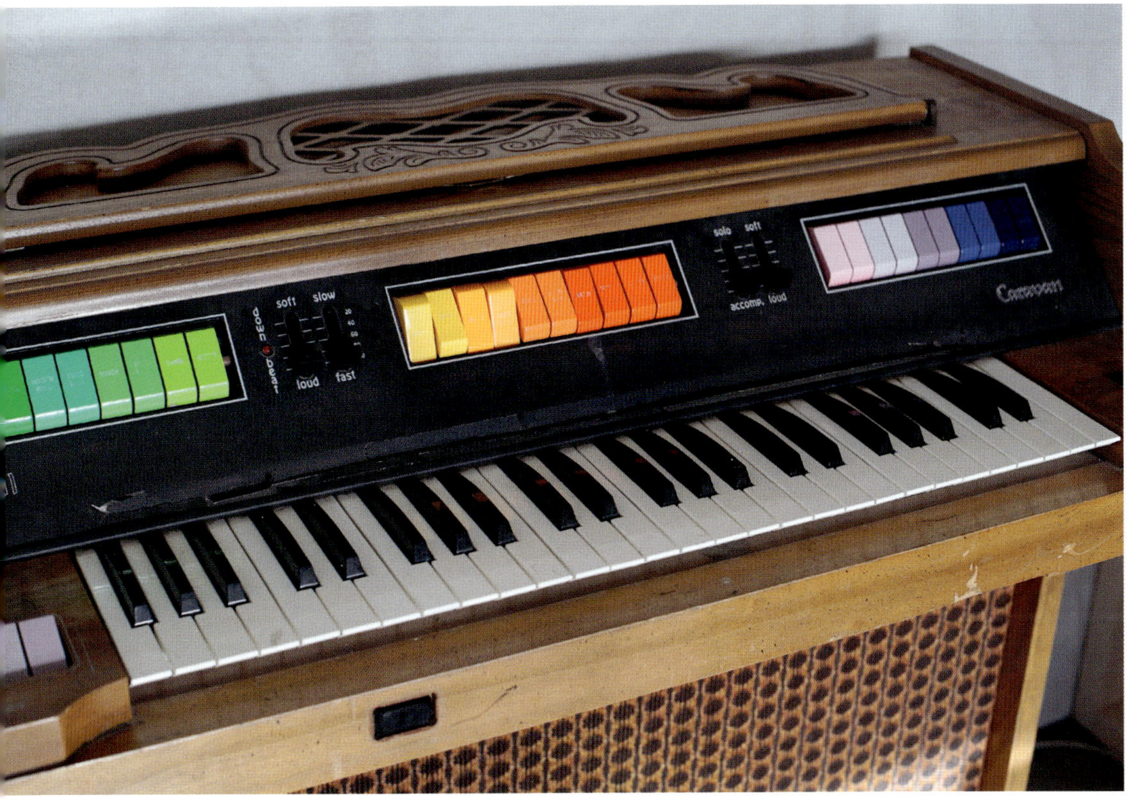
soft
slow
loud
fast
solo
soft
accomp.
loud

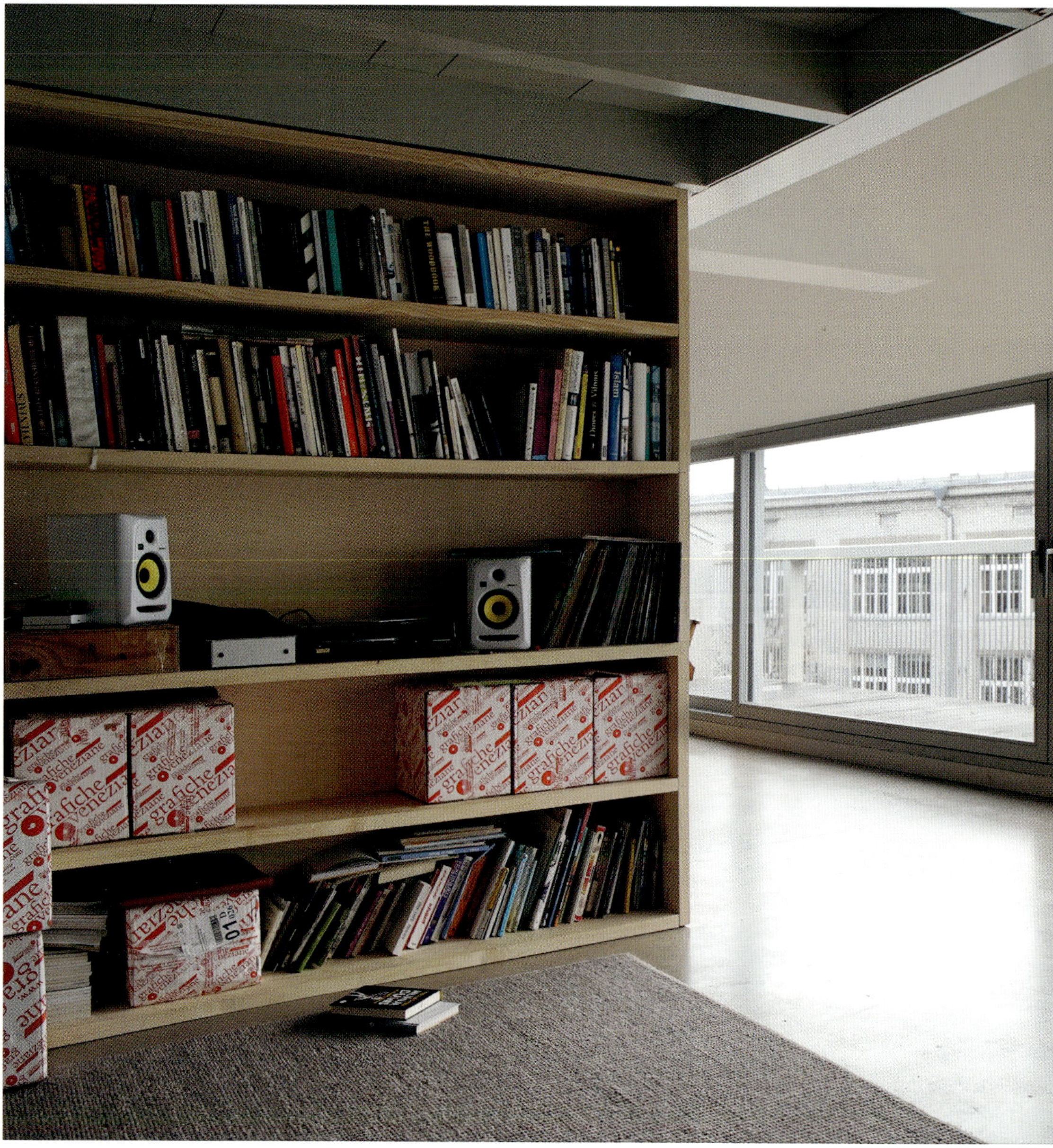
grafiche veneziane

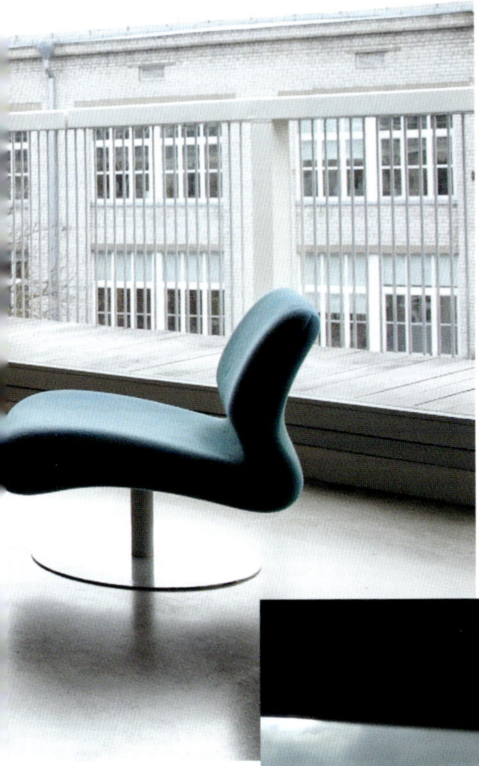
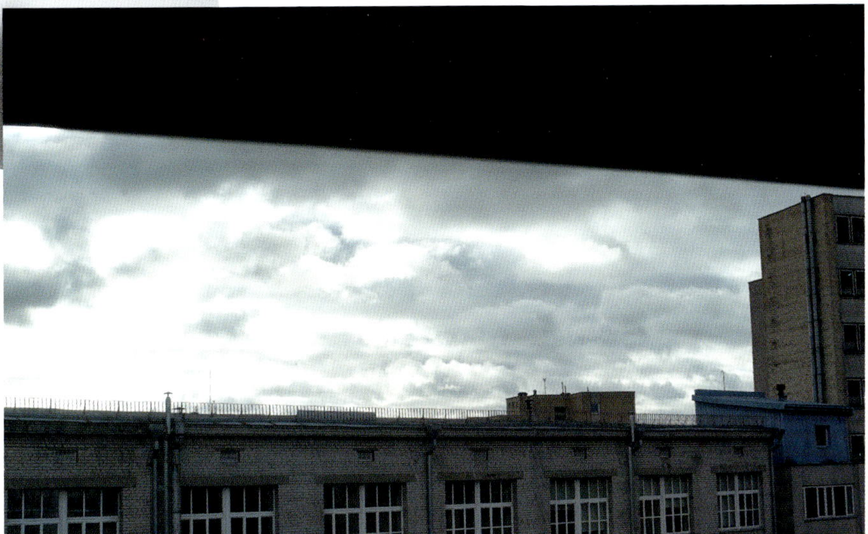

Evita Vasiļjeva

Evita Vasiļjeva (b. 1985, Riga, Latvia) lives and works in Paris. Vasiļjeva works with sculpture, installation, and sound. Having grown up in Latvia in the period of post-Soviet transition, the artist often draws on visual and sonic imagery of generic architecture and rough suburban landscapes. She creates objects, devices, and interactive installations by appropriating materials typically used for construction, such as concrete, armature, metal profiles, lanterns, and various electrical appliances, and by combining them with household objects, including beds and blankets, fridges, microwaves, and soap, but also movement sensors, which were commonly used in Latvia in the 1990s to secure houses. By manipulating and repurposing a large variety of materials, Vasiļjeva invents her own aesthetic, as well as provokes relational dynamics between spaces, architecture, memory, and spectators' bodies. While her works tackle issues of anxiety and control, through ways of coexistence within the present moment, they always remain open for multiple interpretations. Recent exhibitions include: the Lyon Biennial (2022); *Blue Lagoon House* (with Kaspars Groševs), Cēsis Contemporary Art Centre (2022); and Baltic Triennial 14, Vilnius (2021); among others.

Last night I fell asleep in a satellite dish, 2022
Pencil, and ink on paper, 21 x 29.7 cm

For the visual essay, Evita Vasiljeva chose drawings that represent her dreams, which she draws every morning in the cities where she lives, works, or travels to. The artist has captured a subconscious stream of memories, dreams, and frequencies that linger in her room as the day begins. Drawings are part of the installation *Bed-Room-Bed* (2020–).

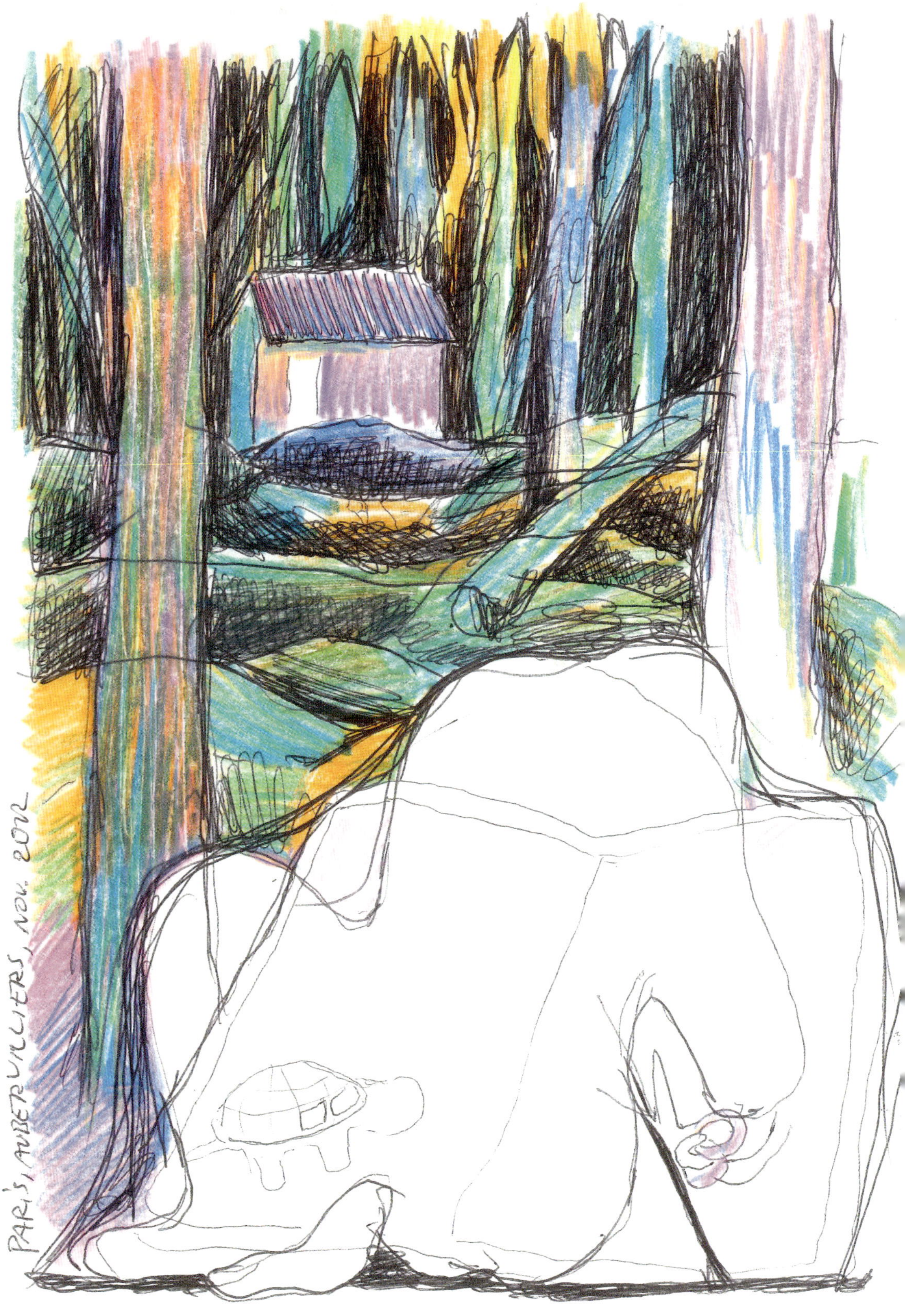
PARIS, AUBERVILLIERS, NOV. 2012

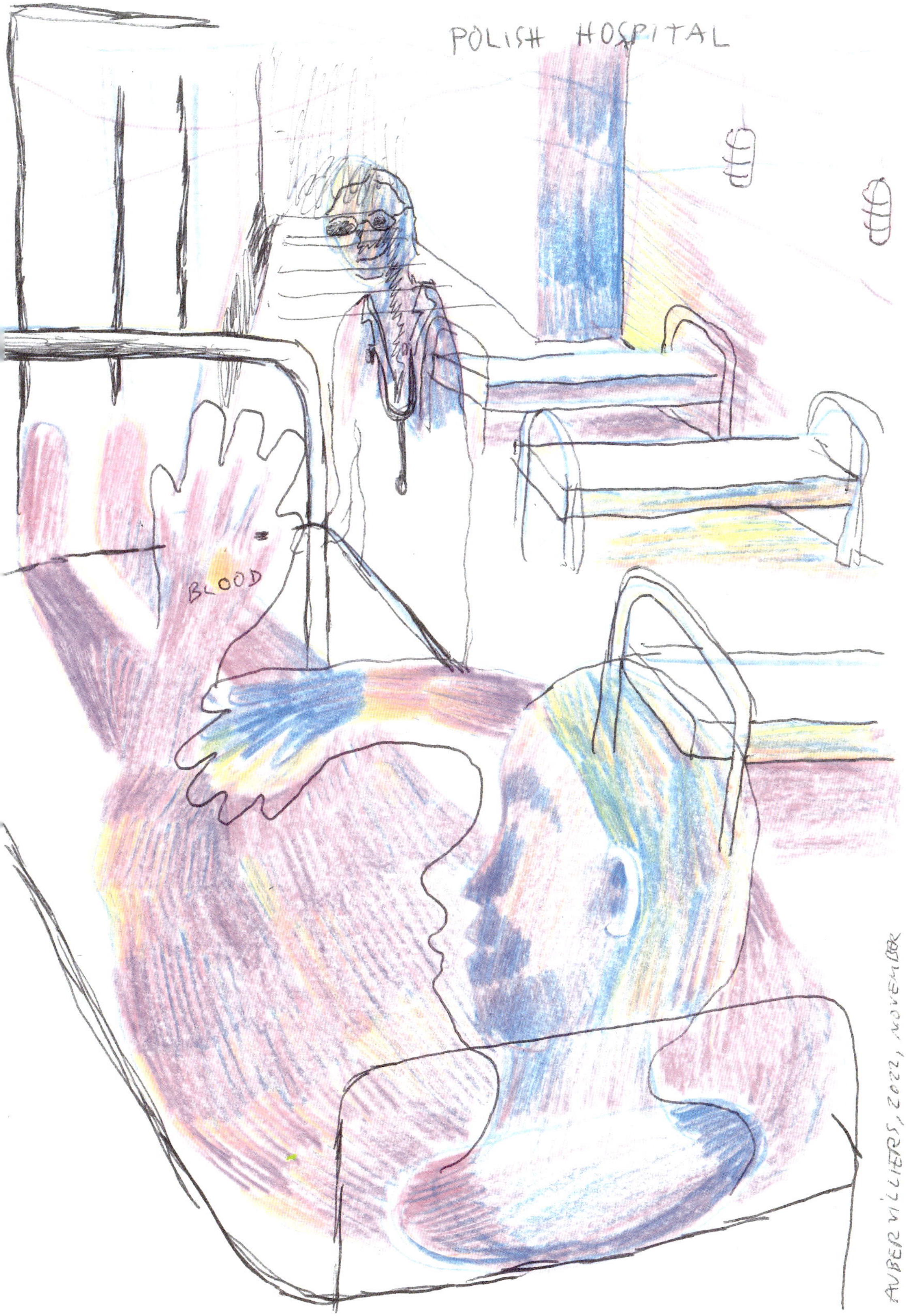
POLISH HOSPITAL
BLOOD
AUBERVILLIERS, 2022, NOVEMBER

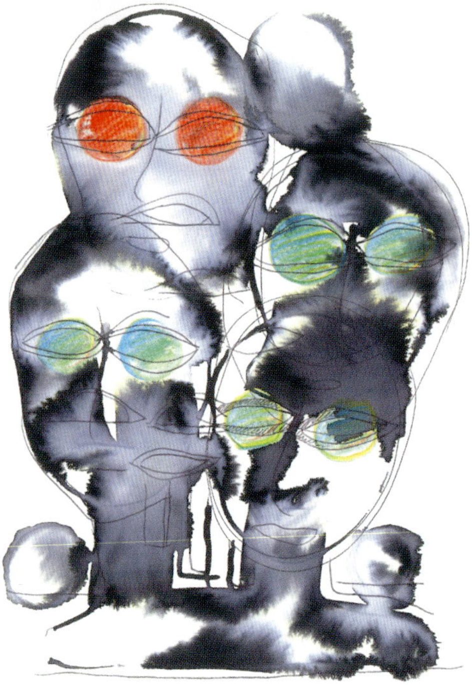

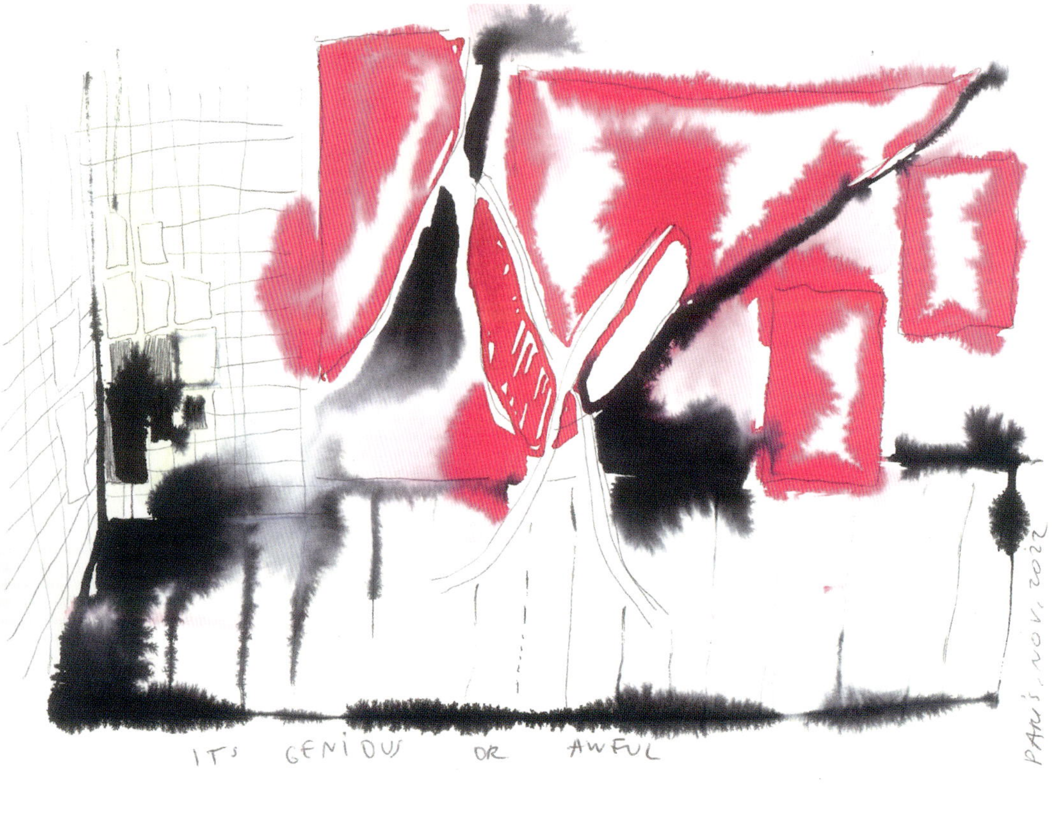
IT'S GENIOUS OR AWFUL
PARIS, NOV. 2022

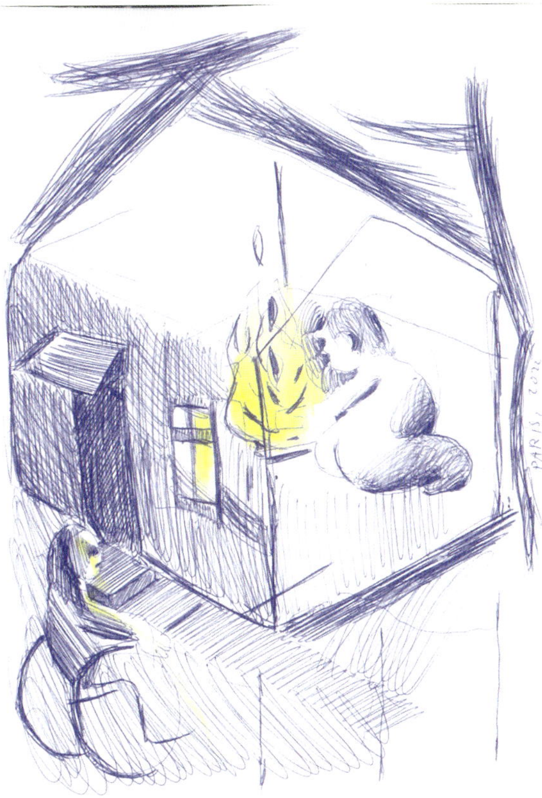
PARIS, 2022

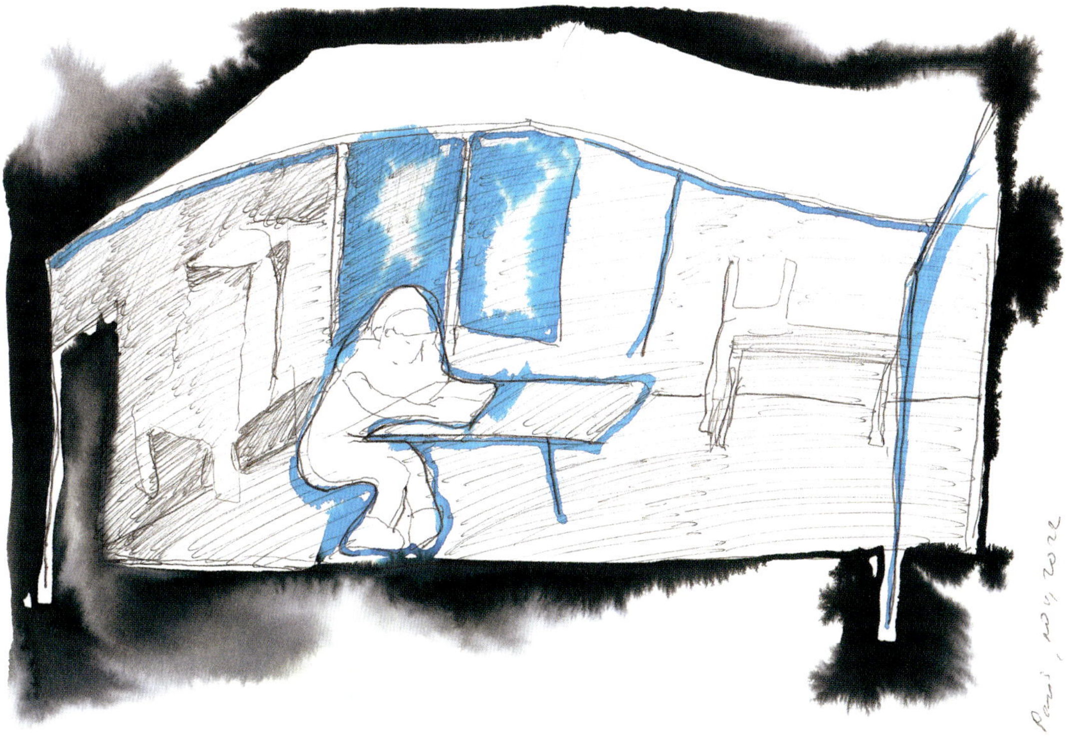
Paris, may 2022

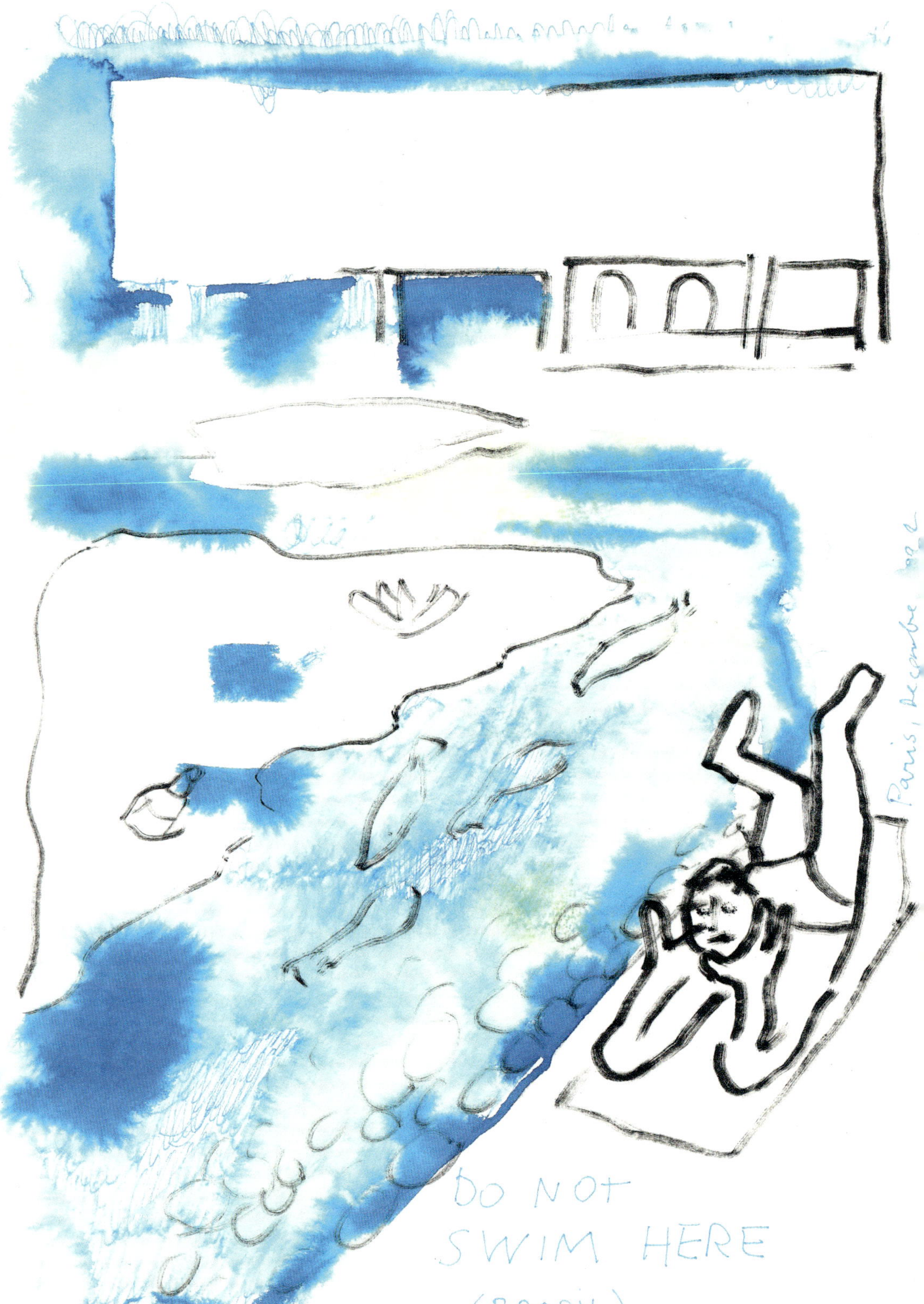
DO NOT
SWIM HERE
(BRASIL)
Paris, decembre 2022

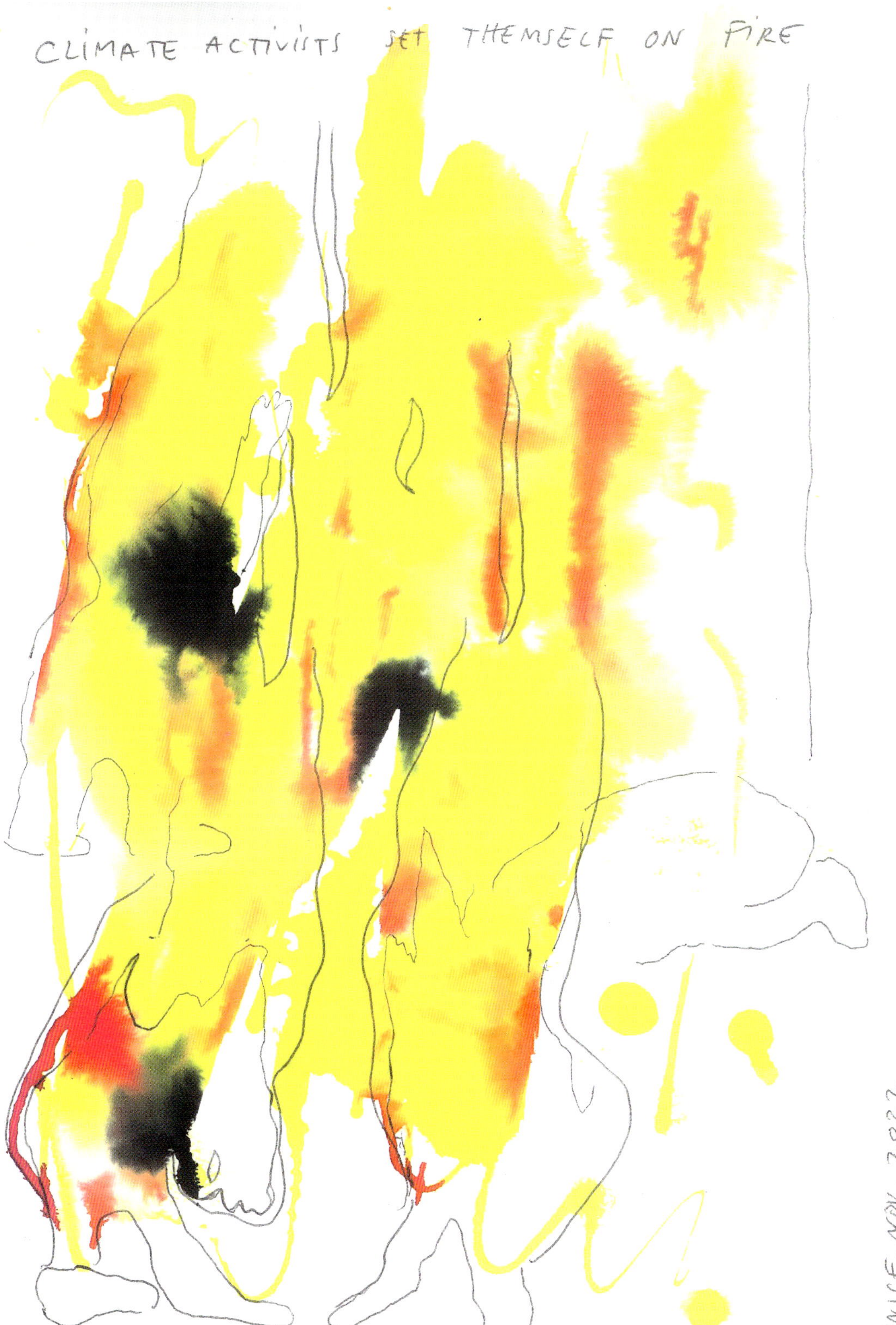
CLIMATE ACTIVISTS SET THEMSELF ON FIRE
VENICE, NOV, 2022

Emilija Škarnulytė

Emilija Škarnulytė (b. 1987, Vilnius, Lithuania) is an artist and filmmaker who lives and works in Vilnius, La Caleta, Spain, and Tromsø. Working between documentary and the imaginary, Škarnulytė makes films and immersive installations exploring deep time and invisible structures, from the cosmic and geologic to the ecological and political—her blind grandmother gently touches the weathered statue of a Soviet dictator; neutrino detectors and particular colliders measure the cosmos with otherworldly architecture; post-human species swim through submarine tunnels above the Arctic Circle and crawl through tectonic fault lines in the Middle Eastern desert. Winner of the 2019 Future Generation Art Prize, Škarnulytė represented Lithuania at the XXII Triennale di Milano (2019). Recent solo exhibitions include Tate Modern, London (2021), Kunsthaus Pasquart, Biel/Bienne (2021), and the National Gallery in Vilnius (2021). Her films are in the collections of the Institut für Auslandsbeziehungen (IFA), Kadist Foundation, and Centre Pompidou, and have been screened at the Serpentine Gallery, London; The Museum of Modern Art, New York; and numerous international film festivals. She is a founder and co-director of Polar Film Lab, and a member of artist duo New Mineral Collective.

Emilija Škarnulytė at Le Corbusier's Cité radieuse de Marseille, 2020

Photos: Aurélien Meimaris

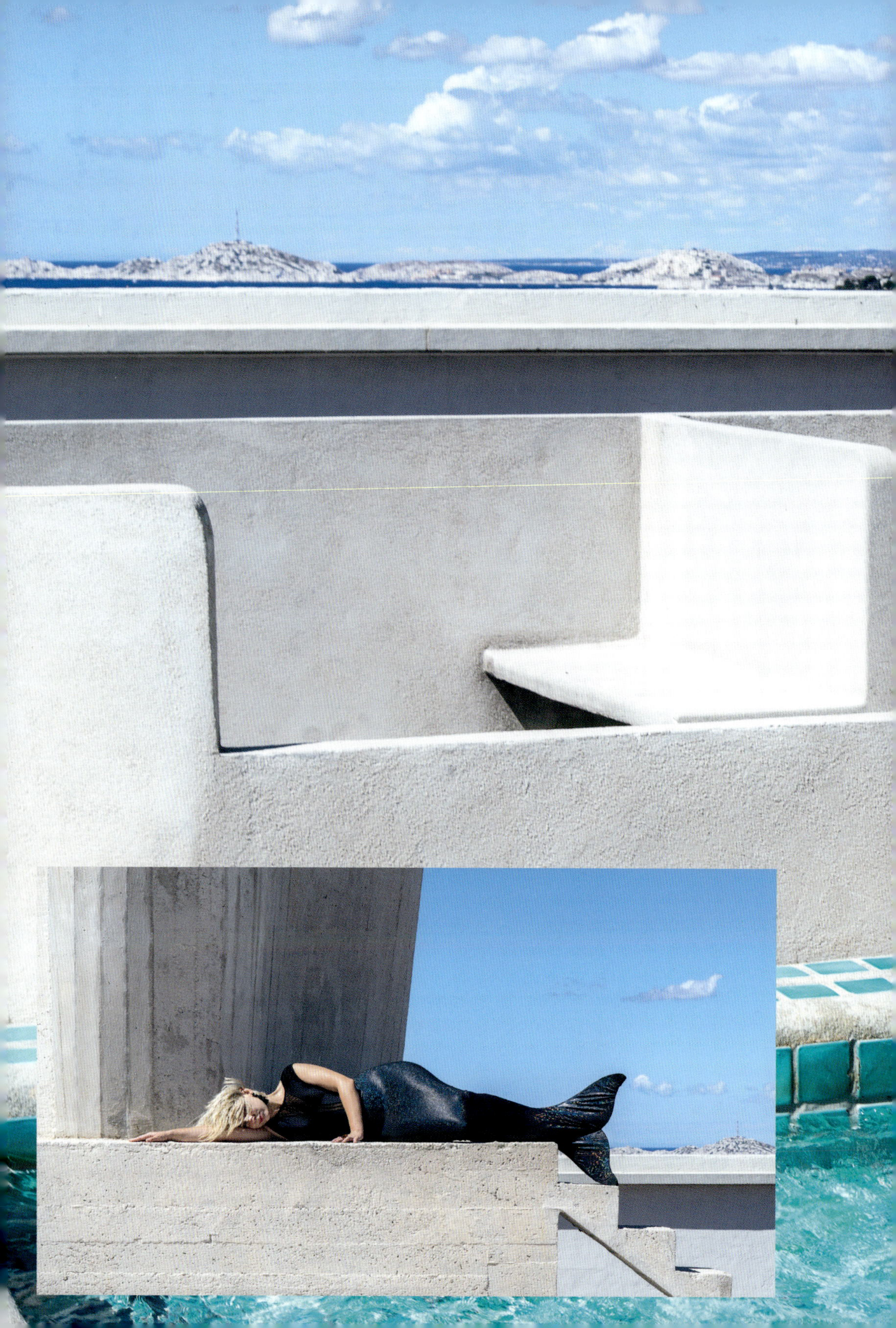

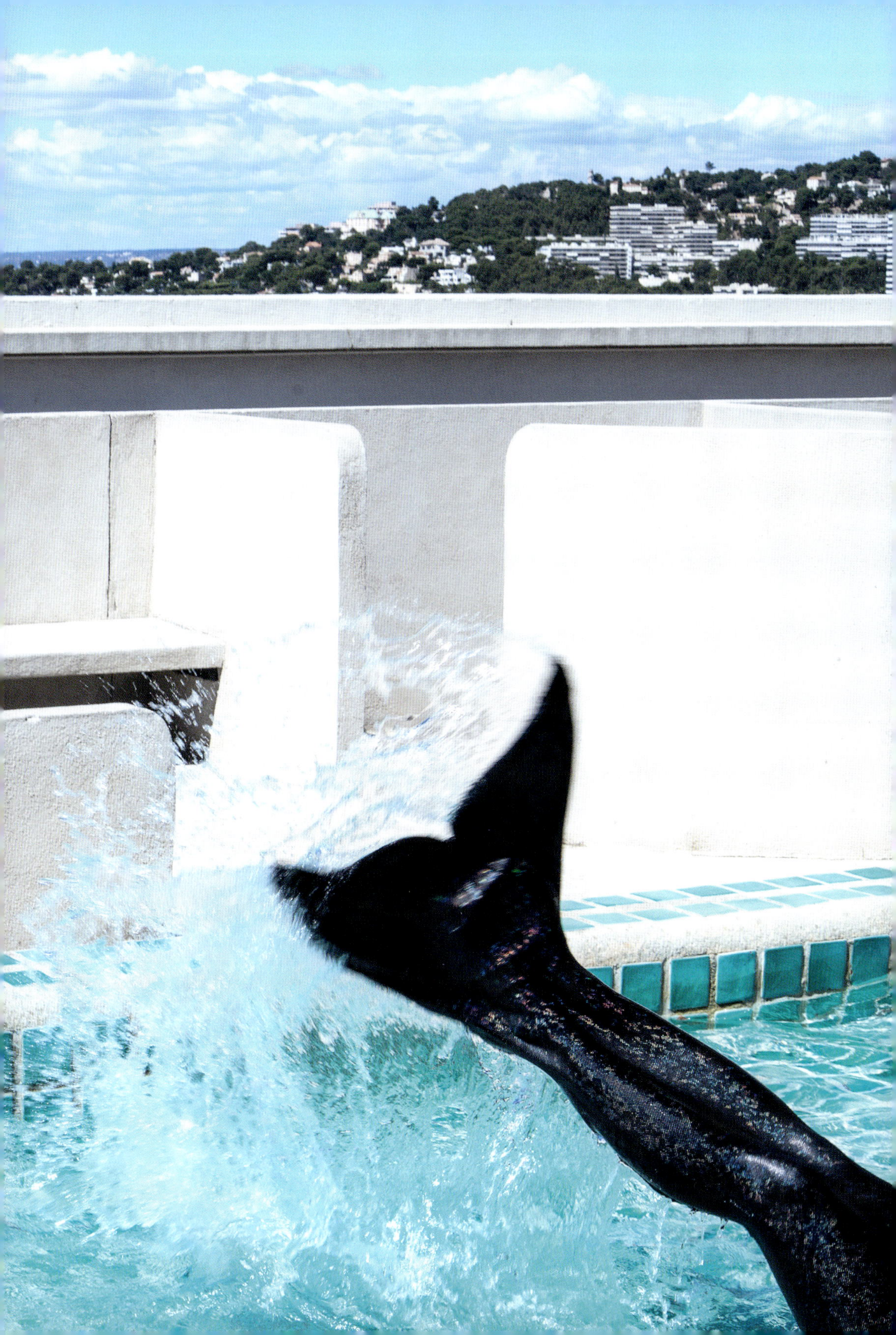

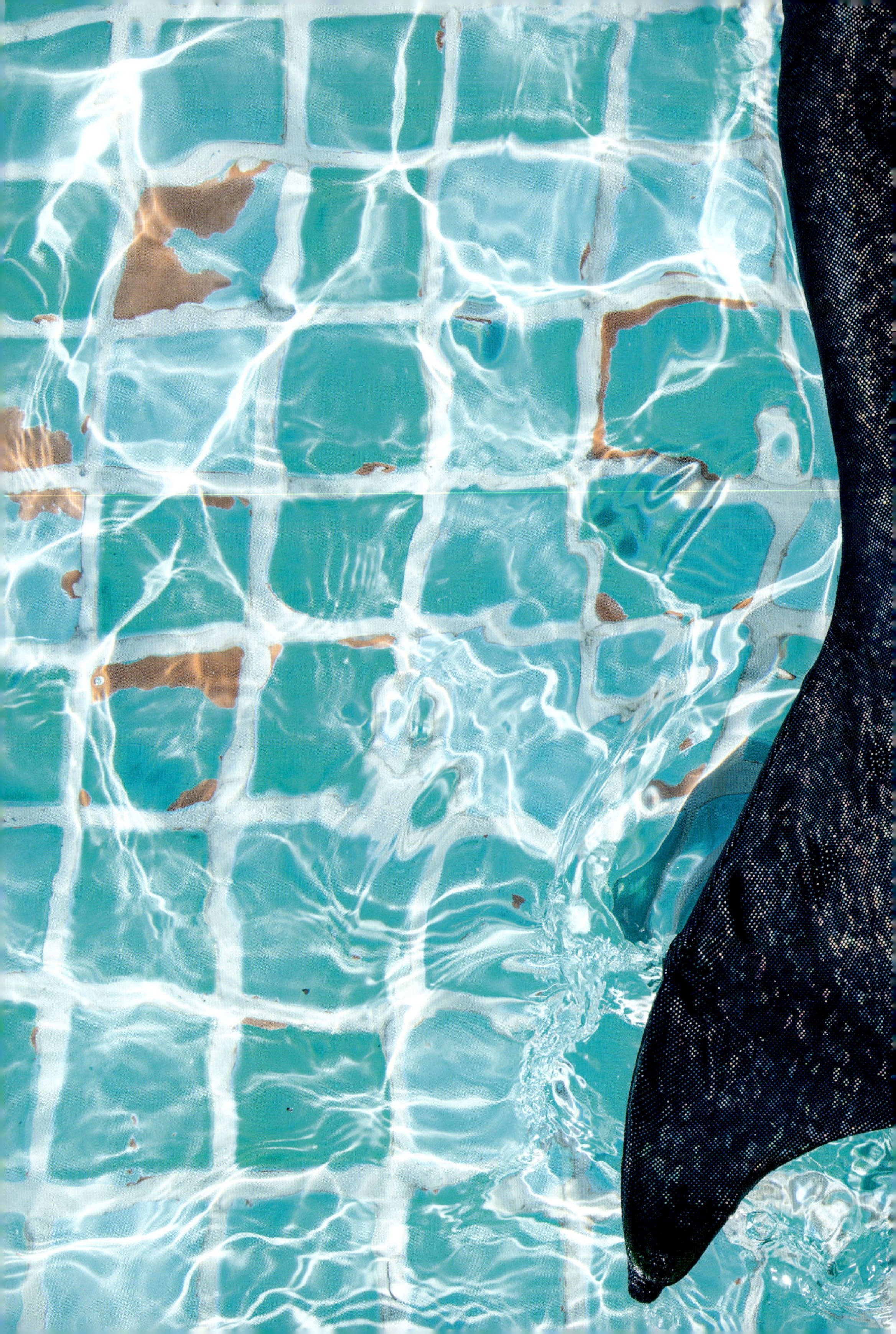

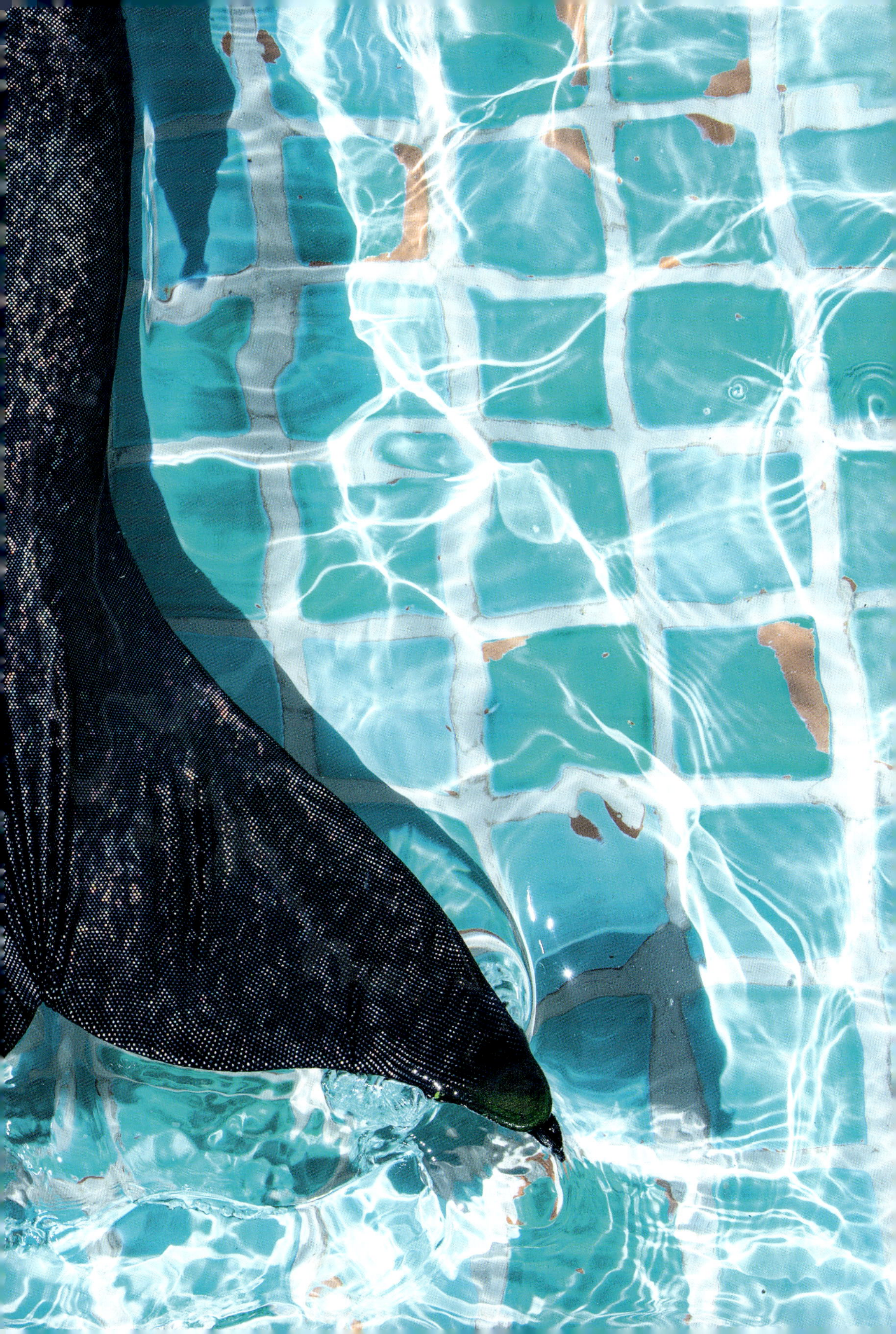

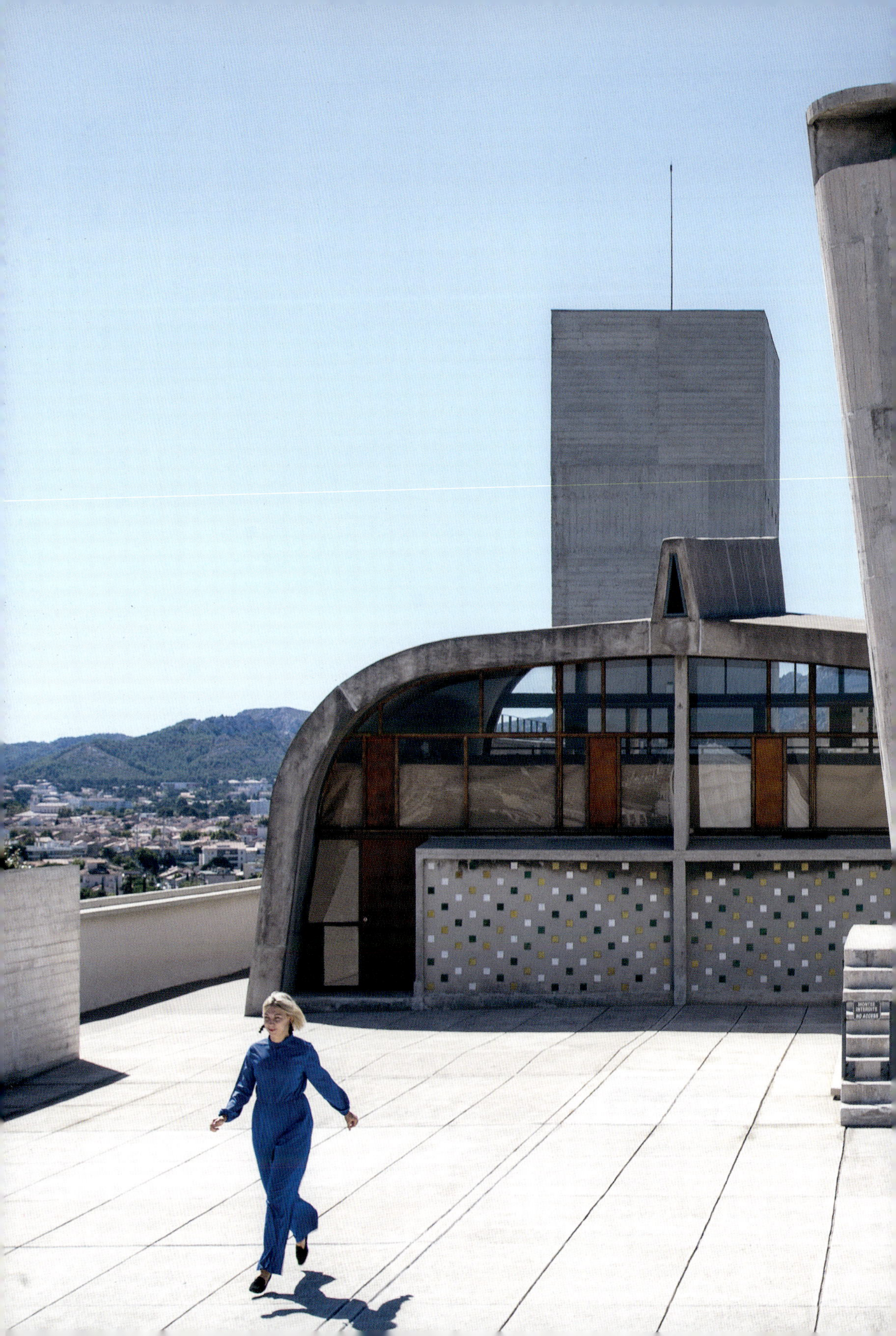

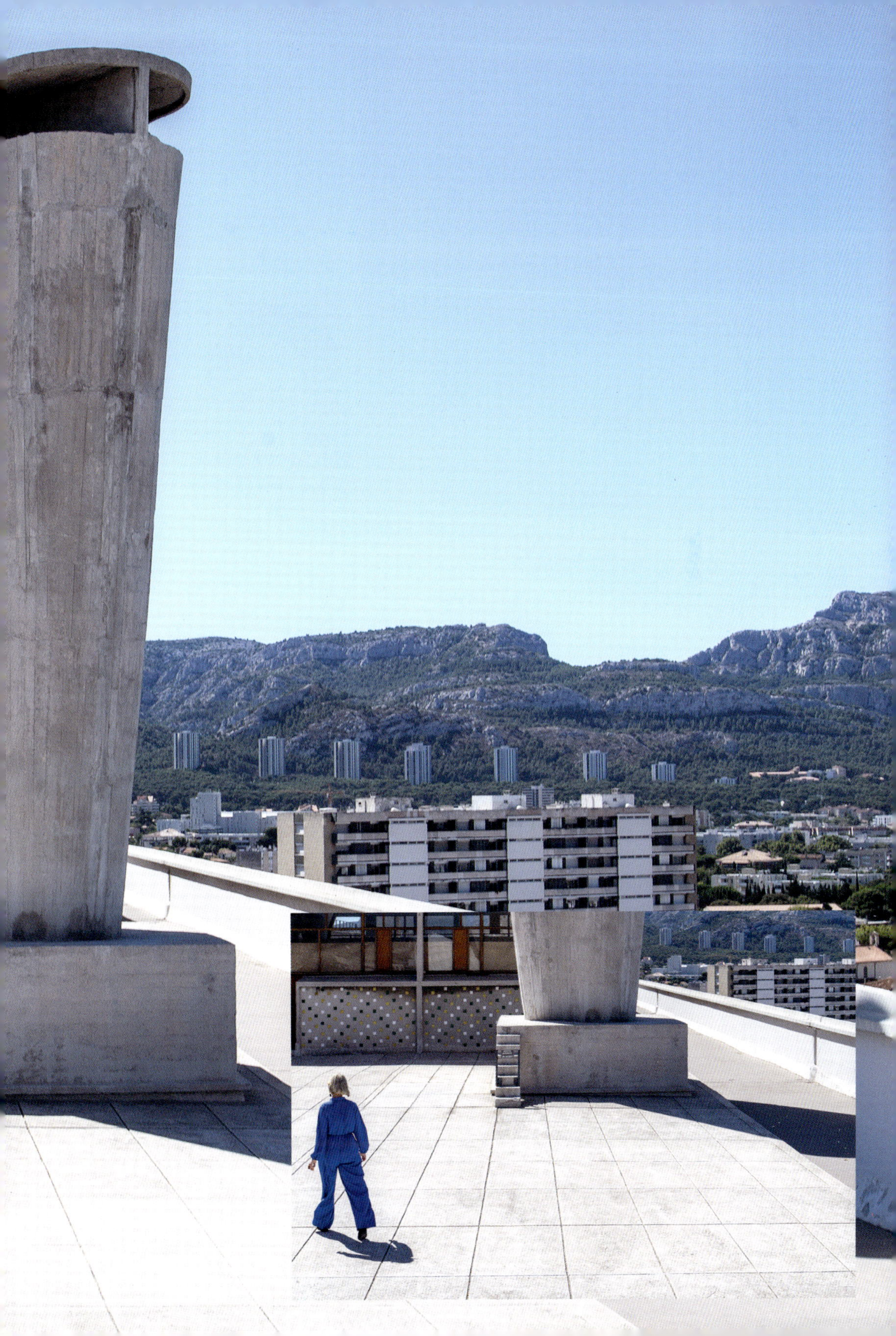

III

The Second Migration

1 *Homing Beyond* (*Põlvkond piiri taga*), directed by Terje Toomistu, (Tallinn: Cece Film, 2022), https://www.terjetoomistu.com/veins-of-the-amazon-copy.

2 University of Art and Design Linz, Department of Sculptural Conceptions and Ceramics, 2018 to 2021.

3 The Estonian Ministry of Culture has been awarding artists' salaries since 2016. From 2022, ten artists' salaries recipients are chosen by a jury. These ten artists receive a monthly salary for three consecutive years.

Interview with Laura Põld

Conducted by Annika Toots & Merilin Talumaa, February 2023

You have been living and working between Tallinn and Vienna for some time now. Not long ago though you mentioned during an interview in the documentary Homing Beyond[1] *that you feel safer in the context of the pandemic in Vienna and you plan to stay in Austria. Currently you are teaching at the Estonian Academy of Arts and living in Tallinn. What has been the reason for this change?*

When Terje Toomistu's film *Homing Beyond* came out, I was even a little startled that I had said something like this on camera and then less than two years later bought an apartment in Tallinn, started working full time at the Estonian Academy of Arts (EKA), and hired a studio assistant to move forward with my work at a good pace. Apparently, one of the reasons was the end of two cycles: in Linz, the school (University of Art and Design Linz)[2] ended and the artist's salary[3] period ran out. Behind this was both longing and fear of coming home. Despite the practical facts that I mentioned, I do not feel that I have locked myself away in a small country or given up anything. EKA's work and artist's salary have created some kind of emotional and financial stability. Preparing projects in Estonia is the most enjoyable and economical at the moment, but exhibitions are often also far away from Estonia, in Austria and elsewhere, also thanks to the Kogo Gallery with whom I work.

It's interesting that you said you were longing to "come home." So home has always been for you here, in Estonia?

Some kind of collective understanding here is what makes you feel at home. In Austria, I waited impatiently for a long time for something to happen. I'm a frank and erratic person by nature. In Austria, with the gallerists and people I worked with, it sometimes seemed to me that we didn't speak the same language. I encountered a certain unequal attitude and contribution to the work done by the artists versus other art professionals. And then I thought I'd go back to Estonia to all these workaholics! For me, perfectionism is also a very homely state.

At the same time, it has certainly given you a better understanding of what living somewhere else can give you and also what it deprives you. Although no place is ever completely perfect, do you feel the right place for you is here and now, back in Estonia? Is this where you feel safe?

It's the same as I said in that documentary—I'm here today. When I applied for an artist's salary, I also wrote that I would like to have the freedom to leave Estonia and work elsewhere when good opportunities arise. While working as a lecturer in EKA, of course, I am more involved. Stability, however, has its downsides when it forces you to stay completely in one place.

4 Fiskars Village Art & Design Biennale 2019, Fiskars, Finland, May 19 to September 15, 2019.

5 *Natural Shelter*, commissioned by the Fiskars Village Art & Design Biennale and curator Ki Nurmenniemi, is a collaboration between artist Laura Põld and poet Katrin Väli.

You studied ceramics and painting, and you are teaching in the ceramics department at EKA. You have always playfully intertwined various mediums in your work. Most recently, textile and wool have taken up more space in your practice. How did you arrive at using these materials?

When I went to study in Austria, ceramics were the material that fascinated me. I was interested in the raw tones of clay. Linz is one of the few places in Europe where you can still study ceramics. I imagined that there is a well-established network with ceramics centres around the world, but that was not the case at all. At the Fiskars Biennale,[4] where I created *Natural Shelter* (2019),[5] I was able to use the powerful spatial and technological capabilities of the studio there, and then I burned out. I had health problems. In the summer, I got a residency in New York and even thought about leaving school because I'd been away for almost a year. In New York, I couldn't make ceramics, I was weaving letters out of thread. If I'm in a shorter residency, where I can't do big things or ship them later, I often work with textiles and fibres. It is a fairly sustainable and flexible, artist-friendly way of creation. In November, I came back, but that was the start of COVID-19 and I decided to stay in Austria. At one point, it was clear that several collaborative projects would be delayed. I started looking for materials to work with at home, continued to study online in the master's programme, and found the method of tufting on YouTube.

Ceramics exhausted me for a moment—it was so resource-intensive. I'm going through these things in waves, exhausting myself. But I decided to finish school, and I quickly had to find material to implement into my graduation project. At that point, my home studio was large enough, the joy of discovery and being in one place were also useful in learning a new technique. Tufting is like a modern folk art, and within this position you can play in interesting ways. It is a fun technique! Also, the choice of colours is greater in textiles, and the softness, the warm touch, is emotionally important to me. Ceramics are delicate, but heavy and cold, so it feels different.

You subtly mentioned how an artist's work is not only mentally but also physically exhausting, and it's something that people don't really perceive. Between ceramics and wool, the physical weight of the latter is probably quite different. Perhaps you can say a little bit more about this wool journey?

In ceramics, firing "makes" the end result. And the white cube "changes" things. In tufting, I can work in large format and rather quickly. At the same time, it also entails climbing on ladders, and a lot of dust is generated. I'm not making yarn myself right now, so for me, the process starts with shopping and combining colours and textures. For example, in the Karnaluks shop in Tallinn where there are shelves up to the ceiling and a very large hall packed with yarns. Then I'm picking them up, carrying them in human-sized bags. The most exhausting thing is the inhalation of dust, and my fingers are constantly broken. Fortunately, I have a really nice assistant who was once a student of mine for a short time. We have a similar background, and she's helped me a lot before. She comes two days a week to my studio and helps me with practical things. She's a real friend and a helper.

Do you feel that you are better suited for collaborative work or rather creating alone?

Going to work at EKA has changed my life a lot. I am very grateful when I get to be alone in the meantime, but there is no feeling of loneliness at all that often haunted me in Vienna, for example. I often work by doing duo exhibitions, and in addition there is a curator, a graphic designer, and a writer involved—this kind of teamwork is a very joyful process. It is nice and exciting to do projects in a small collective. And there is never a need to continue working together if it doesn't suit somehow.

I've found a lot of collaborators through residencies I've been to. A few years ago, I guess I said yes to every offer I had in front of me. Now I'm more often wondering if I'll have time and energy, and sometimes I try to say no to collaborations.

Being able to say "no" is a great skill.

I'm still often quite shocked when someone says that he or she won't have time to take on any new projects for the next few years—how can you be sure of this? Maybe I should have said no to some things too. I'd actually rather do one bigger and more thorough exhibition than five smaller ones at once.

Do travel and movement keep your mind awake? When you're in one place, do you get tired?

I usually don't feel that I definitely have to go away somewhere. I rather feel that since I've been able to travel so much, I would only like to travel under certain circumstances. If I can stay a little longer and do my work. I feel that when it comes to an international career, it's better for me to make my works in Estonia and send them abroad. At the same time, I do not rule out that in the future I will be away for a year, doing a PhD or teaching somewhere. Now I'm no longer a "homeless traveller." I've bought a home with a mortgage, so maybe I can be a "traveller with home." While moving between different residency programmes, mental crises are more prone to arise, so this is not the best option. Even if it's nice, it hurts that the clock is ticking and you'll probably never meet your new "best friends" again.

You started making paintings and installations referring to a sense of home and living abroad in the 2010s. How has moving back and forth between different places affected your practice?

I'm sure my story is also a bit of the story of my generation, quite typical. When you are young, you go abroad to study or do residencies (in my case, the latter), your schoolmates become collaborative partners. Moving between several so-called homes is quite common among artists in their twenties and thirties today, bringing alongside certain difficulties but also charms. When the first enthusiasm for the new life found abroad has ceased, the habits you have come to miss can be digested in the form of art for a long time. As a result, there have been quite a lot of subjects that have come to the surface, which have been addressed in my works for several years. Perception of space and landscape, anonymity, relationships, cultural misunderstandings, seeking one's own place, being stamped as an Eastern European, etc., are the framework topics for many young people commuting between Estonia and some foreign countries, and also for me. I have realised that commuting for a long period of time can become quite emotionally exhausting. This feeling has also pushed me towards techniques that are built on repetition, handcraft, and that are well-grounded, like working with wool and clay. The experience of living between several countries also gives me the ability to plan work cycles and logistics better in advance, work and private trips intertwine, life is art.

In your latest works and exhibitions you have been revolving around Estonia's recent history. Can you point out some of the projects you are working on?

Some of the projects that are currently in the works are the ones that have made me to turn to our recent history. For example, as part of the Kumu exhibition *Art in the Age of the Anthropocene*, I am working with Canadian artist Lou Sheppard on the work *Sweeping the Sea + Large Oak + Strange House*. It's a bit like a sequel to the installation *Wasteland. The Phosphorite War* (2021–2023), inspired by Lennart Meri's notes describing the desolate landscape seen in the abandoned phosphorite mines of Ülgase and Maardu.

In cooperation with Lou, we focus on the Kunda Aru limestone quarry. The installation will look at quarries after the excavation of rocks and minerals has been completed and a large gap remains. Different histories meet in Aru: the geological depth, the millions of years of rock formation, the newer history of mining and wealth creation, the end of mining and its afterlife, the new possible future that will begin to emerge when nature re-establishes itself, today and tomorrow. In our work, the usual quarry pit becomes an amphitheatre, where stories are told. The stone cavities echo a polyphonic melody inspired by the Estonian folk song "Sweeping the Sea + Large Oak + Strange House," which Lou found in the folklore archive of the Tartu Literary Museum on a research trip. We invite viewers to the future of Aru mine and to think about the abundance that this quarry can feed and the communities that can form in these crevices at a time when this rock landscape no longer has value in the cycle of wealth creation.

Also, another exhibition that grew out of thinking about local history and my hometown Tallinn, was the duo exhibition with the works of Andres Tolts at Kogo Gallery in Tartu. The exhibition made me think of Tallinn as a living environment, and of the similarities in our life story, balancing between design and art. These projects have also made it very interesting to come back to Estonia spiritually. I feel like there's so much to dive into, and I can ask questions and read in my mother tongue. And just be here.

Interview with Maria Kapajeva

Conducted by Annika Toots & Merilin Talumaa, January 2023

You lived in London for around fourteen years. When did you return to Tallinn?

I came back with the first wave of COVID in mid-June 2020. On May 15, I was asked to move out of the place I lived in London and a month later I was on a plane to Estonia. Within one month my life changed totally.

So moving back to Estonia was not planned?

It wasn't. But during the final two or three years I was thinking about it without making any decisions. It is true what is often said about London, that after ten years you start to question whether you should get settled here or move out. London is great, it's a unique place, but it also demands a lot from a person. Being an artist means choosing financial insecurity, unfortunately, and it means you will never be able to afford to buy a flat in London and you always have to compromise between your practice and jobs that pay your rent. It becomes tiring at some point. My ten years also clashed with the vote for Brexit, which did not help the overall situation. Before the referendum I was considering living in another city in England. After the referendum we all realised that only London (and Scotland) voted against Brexit; the rest of the country voted for it. So it became harder to imagine living anywhere else in the UK as a foreigner.

I was trying to think of other scenarios that could be possible for me. As I had been in London for fourteen years, I realised that I am quite heavy in terms of moving around because I had lots of research materials and books. So I started to think about how I could change that. In a way all those books were kind of my anchor. The only anchor I had in my life.

As I have a small flat in Tallinn where I am still paying the mortgage, I started to think, what if I move all my belongings to Tallinn and then come back to London again with only one suitcase? All these years when I visited Tallinn I had to stay with friends as my flat was rented out. So it made me feel like a visitor, who sleeps on someone else's couch, in my own home country.

It is interesting that after living in London for more than a decade you still thought of Tallinn as home. Wasn't it difficult to leave your friends, job, activities in London?

Moving back to Estonia was one of the scenarios I considered, but I did not know if this would work because financially it meant I had to take care of both places. During the pandemic I was asked to move out as soon as possible by my landlords. It was a very stressful moment: my employment contract was about to end in June and no new jobs were in the market. It was impossible to find a new place to live and I had no savings.

Also, after fourteen years of shared living with other people, I was exhausted. I was desperate for my own space. The idea to move all my belongings to Estonia was already planted in my head, so I decided to go back and see what happens. In total I had 700 kilograms to move, which made me think of my possessions—50 kilograms per year.

Later that summer, my contract as Project Manager for *Fast Forward: Women in Photography* was extended and now I work on a freelance basis, which has made it possible for me to live in Estonia but continue my job in the UK.

Did you ever have a studio in London, where you could concentrate on your artistic work?

I once tried to have a studio, but it did not work because the space I could afford was too small and quite far away from where I lived. So for all these years I ended up working, living, doing everything in one bedroom, not even a flat.

Out of all the other options you had in mind, where else would you have moved after London?

One place I thought about was Gdańsk because it is a city by the sea. I realised that I am mostly homesick for the sea, the Baltic Sea, nothing else. The sea and pine trees are what I really have to breathe in at least once a year. It is quite physical and therapeutic: I do not feel well if I cannot visit the Baltic Sea coast regularly. It's a combination that allows me to breathe in fully as a human being. But to move to Poland also meant to move to a new country and a new culture. Whether

1 Maria Kapajeva, *When the World Blows Up, I Hope to Go Down Dancing* (curated by Siim Preiman), Tallinn Art Hall, Tallinn, Estonia, September 17 to November 8, 2020.

you feel you are close to a culture or not, the migration process is very complex. I was not sure I had enough strength in me to handle it again.

The pine trees and sea that you talked about give you a feeling of home, are they from Narva-Jõesuu? Is this something from your childhood?

Narva-Jõesuu is a place of power for me. I only realised that after I moved to London. There were people always asking: Are you homesick? What do you miss the most from home? Often these kinds of conversations end up in talking about food. For me, for instance, there are forest blueberries and lingonberries that are not available in London. I always tried to bring their jams from Estonia. I could easily live without those, but it was just a bonus I could bring with me. What I truly missed was my walk, my being in Narva-Jõesuu, and I noticed that every time I visited Estonia I tried to go there as my own "must." It made me think about this place as rather special to me and how physically I need to visit it annually and breathe its air.

How was the transition process for you? Did you have a strong community in Estonia?

I think I am still in a transition, at least I feel like that. Being in transition is something beyond just another move from the UK to Estonia; it is a part of who I am, part of my identity that includes a difficulty to be anchored or to feel anchored in one place. In 2020, when I was moving back to Estonia, I already had a plan for a solo exhibition at Tallinn Art Hall.[1] That exhibition was like re-entering the art scene in Estonia, it helped me to get back into the local art community. I still felt my relationship with people here had to be built up almost from scratch, though, because the dynamics had changed: I am not doing short visits anymore, I live here.

So would you describe home as something that is based on human relationships rather than physical or geographical locations?

Well, I keep joking that home is where my bed is. It might sound like a very specific definition, but at this moment of my life I cannot define home as anything bigger than my bed. Knowing the place and being connected to the people definitely helps. Now when I go back to London it is a strange feeling as everything is very familiar, but at the same time I am sleeping on someone else's couch. When I'm on the streets, when I meet people, I feel like I'm coming back to where I used to be. But when I'm going back to a friend's place to sleep, I feel I'm a guest because this is not my bed.

The constant feeling of transition is a part of you?

Transition hasn't been so much discussed in my work, but I think it is somehow the keyword for me even in my practice. In my work *Dream is Wonderful, Yet Unclear* (2014–2020), about a former community of textile workers, I am talking about a transition from the Soviet regime and state-owned economy to a market economy and capitalism. In my exhibition at Tallinn Art Hall, *When The World Blows Up, I Hope to Go Down Dancing,* I looked at women after age forty, who are less visible in our society, as if they move, so to speak, from a role of "young, beautiful and promising" for bearing children into a role of a "grandmother" with the expectation of taking care of grandchildren at the price of her own wishes and interests. That transition is defined by the patriarchal society we live in, which values and appreciates women less, especially if they don't fit into these two categories. So with my work, as a middle-aged woman, I am trying to question that duality and also give a space for women like me to express themselves. My earlier work also looked at the complex relations and transitions between the cultures and how they affect women and what the stigmas are around them. Transition is a process, right? I am not sure if there is even a final destination, but I can see why these topics attract my attention as an artist and why I am developing works around them. At my own core, I do feel that being in transition, being on the border, at the borderlands, is part of who I am and how I live and work.

Neringa Černiauskaitė has written in her essay "A Love Letter to the Non-Belonger" that non-belonging is something that is inherent to the people from the Baltics. Non-belonging is a constant feeling because we don't really belong to the East or the West or the North.

It is a very complex topic to discuss. West and East are artificially formed definitions of some territories and they are always quite relative—for some countries we are located in the East, for others, in the West. I won't get into the discussion about the Eurocentric narratives that dominate our world. Nevertheless, a need to belong, a feeling of belonging is definitely more archaic and lives in us as a basic need. We need to feel we belong to something bigger than just us—to the land, to a family, to a community, to a country. We also feel a need to contribute to something bigger. It might also be a chosen family, but the feeling that you belong to this community is essential to our well-being.

So when I think about transition and my art practice, I can see that with all I do I am searching for that feeling of belonging. It might be reflected in my work as opposing myself to something I was told I should belong to. For instance, I have done many works on stereotypes about women and how they are expected to behave or look, who they should be, which also has implications for me as I am part of this patriarchal society. By producing work about these stereotypes, I make a statement thatl refuse to be subject to the imagery you expect me (and many other women) to be. The same applies for the geographical dislocation. While I was in the UK, I tried to observe and reflect on the expectations of me as a woman, as a Russian speaker, as an Eastern European, whatever these definitions mean.

Coming back to Estonia is not really coming back. It is, as a friend of mine said, “the second migration” for me. I’m again going through something that roughly feels like a migration. Coming back home without feeling fully at home is a bit paradoxical. Previously I lived in Estonia as an office worker not as an artist, so my community varied a lot. I established new contacts and relations in an art circle while I was visiting Estonia regularly, but the relations were based on my rare visits only, not on the fact of living in one city or country. So it is understandable that the relations take time to grow into long friendship and trust. Also, for fourteen years, I lived in a very different cultural context, and it took lots of internal resources for me to try to understand it. I returned to a country that has changed. I am again trying to find my own place in a society and an art community, trying to find my own “flock,” so to speak, my people, who I feel I can belong to, and trying to figure out how I can contribute to this society, what are the needs here and how can my skills and knowledge be useful. It all comes with incredible stress around Estonian language for me also as I haven't used it for fourteen years and even before that speaking it never felt easy. I do believe that if you live in the country, you must speak its language. So I am trying and slowly getting there, but it is harder than I thought, especially knowing by now that I have dyslexia and studying a foreign language for a dyslexic can be a difficult task. But I am grateful to the universe that I found art as a language through which I can communicate, so I hope all those thoughts, frustrations, questions will result in some kind of artworks that I will develop while I am here, in Estonia.

Currently you are doing a PhD at the Estonian Academy of Arts (EKA). How is that for you as an artist? Has this also helped to find your community?

Actually, until the end of last term I was really struggling, asking myself, where is the joy in it all, because I didn't want to have the same experience as I had while studying economics—you do it out of obligation, not your own willingness and joy. At the moment, I'm again in this uncertainty but I'm also in a much calmer place, understanding that it is a process that I need to work through and that I might find something rewarding about that journey. I am getting great support from my supervisors, Redi Koobak and Annika von Hausswolff, and PhD colleagues and tutors. Community is vital in this process, even though doing PhD is a rather lonely journey, as many people will tell you.

I need to also say that the decision to apply for a PhD was largely conditioned by my financial situation. I basically applied to receive health insurance, which I am eligible for as a student. I'm joking about it, but this is the precarious reality for many artists. Of course, I have been teaching in different universities for the past ten years and I was thinking about a PhD as my next step. Of course, it is an important privilege to be able to join an academic society and potentially to contribute to a shared knowledge. I do appreciate that I was given this opportunity. But again, in the non-existent world where artists are paid, including the provision of all social insurances, I might not have considered an academic career at all. By my own nature I am not an academic and I am not sure if I can belong to that world fully. But I need to make those kinds of choices to be able to survive as an artist and continue my own practice.

In addition, the war in Ukraine totally changed everything for me, not just in real life, but in terms of a subject for my PhD. I was planning to go to Russia for some of my fieldwork and I cannot imagine doing that now. I think for Russian speakers in Estonia it is quite a complex situation, which is not discussed enough in public. There is a lot of anger towards Russian speakers but the complexity for us definitely goes beyond language: most of us have close connections in Russia and some of us have connections in Ukraine. It becomes very complex and painful on so many levels that it is quite hard to articulate it in one short sentence.

Your practice can be described as artistic research. Is it the purpose of your project that it would explain something to the audience? Is knowledge accumulation something that you keep in mind when you are working on a project?

I'm not trying to explain anything, that's for sure. Since I started my PhD at EKA, I am in a more complex relation-

2 Maria Kapajeva, *Dream is Wonderful, Yet Unclear* (curator Liisa Kaljula), Narva Art Residency, Narva, Estonia, September 9 to October 8, 2017; also published as the book *Dream is Wonderful, Yet Unclear* (Milda Books, 2020).

ship with the term "artistic research" than before as academic research and artistic research can be understood differently. I guess what you are asking me is if background research for a work production is as important as the final work for me. I think it might come from a conscious or unconscious decision to tell a slightly different story of something that people have heard before. So I do research on what is known, and I am also trying to discover what might be not known yet. I like to offer a slightly peripheral view on things, similar to what happens with our vision: we can grasp in sharp view only what is in front of our eyes. We can still see quite a lot through peripheral vision, but these things remain out of focus. This is where I am trying, metaphorically speaking, to turn heads, to see what is out there, whose stories are missing in the bigger picture, who is left behind at the periphery. I believe that everyone's story deserves to be heard.

For instance, my work about the Kreenholm community in Narva.[2] I really felt like everyone knows the facts about the famous textile mill—when Kreenholm was established, who the directors were, and when it went bankrupt. It is often said that the story of Narva is tightly connected to the women who worked at the mill as most families had someone working there. But why don't we hear the stories of these women? As a member of that community, I decided to try to give visibility to these women who still live in Narva. In my book I didn't even include any dates or facts about the mill; these can be found in other books or Wikipedia. I only put the figures of how many people worked and how many people went through a governmental program for re-qualification,

3 Maria Kapajeva, *Loose Photos, Odds and Ends*, Kumu Art Museum, Tallinn, Estonia, June 16 to December 30, 2022.

which was organised at a later stage of the mill closure. This number was extremely small in comparison to the total number of the workers, and it is a rather devastating part of the story. With this work, I was trying to offer untold stories about the mill through the perspective of this community I am part of, and of these women who felt forgotten and left behind.

I guess it might be similar to the approach I used for my recent exhibition at Kumu,[3] which I produced especially for the museum. The core and starting point of my installation is a collection of 105 photographs that I purchased 8 years ago from an American dealer who found them in some kind of a flea market and was trying to sell them online. By bringing those images to an exhibition space I am asking if they are worth something, if the stories of these people in the photos, or the photographers who took them, are also part of our history.

It seems you have had a strong attachment and commitment to the Narva community and region. Why did you move to London in the first place?

The short answer is to get a photography degree. The longer answer is that there was a moment in my life when everything came together and the move was just the most logical next step. I have a degree in economics, and I had marketing jobs at different companies. The last job I had before moving to the UK was as a purchase manager, with a decent salary, at a company that dealt with steel. But my studies in economics were quite a difficult and traumatic experience for me. At the same time, I had an ambition inside of me, a wish to grow professionally and as an individual, so the thought of staying at that job until retirement, which for me meant the next forty years, totally freaked me out and made me change my life completely.

Photography had entered into my life as a hobby a few years before that and I was spending all my free time reading about, looking at, and making photographs. At that time, I also felt there was a bigger world out there that I wanted to see. It was almost a physical feeling of not being able to breathe fully in Estonia. All those small factors made me apply to study in the UK. I randomly picked the University for the Creative Arts in Farnham as I knew nothing about art universities. But it became a destiny, I guess, as I never left this university and I still work for them now.

In my experience—and I know a lot of people of my generation can relate to this—joy and studies don't usually go together. We didn't even question the necessity of education and the importance of enjoying while studying; we just did it because that's what you are supposed to do. That was my experience while studying economics at University of Tartu—you have to have a higher education for a better future, and no one really bothers to ask if you like what you study. So photography was a very different and truly incredible experience; I realised studying something can be enjoyable and it only matters if you love and have passion about it.

I keep thanking myself for being able to leave everything behind and follow my interests. I made this decision on my own and I was freaked out by the uncertainty of the future. But it also excited me a lot, and still does. I am full of hope and adrenaline.

Laura Põld

Laura Põld (b. 1984, Tallinn, Estonia) lives and works in Tallinn. Põld is an installation artist whose practice is distinctive for its symbiosis of sculptural and traditional craft, with questions of material and its agency emerging in contemporary art and philosophy. Her large-scale constructions and installations often take over or intervene in a given site and/or its context and material complexity. Her work draws on environmental history, including the behaviour of birds, animals, and plants. Many of her projects have their origins in a residency experience, which allows for immersion in new subjects and consultation with various experts, exploring materials or techniques found on site, and which has developed into long-term collaborations with other artists, writers, musicians, and performance artists. In her most recent works, Põld focuses on the choice of materials and their historical and political context, environmental history, and activism practices. She is currently applying traditional and innovative craft and construction techniques in ceramics, embroidery, tufting, and weaving, the latter of which interests her as a traditionally feminine method of preserving stories, memory, and skills.

Woolen, 2022–2023

Photos: Laura Põld & Leelo-Mai Aunbaum

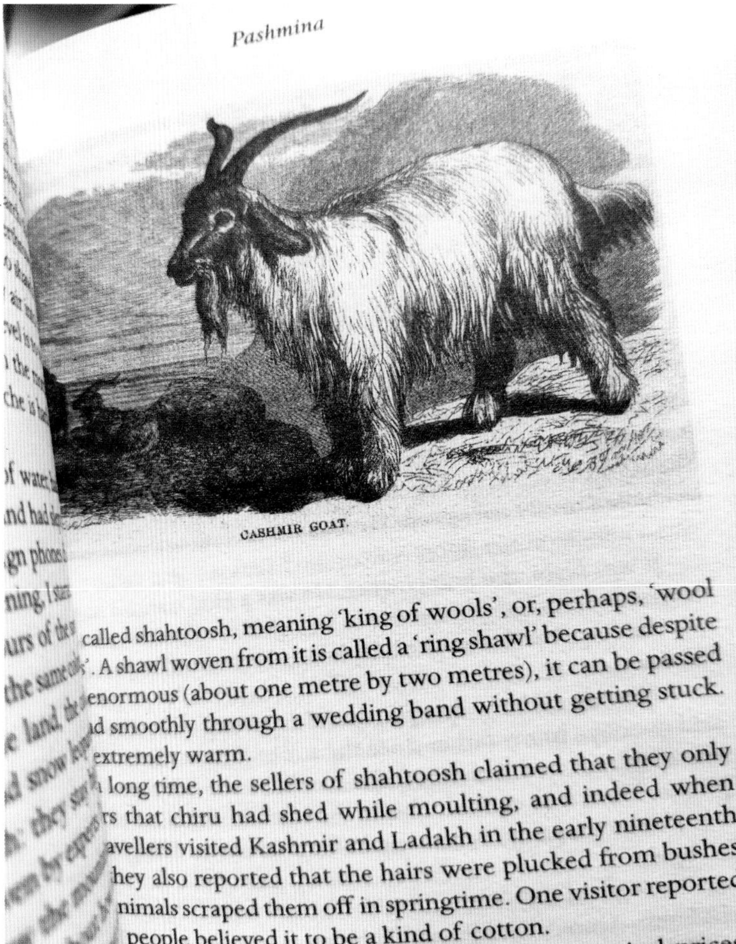
Pashmina

CASHMIR GOAT.

called shahtoosh, meaning 'king of wools', or, perhaps, 'wool
'. A shawl woven from it is called a 'ring shawl' because despite
enormous (about one metre by two metres), it can be passed
d smoothly through a wedding band without getting stuck.
extremely warm.
long time, the sellers of shahtoosh claimed that they only
rs that chiru had shed while moulting, and indeed when
avellers visited Kashmir and Ladakh in the early nineteenth
hey also reported that the hairs were plucked from bushes
nimals scraped them off in springtime. One visitor reported
people believed it to be a kind of cotton.

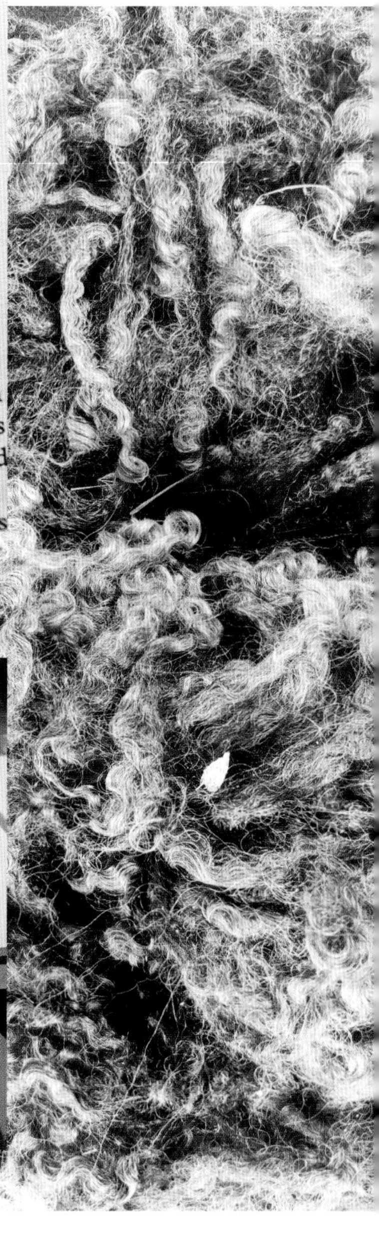

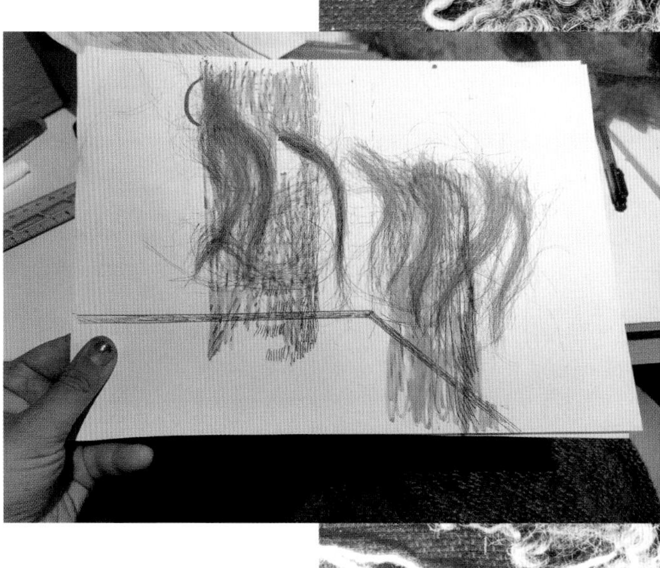

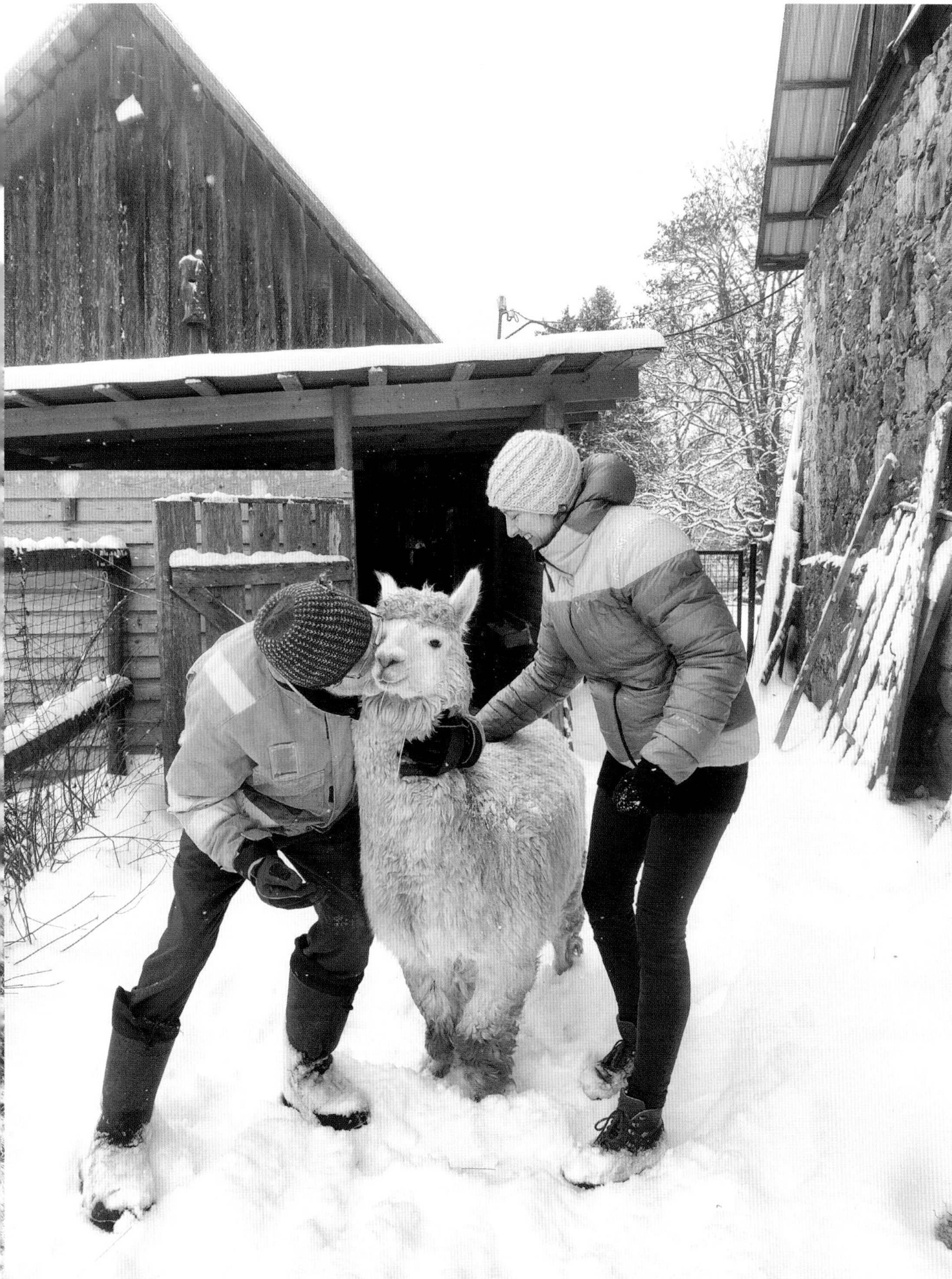

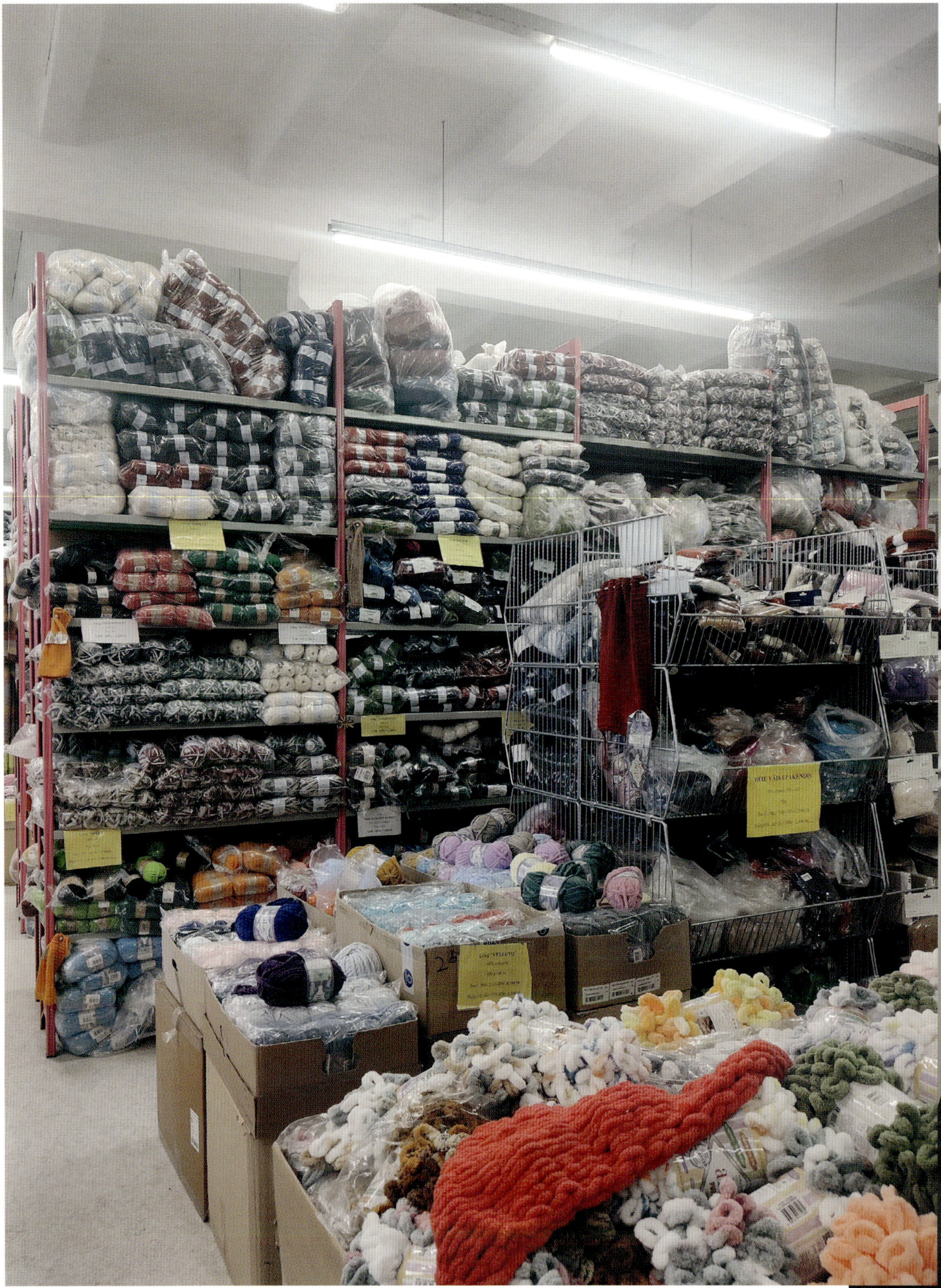

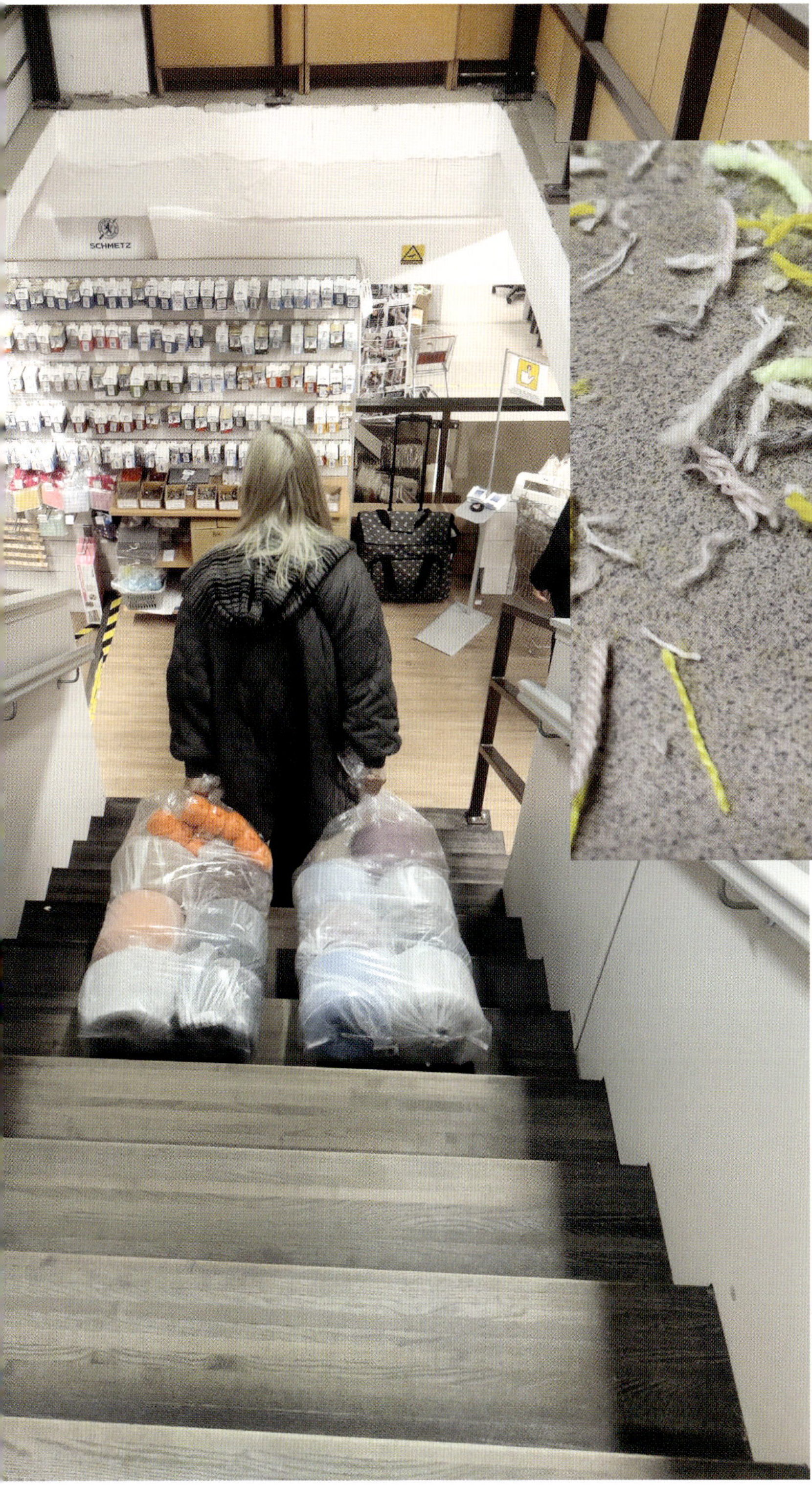
SCHMETZ

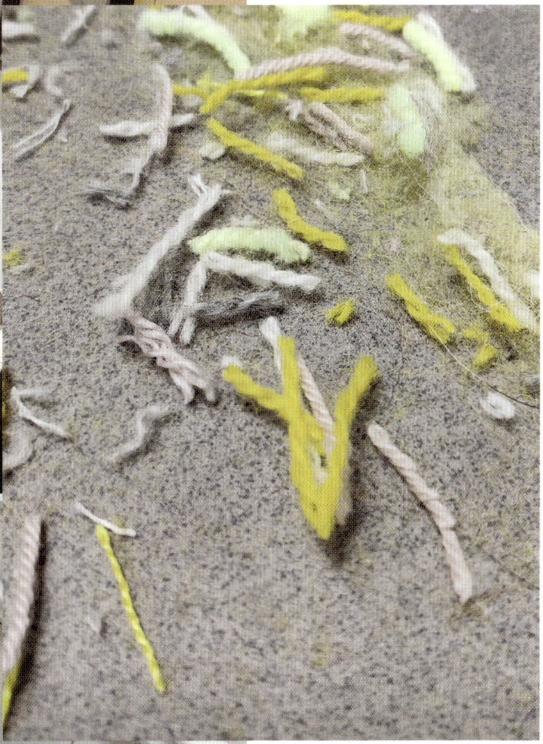

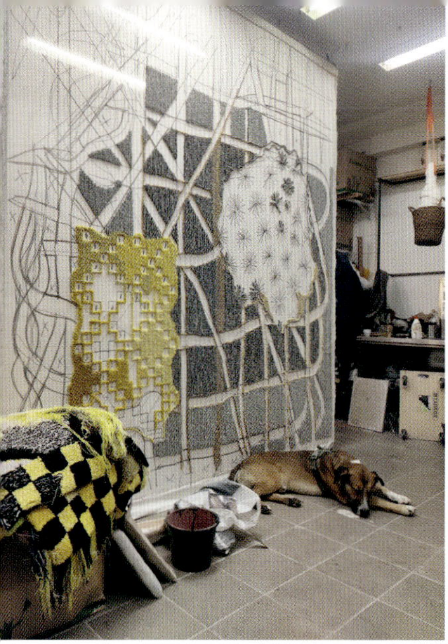
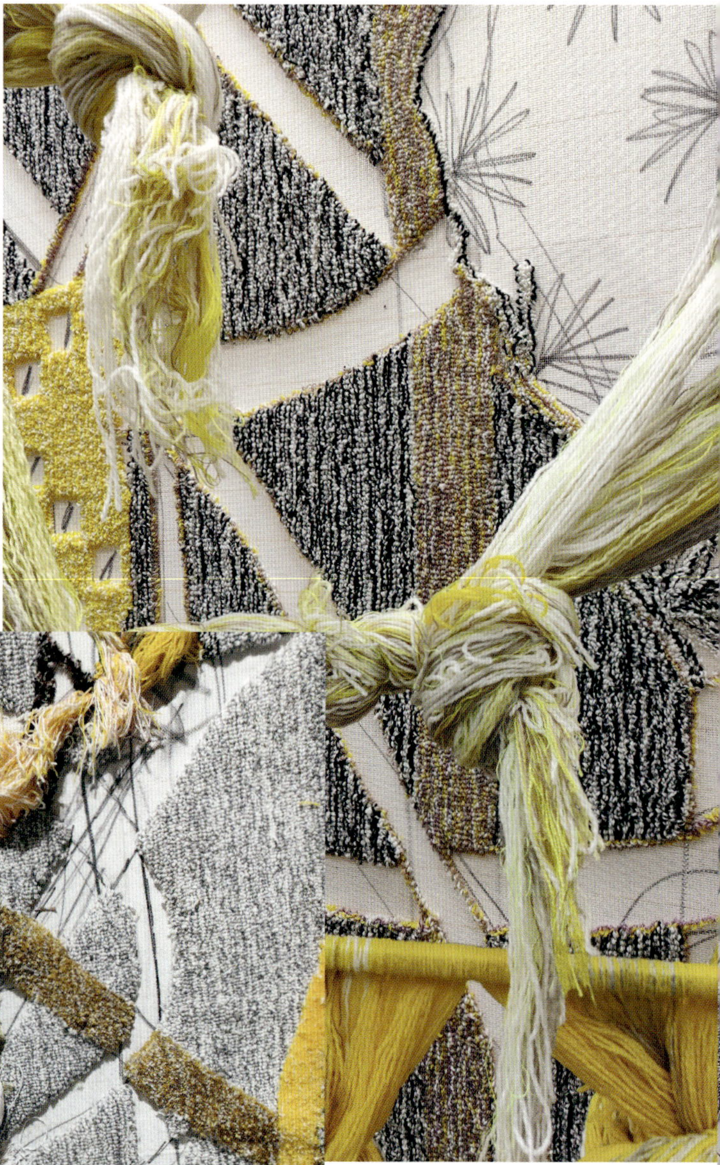
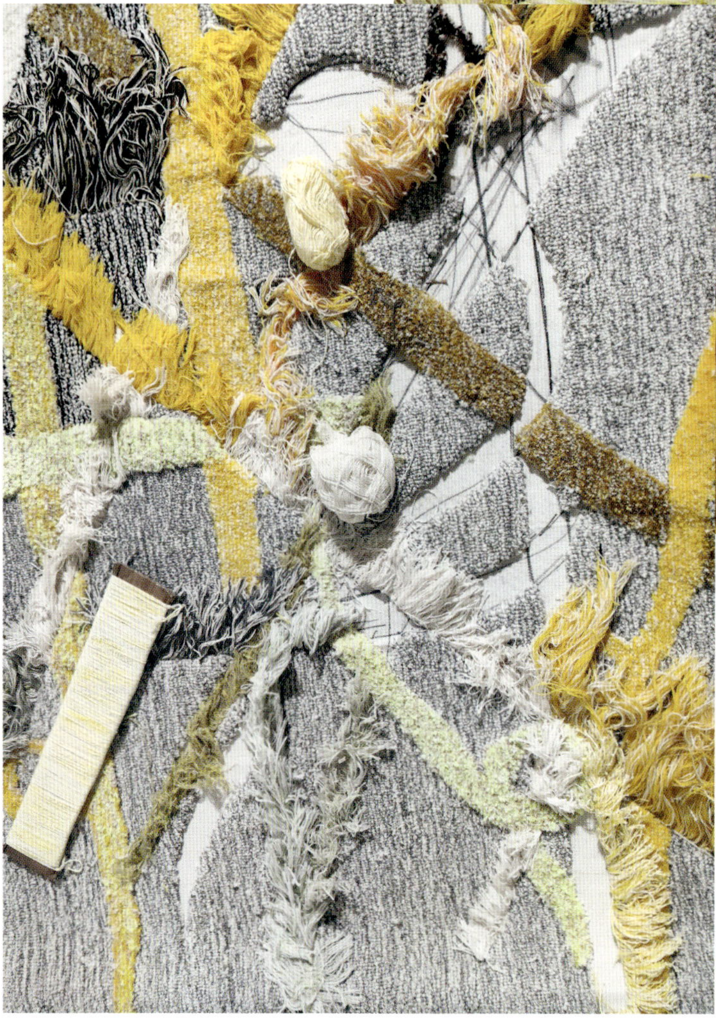

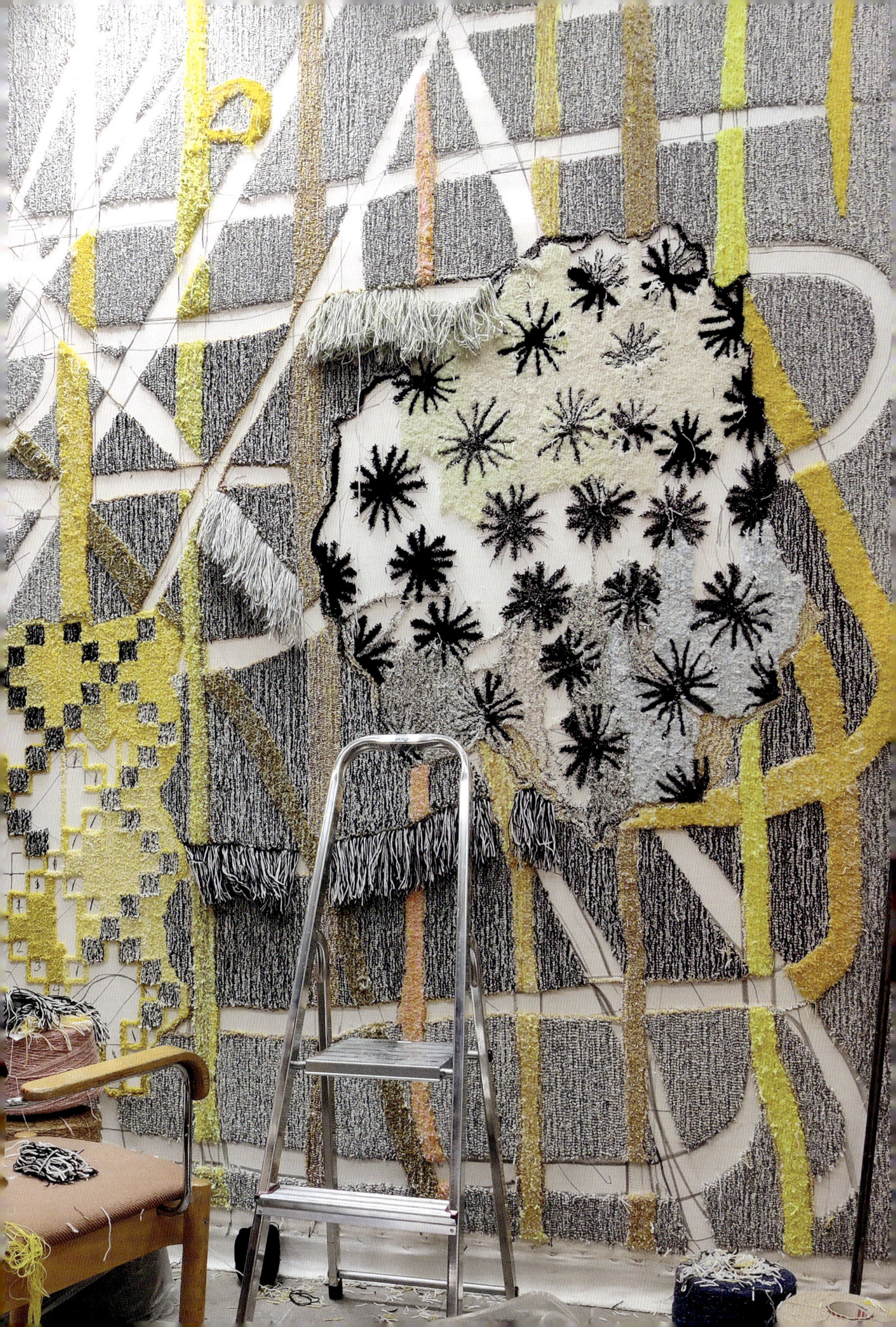

Maria Kapajeva

Maria Kapajeva (b. 1976, Narva, Estonia) lives and works in Tallinn. Kapajeva is an artist whose work often explores a diverse spectrum of cultural identity and gender issues within historical and contemporary contexts. She uses various mediums, such as video, photography, textile, and installations to bring to the focus what is often left invisible or stays in peripheral vision. Kapajeva's artist book *Dream Is Wonderful, Yet Unclear* (Milda Books, 2020) received the Kraszna-Krausz Photo Book Award 2021. Her first book *You can call him another man* (Kaunas Photography Gallery, 2018) was shortlisted for the Aperture Photobook Award. Kapajeva's works have been exhibited internationally, including the KUMU Art Museum, Tallinn (2022); F3 freiraum für fotografie, Berlin (2022); Finnish Museum of Photography, Helsinki (2021); Lithuanian Gallery of Photography, Vilnius (2020); and Tallinn Art Hall (2020). Kapajeva is currently pursuing a practice-based PhD at Estonian Academy of Arts.

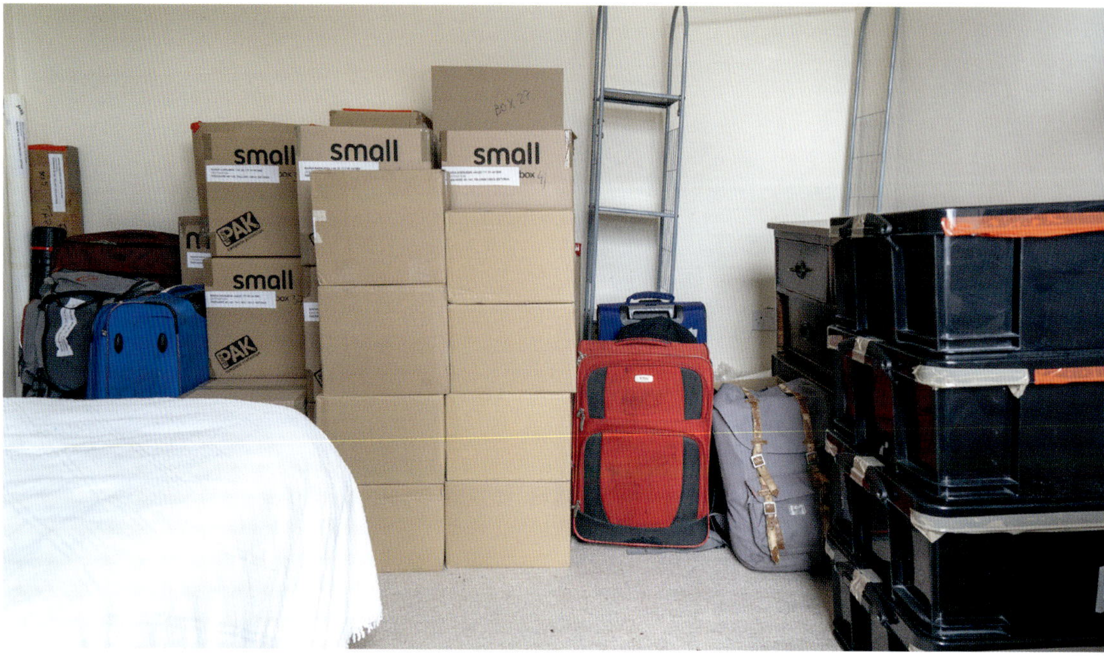
small
small
small
small
PAK
PAK

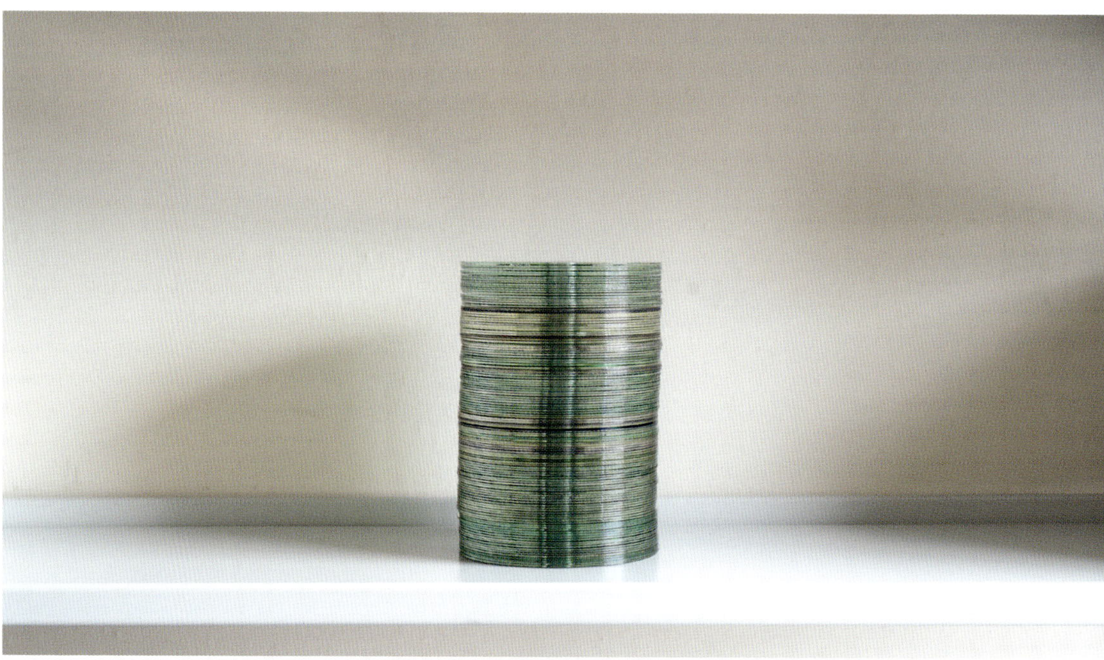

fourteen years of my life
seven hundred kilos

eigth years of my life
one hundred twenty-three co-roms

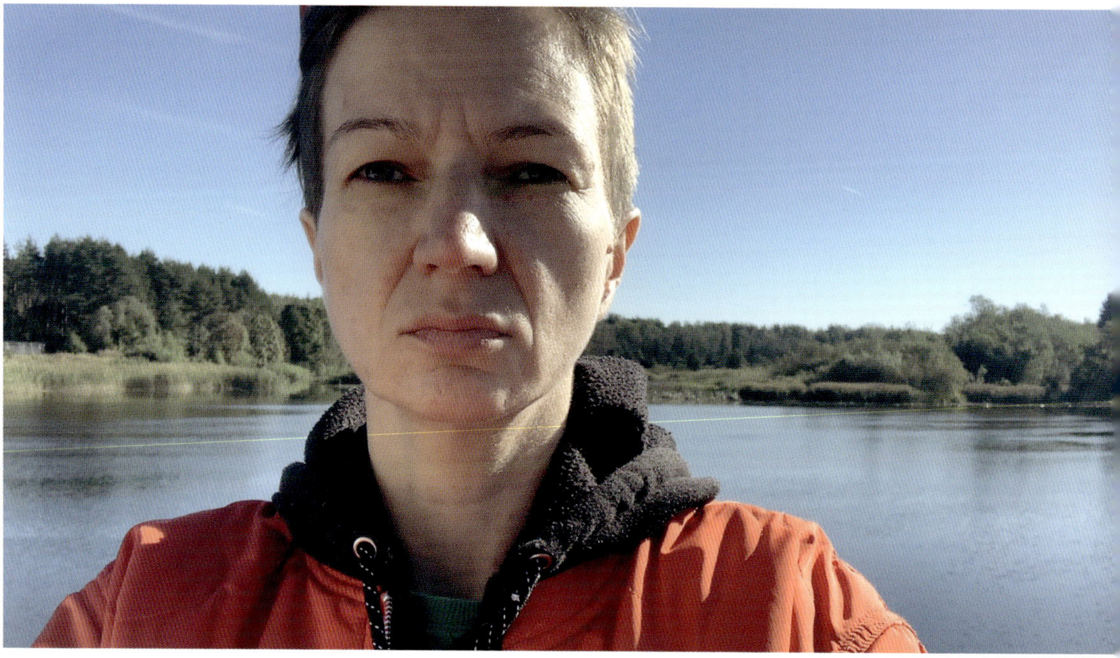

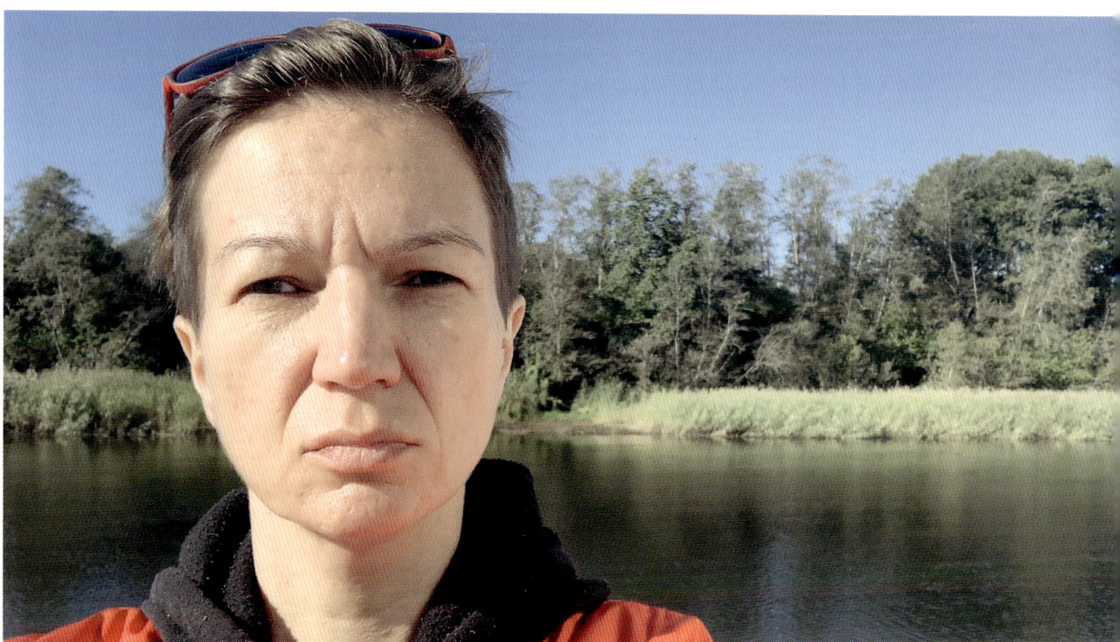

11.09.2022

паром	ferry
в тишине ехать офигительно	taking it in full quietness is magical
внутри меня	inside me
как будто вода	some kind of water
поднимается	rises up
и соединяется	and connects
с этой водой	to this water
по которой я иду	that i'm riding on
как будто через нее	as if go through it
через ее непрерывное	through its continuous
движение	current
я слышу свои корни	i hear my roots
в движении	in its movement
я связываюсь с каждой водорослей	i get connected with every algae
в этой реке	in this river
я понимаю каждую рыбу	i understand every fish
там в ней	there
какая-то мощь	is some kind of power
и она во мне тоже есть	and it's in me, too
а я и не знала.	and i wasn't aware of it.
за мной	behind me
твоя земля	your land
я смотрю	i'm looking
на свою землю	at my land
а теперь	and now
за мной	behind me
моя земля	my land
а я смотрю	and i'm looking
на твою землю.	at your land.
мои предки	my ancestors
с моей земли	from my land
та что на другом берегу	the one on the other side of the river
другие мои предки	my other ancestors
с твоей земли	from your land
тоже на том берегу	also on the other shore
а мой берег только мой	my shore is mine alone
и я плыву в реке	and i'm floating down the river
между	between
этим и другим	this and the other
берегами	shores
и я часть этой воды	and i'm part of that water
я это знаю	i know that
но научно не объясню	but scientifically i can't explain it

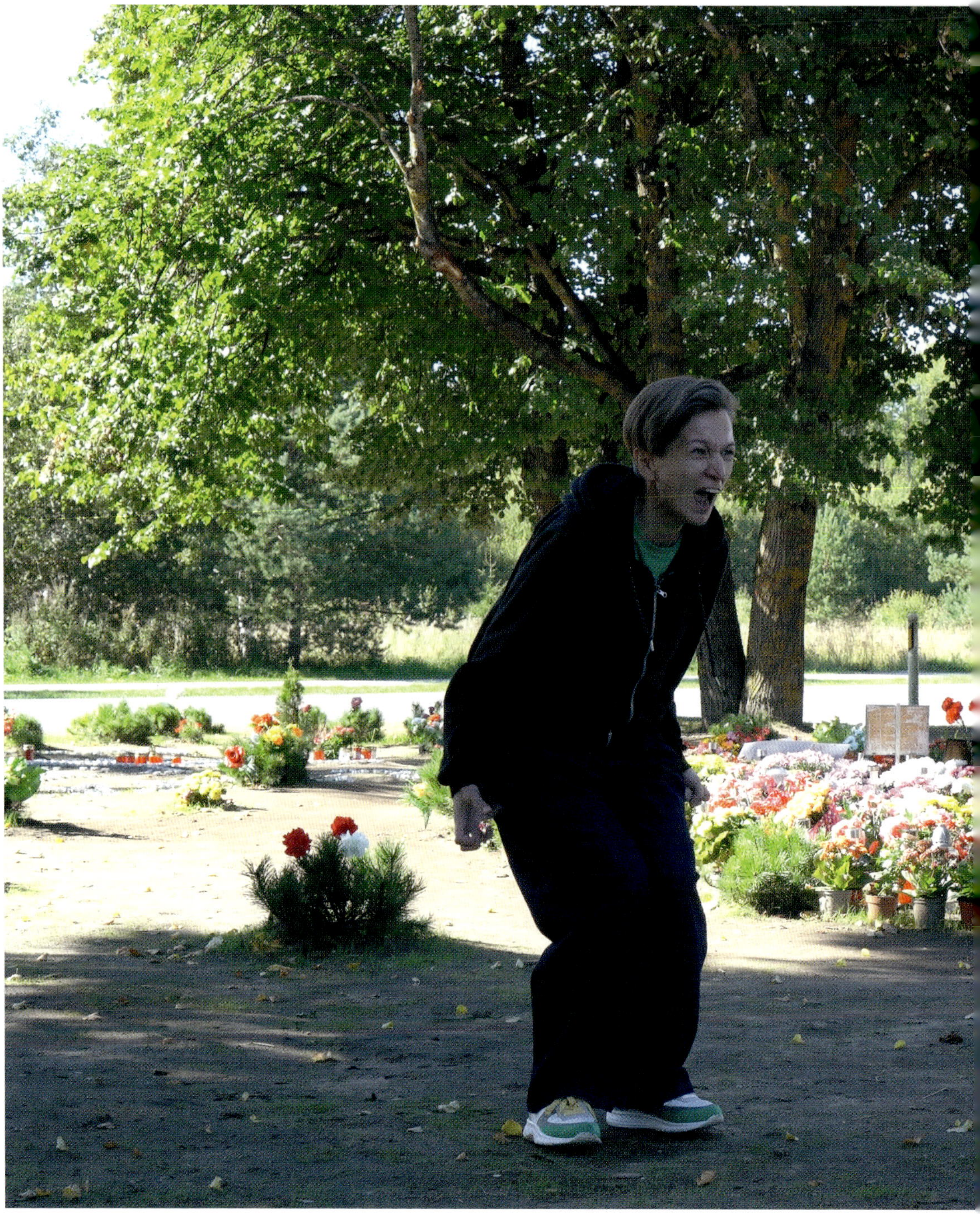

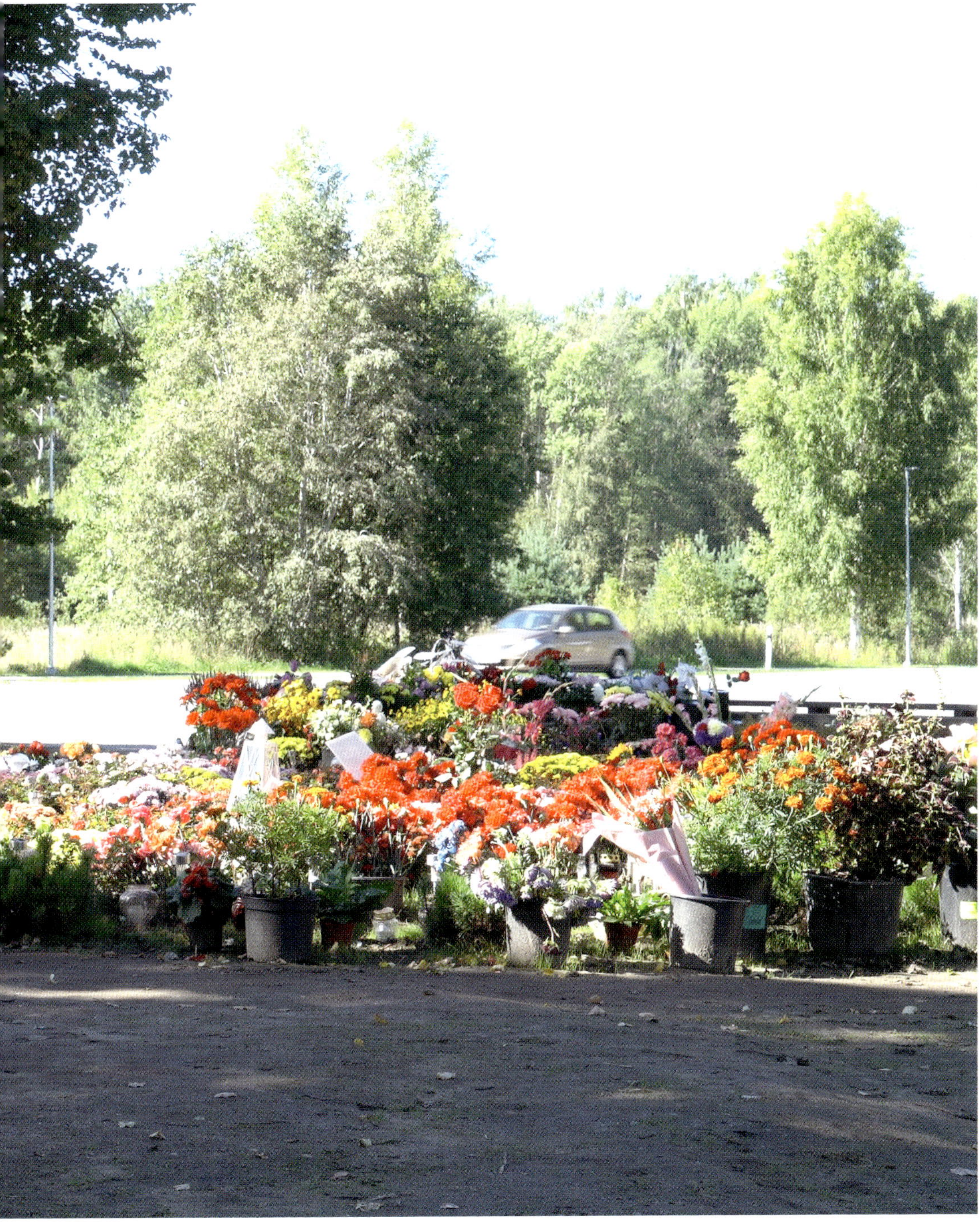

Still from video work *the enforced memory*, 2022

Annika Toots (b. 1985, Tartu, Estonia) is an art and photography historian, curator, and editor living and working in Tallinn. In her research she is mainly interested in artistic practices that deal with materialising the past and representations of landscape, focusing mainly on photography. She is a lecturer on photo theory and history at the Estonian Academy of Arts. Her more recent research projects include working with the vast number of glass negatives by Estonian photographer Jaan Riet (1873–1952) at the Film Archive of the National Archives of Estonia, and exploring questions of digital photographic heritage. She has edited art-related magazines such as *Estonian Art* (2019–2021) and *Studies on Art and Architecture* (2021–present) as well as the books *Artists' Spaces: 16 studio visits* (with Merilin Talumaa, 2017) and *Displaced Time* (with Aap Tepper, 2021).

Merilin Talumaa (b. 1986, Tallinn, Estonia) is a curator, art historian, and cultural manager who lives and works in Paris and Tallinn. She has graduated from the Department of Art History and Visual Culture at the Estonian Academy of Arts. She is also a graduate of Environmental Studies from the University of Tartu. Her practice has evolved around research about artists' studio and work environments and notions of migration and belonging. Ongoing projects include *Roots to Routes* (since 2020), a curatorial initiative gathering a community of artists, curators, and cultural producers. Prior to the book *Your Time Is My Time* (Mousse, 2023) she compiled and edited (with Annika Toots) the book *Artists' Spaces: 16 studio visits* (Estonian Academy of Arts Press, 2017).

Inga Lāce (b. 1986, Jurmala, Latvia) is C-MAP Central and Eastern Europe Fellow at the Museum of Modern Art, New York. She has been curator at the Latvian Centre for Contemporary Art since 2012 and was co-curator (with Valentinas Klimašauskas) of the Latvian Pavilion, featuring the artist Daiga Grantiņa, at the Venice Biennale in 2019. She was also co-curator of the Kyiv Biennial 2021 (as part of the East Europe Biennial Alliance) and co-curator of the 7th to 10th editions of the contemporary art festival SURVIVAL KIT. She is co-curator of a research and exhibition project *Portable Landscapes* which examined art and life of the Latvian exile and emigrant communities throughout the twentieth century with exhibitions at James Gallery at CUNY, New York (2019); Latvian National Art Museum, Riga (2018); Villa Vassilieff, Paris (2018); and an upcoming publication. Lāce has (co-)curated exhibitions at the Henie Onstad Kunstenter, Oslo (2023); Malmö Konstmuseum (2022); Pori Art Museum, Finland (2021); Konsthall C, Stockholm (2020); Muzeum Sztuki, Łódź (2019); and Framer Framed, Amsterdam (2017).

Sandra Skurvida (Vilnius, Lithuania) is a cultural critic, curator, and scholar specializing in interdisciplinary, transnational, feminist, and environmental histories, theories, and practices of contemporary art. She emerged as an independent curator in Lithuania and relocated to New York City in 1996. Among her many bilingual publications are essays for the catalogues of retrospective exhibitions of Kestutis Zapkus (2014) and Aleksandra Kasuba (2020), both at the Lithuanian National Museum of Art, Vilnus, and Jasper Johns (2021) at the Whitney Museum of American Art and Philadelphia Museum of Art. She is currently completing the book *John Cage: Composing the Common.* Since 2010, Skurvida has engaged with media art of Iran and curated video programs at many venues worldwide, organized symposia, and published numerous texts. She teaches at the Fashion Institute of Technology at the State University of New York.